CONTENTS

FOOD

FOR THE BODY

FOR THE SOUL

We Believe in the Dignity and Importance of Women —

We Believe that Everything Woman Touches should be Ennobled by that Touch —

We Believe that the Home is the Greatest Influence on the Character of Mankind—

We Believe the Home Should be a Haven . . .

A Place of Refuge
A Place of Peace
A Place of Harmony
A Place of Beauty

No Home in America ever need be Dull and Unattractive. We are Dedicated to doing our part to make every Home have Attraction Power.

"Let Us
Give Thanks"

......For the providence of our loving Heavenly Father who has
given us the resources to grow bountiful harvests of foods -
and the creative imagination to prepare and serve them beautifully
and colorfully.

......For the satisfaction and fellowship of "breaking bread
together.

......For the "home" - Love has a locale on earth, it is called
"home" - Here it:

        Most deeply expresses itself,

        Most surely receives its nourishment

        Most purely radiates its power.

Every one of us, whether we are single or married, are in some
stage of building a home. Houses are made of wood and stone,
only love can make a home.

......and for our very important HOME INTERIORS & GIFTS,
HOSTESSES, who have contributed so very much to our success
as a company, and who have contributed their favorite recipies
for this book -

We give thanks --- for 20 years of mutually joyous relationships
and pledge ourselves to continue to serve with love, dignity and
excellence.

Mary C. Crowley

Mary C. Crowley, President

Home Interiors & Gifts, Inc.

Make Your World More Beautiful

Make your world more beautiful for everyone,
Let your light shine brighter everyday —
For you're someone, especially to those you love,
And love will always find a way . . .
To make your life a lovely place for all to share;
Make your heart a shelter of God's love,
Make your home a refuge for your family —
A place of happiness for everyone!

Make your life a lovely place for all to share;
Make your heart a shelter of God's love,
Make your home a refuge for your family —
A place of happiness for everyone!

MARY CROWLEY'S YUMMY CAKE

Pour 1 1/4 cup boiling water over 1 cup oatmeal and one (1/4 pound) stick of butter (or margarine) Let stand 10-20 minutes. Add:

1 cup brown sugar
1 cup white sugar
1 1/3 cup sifted flour
1 teaspoon soda
1 teaspoon cinnamon
1/2 teaspoon salt
1/2 teaspoon nutmeg

Stir gently - do NOT use mixer.   Pour in buttered pan and bake 35 minutes at 350 degrees.

ICING:
3/4 stick butter, or margarine
1/2 cup brown sugar
1/2 cup white sugar
1/4 cup canned milk
1 teaspoon vanilla
1 cup shredded coconut and nut meats mixed (I use pecans)

Mix icing and pour on cake after cake has baked, and brown under broiler --- about 10 minutes.

Leave in pan and serve -- cut in squares.

WARNING: Absolutely delicious.   FAMILY WILL RAID!!

I won the Stokley Van Camp "Best Cook Award" several years ago.

7-UP POUND CAKE

3 cups sugar
3 sticks margarine
5 eggs
1 teaspoon lemon extract
1 teaspoon butter flavoring
1 teaspoon coconut flavoring
1 teaspoon vanilla extract
1/2 teaspoon salt
3 cups flour
7 ounces 7-Up

Mix well and bake at 300 degrees in well greased and floured tube or bundt pan 1 1/2 hours or until done, starting in <u>cold</u> oven. Cool on wire rack before removing from pan.

Mrs. Frances Folkes

****

ALL ABOUT CAKE PANS

Cakes may be baked in loaves, sheets, cupcakes, tubes or the ever popular layers. Many recipes cannot be interchanged, however. If the recipe specifies a tube pan, the cake must be baked in a tube pan for best results.

Cake pans may be made of aluminum, heavy tin or oven-proof glass. Use the pan size recommended in the recipe. Check the pan size by measuring it across the top.

Use bright shiny pans. Discolored pans cause uneven browning. Avoid warped pans, too. They will cause uneven baking. If glass pans are used, follow the manufacturer's directions. Glass usually requires a lower baking temperature.

This is my very first Home Interiors Hostess, and a precious
friend.

I held an introductory Home Interiors and Gifts show December 12,
1957 at the home of Frances (Mrs. Glenn) Folks. She was gracious
enough to be the FIRST. We had put together a line consisting of
only twenty seven pieces of gifts and accessories, and at that
time did not have an office or warehouse yet. (That came January 1,
1958.) But my son Don, and daughter Ruth, and I were working from
the garage. Truly "little is much when God is in it." For from
the very beginning we wanted to honor Him in all of our lives -
and that certainly included the new business venture.

NOTES

FRESH APPLE CAKE

2 cups sugar
1 cup shortening or butter
4 eggs
2 1/2 cups flour
1/2 cup cold water
1 tablespoon, cloves, cinnamon, nutmeg
1 tablespoon soda
1 tablespoon salt
1 cup nuts
2 cups fresh apples chopped finely

Mix sugar and shortening until creamy. Add eggs, then add
water and vanilla. Sift flour, spices and salt together. Add
to sugar mix then add apples and chopped nuts. Bake at
350 degrees for 45 minutes to 1 hour.

Hostess: Katie Havard
Displayer: Mary Stockard

MANDARIN ORANGE CAKE

1 yellow cake mix (disregard instructions on box)
1 cup oil
4 eggs
1 small can Mandarin oranges, juice and all

Mix all together well, and put in greased and floured pan, 9 x 13"
Bake at 350 degrees for 35 minutes.

TOPPING:
1 large can crushed pineapple, with juice
1 package instant vanilla pudding
1 9 ounce Cool Whip

Stir together with spoon until thoroughly mixed. Spread on cake.
Keep refrigerated.

Hostess: Sharon Anderson

SUMMER CAKE

1 large box jello (any flavor, but red is best)
1 Duncan Hines White Cake Mix (prepared as directed)
Cool Whip
Prepare jello as directed, but omit the cold water, do NOT
refrigerate, let set at room temperature. Bake cake, using
a 13 x 9" pan. Let cool. Poke holes in cake. Pour jello
overall. Refrigerate at least two hours. Frost with Cool
Whip before serving.

Hostess: Darlyne Hastins
Displayer: Nancy Evans

JUICE CAKE

1 box Duncan Hines Yellow Cake Mix
3 Eggs
1 1/2 cans Apricot Nectarine

Empty contents of cake mix into mixing bowl, add eggs, and
apricot nectarine. Preheat oven at 350 degrees. Beat ingredients
at medium speed for 3-5 minutes. Pour ingredients into cake pan,
bake for 45 minutes.

ICING:
1 1/2 cups powdered sugar
1 8 ounce can apricot nectarine

Pour into sauce pan 1 1/2 cups powdered sugar. Add nectarine.
Bring to boil, stir until thick, let cool, pour over cool cake.

Hostess: Pearlie Williams

FRUIT CAKE

1 cup sugar
1 1/2 cups flour
1/2 teaspoon salt
1 teaspoon baking powder
4 eggs
1 pound candied cherries
1 pound candied pineapples
1 pound pitted dates
1 pound pecans

Chop fruit and nuts and mix with 1/2 cup flour. Mix together
other dry ingredients. Add eggs to make a batter. Mix batter
mixture with fruit and nut mixture. Bake at 325 degrees for
1 1/2 hours.

Hostess: Gladys B. Phelps
Displayer: Izella Allen

****

MAY WE RESOLVE ALWAYS

May we be a little less impatient with those we deem too slow,
A little less arrogant because of all we know,
A little more forgiving and swifter to be kind
And a little more eagerness - to be sweeter all the time!

****

7

BELVILLE GOOEY BUTTER CAKE

1 box yellow butter cake mix (Duncan Hines)
1 stick butter
1 egg

Mix by hand and press in baking dish.

8 ounce package cream cheese
2 eggs
3/4 box confectioners sugar

Beat in mixer until creamy; pour over first mixture in dish.
Bake at 350 degrees, 30-35 minutes in an 8 x 12" dish. Sprinkle
confectioners sugar over hot cake when baked. Cool. Refrigerate,
better overnight, cut in bars or squares.

Hostess: Rosalyn Dowling
Displayer: Rita Brown

LEMON CHEESE CAKE

1   3 ounce package lemon jello
1 cup boiling water
3 tablespoons lemon juice
1   8 ounce pakcage Philadelphia Cream Cheese
1 cup granulated sugar
1 teaspoon vanilla
Combine and chill above ingredietns.
13 ounce can Milnot (or evaporated milk)
Beat Milnot and add partially thickened jello, cheese, and
sugar mixture. Then pour over graham cracker crust and chill.

GRAHAM CRACKER CRUST:
1/2 pound graham crackers
1/2 stick oleo
Crush graham crackers and pour melted better over them,
Mix well and press into bottom of pan.

Hostess: Crystal Sronce
Displayer: Janet Sroka

****

HUSBANDS HOMECOMING
I scrubbed the kitchen floor today, and washed the woodwork too...
I refereed the childrens play, until I'm black and blue...
I washed the dishes, and baked a cake, and cleaned the linen chest,
And now I'll just lie down and take a little, teeny rest. That's
just when you walk in and say, "So this is what you do all day?"

****

8

MAYONNAISE CAKE

2 cups flour
1 cup sugar
1/2 teaspoon salt
1 teaspoon soda
1 teaspoon vanilla
1 teaspoon baking powder
4 tablespoons cocoa
1 small jar or 1/2 cup mayonnaise
1 cup water

Mix all dry ingredients together, add mayonnaise, vanilla and
water. Mix until smooth. Bake at 350 degrees for 30 minutes.
To make sheet cake, double recipe and bake about one hour.

Hostess: Linda McGuckin
Displayer: Gesele Ross

"RED RED" CHRISTMAS CAKE

1/2 cup crisco or oleo
1 1/2 cups sugar
2 eggs
2 cups flour
2 tablespoons cocoa
1 teaspoon salt
1 tablespoon vinegar (reserve)
1 teaspoon salt (reserve)
1 cup buttermilk
1 teaspoon vanilla
1 2 ounce bottle red food coloring

Sift together flour, cocoa, and salt. Cream crisco and sugar.
Add eggs one at a time. Beat until fluffy. Add sifted dry
ingredients alternately with buttermilk. Add vanilla and food
coloring. Beat well. Fold in soda and vinegar, which have been
mixed together. Bake at 350 degrees for 30 minutes if two round
pans have been used, 35 minutes for oblong pan.

CREAMY WHITE FROSTING:

1 cup milk
1/4 cup flour
Cook until thick, let cool.

1 cup sugar
1 stick oleo
1 cup crisco
Beat until fluffy. Add to first mixture and beat until ready
to spread. Cover with red coconut if desired. To color
coconut just add a couple of drops of red coloring to a bowl of
coconut and stir until well coated.

Hostess: Joan Van Dyke
Displayer: Doris Roper

9

MELT IN YOUR MOUTH BLUEBERRY CAKE

2 eggs separated
1 cup sugar
1/4 teaspoon salt
1/2 cup shortening
1 teaspoon vanilla
1 1/2 cups sifted all purpose flour
1 teaspoon baking powder
1/3 cup milk
1 1/2 cups blueberries

Beat egg whites until stiff. Add about 1/2 cup of the sugar to keep them stiff. Cream shortening and add salt and vanilla. Add remaining sugar gradually. Add unbeaten egg yolks and beat until light and creamy. Add sifted dry ingredients alternately with the milk. Fold in the beaten whites. Fold in the fresh blueberries. Take a bit of the flour called for in recipe and coat berries so they won't settle. May also use canned berries. Turn into a greased 8 x 8" pan. Sprinkle top of batter lightly with granulated sugar. Bake 50-60 minutes at 350 degrees.

Hostess: Linda Pelotte
Displayer: Jean Brown

STRAWBERRY CAKE

1 box white cake mix
10 ounces strawberries (thawed)
3 ounce box wild strawberry jello
3/4 cup oil
1/2 cup water
3 tablespoons flour
3 eggs
Mix together, bake at 350 degrees for 40-45 minutes.

STRAWBERRY FROSTING
10 ounces cool whip
10 ounces strawberries (thawed)
Mix with spoon, juice and all. Spread on cooled cake. Keep refrigerated

Hostess: Sue Chandler

****

Luck is preparation meeting opportunity.......

The harder I work......the luckier I get!

From "Be Somebody" by Mary Crowley.

****

10

PINEAPPLE DREAM CAKE

2 cups flour
2 cups sugar
1 teaspoon vanilla
2 teaspoons baking soda
2 eggs
1 large can crushed pineapple

Mix all ingredients, pour in baking pan and bake at 350 degrees
for 1 hour or til done. Very moist and rich and EASY.

ICING:
8 ounces philadelphia cream cheese
1/2 stick oleo
1 teaspoon vanilla
1/2 to 3/4 box powdered sugar

Hostess: Mary Jane Spencer
Displayer: Virginia Patterson

PINEAPPLE CAKE

3 eggs
2 cups sugar
1 teaspoon vanilla
1 #2 can crushed pineapple with juice
2 cups flour
2 teaspoons soda
1/2 teaspoon salt

Beat eggs, add sugar and mix well. Add vanilla, then pineapple
and juice. Add flour sifted with soda and salt. Pour into
large greased and floured pan - bake 45 minutes at 350 degrees.
(Batter should not be more than 1 inch thick.)

ICING:
1 1/2 cups sugar
1 cup evaporated milk
3/4 stick butter
1 1/2 cups flake coconut
1 cup nuts
Ten minutes before cake is done begin icing. Mix sugar, milk,
and butter, bring to a boil, cook 2 minutes. Add coconut, and
nuts, spread on hot cake and return to oven 10 minutes or under
broiler 2 or 3 minutes.

Hostess: Ann Burkes
Displayer: Shirely Meador

POPPY SEED CAKE

1 package white cake mix
1 ounce poppy seed
1 tablespoon cooking oil
2 tablespoons more moisture than recipe calls for
Vanilla filling
Whipped cream or whipped topping

Bake cake in 2 layers 30 minutes at 350 degrees. Put layers
together with favorite vanilla filling. Top with whipped cream
or other whipped topping just before serving.

Hostess: Kay Oberlitner
Displayer: Edith Cummings

SWEET AND SOURKRAUT CAKE

1/2 cup butter or margarine
1 1/2 cups sugar
3 eggs
1 teaspoon vanilla
2 cups sifted all purpose flour
1 teaspoon baking powder
1 teaspoon baking soda
1/4 teaspoon salt
1/2 cup cocoa powder
1 8 ounce can (1 cup) sourkraut (drained, rinsed, finely chopped)
1 cup water

In large mixing bowl, cream butter or margarine, and sugar
till light. Beat in eggs one at a time, add vanilla. Sift
together flour, baking powder, soda, salt and cocoa. Add to
creamed mixture alternately with water, beating after each
addition. Stir in kraut. Turn into greased and floured
13 x 9 x 2" baking pan. Bake at 350 degrees for 35-40 minutes.

Hostess: Bethany Fowler
Displayer: Sandra Hayes, Mgr.

****

I have just a minute...with sixty seconds in it...forced upon
me...can't refuse it...Didn't seek it...didn't choose it....
But...it's up to me to use it...I must suffer if I lose it...
Give account if I abuse it. Just a tiny little minute....But...
ETERNITY is in it.   Author unknown
From "Be Somebody" by Mary Crowley

****

DREAM CAKE

1 angel food cake, broken into pieces
2 packages Dream Whip
1 cup cold milk
1 cup confectioners sugar
1 8 ounce package cream cheese
1 can cherry pie filling

Beat Dream Whip and milk together. Add sugar, mix. Beat cream cheese until smooth. Add Dream Whip mixture to cream cheese a little at a time. Place layer of cake pieces in 13 x 9" pan, then layer of Dream Whip mixture, another layer of cake, then Dream Whip mixture. Put cherry pie filling on top and chill over night. Serves about 12.

Hostess: Connie Henry
Displayer: Linda Gordon

SOUR CREAM CAKE

1/2 cup wesson oil
1 cup butter
3 cups sugar
6 eggs
3 cups flour
1 cup sour cream
1 teaspoon vanilla
1 teaspoon baking powder
pinch of salt

Cream oil, butter, and sugar - add eggs one at a time. Add flour with sour cream to first mixture. Mix well. Add flavoring and bake one hour in greased tube pan at 350 degrees.

GLAZE:
1 cup confectioners sugar
2 tablespoons lemon juice or milk

Hostess: Faye Hoke
Displayer: Marie Keel

****

Where we are wrong, make us willing to change; and where we are right, make us easy to live with. Deliver us, we pray, from the tyranny of trifles. Teach us how to listen to the prompting of thy Spirit, and thus save us from floundering in indecision that wastes time, subtracts from our peace, divides our efficiency and multiplies our troubles.   Peter Marshall

****

POLKA DOT CAKE

3 cups flour
1 teaspoon vanilla
2 tablespoons white vinegar
2 cups sugar
1 teaspoon salt
1/2 cup cocoa
2 cups cold water
2 teaspoons baking soda
2/3 cup oil

Mix all dry ingredients, add liquids. Mix well. Pour into greased and floured pan, 13 x 9 x 2". Bake at 350 degrees for 45-60 minutes. Maybe needed to bake a little longer. But it is worth the time because this is a delicious cake.

TOPPING:
1 8 ounce package cream cheese
1 egg
1/3 cup sugar
1/2 teaspoon vanilla
1 6 ounce cup of chocolate bits
Combine and stir in chocolate bits last, drop by spoonsfull over the cake.

Hostess: Patricia Boyer
Displayer: Bessie Queen

LEMON CHEESE CAKE

FILLING:
2 8 ounce packages of cream cheese
1 6 ounce box of lemon jello
1 large can crushed pineapple
1 large Cool Whip
2 cups sugar

Make jello with 2 cups of very hot (but not boiling) water. Set aside to cool. Drain crushed pineapple. Cream together cheese and sugar. Add cooled jello and mix until well blended, add pineapple. Fold in Cool Whip. Pour into prepared crust.

CRUST:
2 1/2 sticks oleo, melted
2 packages graham crackers, crushed

Press 2/3 of mixture into bottom of oblong cake pan. Pour in cream cheese mixture. Sprinkle remaining graham cracker mixture on top. Chill well before serving. Can be made the day before.

Hostess: Virginia Roslonicc
Displayer: Doris Roper

MILNOT CHEESE CAKE

1   3 ounce package lemon jello
1 cup boiling water
1   8 ounce package cream cheese
1/2 cup sugar
1 teaspoon vanilla
1   13 ounce can of milnot
3 cups graham cracker crumbs
1/2 cup butter or margarine, melted

Dissolve gelatin in boiling water. Chill until slightly thickened.
Cream together cheese, sugar, and vanilla; Add gelatin and blend
well. Fold in stiffly whipped Milnot. (this can be done with
electric mixer.) Mix graham cracker crumbs and melted butter.
Pack 2/3 of mixture on bottom and sides of 9 x 13 x 2" pan, or
lager. Add filling and sprinkle with remaining crumbs. Chill
over night. Cut in squares and serve plain or garnish with fruit.
Serves 12-16.

Hostess: Lee and Mary Chorey
Displayer: Susie Haworth

PINEAPPLE CREAM CAKE

PINEAPPLE CREAM TOPPING:

1 large package lemon jello
1 1/2 cups boiling water
2 cans 8 1/2 ounces each crushed pineapple with juice
3 egg yolks
3/4 cup sifted powdered sugar
1 1/2 cups heavy cream

Dissolve jello in water. Add pineapple, chill till slightly
thickened. Beat egg yolks, gradually adding sugar. Beat
until thick and yellow colored. Whip cream. Folk in egg
mixture and cream into jello. Chill until of spreading
consistency.

Purchase or make an angel food cake. With a sharp knife, cut into
three even layers. Spread topping between layers and over top and
sides. Chill until ready to serve.

Hostess: Alberta Crowell
Displayer: Darlene Simpson

****

Judge not another - from your high and lofty seat, step down into
the arena, where he and his problems meet. "Be Somebody"

****

PISTACHIO INSIDE OUTSIDE CAKE

1 package (2 layer size) white or yellow cake mix
1 package Jello pistachio flavor instant pudding
3 eggs
1 cup club soda
1 cup oil
1/2 cup chopped nuts

Blend all ingredients. Bake in greased floured 10" bundt pan at
350 degrees for 50 minutes. Cool 15 minutes. Remove from pan
and cool. Split into 3 layers. Spread about 1 cup of frosting
between layers. Spoon rest into center. Chill, garnish with
chopped nuts.

FROSTING:
1 1/2 cups cold milk
1 envelope Dream Whip
1 package Jello pistachio flavor instant pudding

Blend ingredients together and whip until thickened. About 5 min.

Hostess: Susan Sherman
Displayer: Dodie Carpenter

PISTACHIO CAKE

1 large box of yellow cake mix
1 3 1/2 ounce box instant pistachio pudding
1 cup oil
1/2 pint sour cream
4 eggs
1/2 cup chopped nuts
1 tablespoon cinnamon
1 teaspoon nutmeg
1/2 cup sugar

Combine cake mix, pudding, oil, sour cream and add eggs in large
mixing bowl. (Combine well.) Pour 1/2 cake batter into greased
and floured 10" tube pan. Combine nuts, sugar and spice mixture
sprinkle 1/2 the nut mixture evenly over batter. Pour in remaining batter, top with remaining nut mixture. Press nut mixture into
batter with back of spoon. Bake at 350 degrees for 50-60 minutes.
Let cake cool at least 30 minutes before removing from pan.

Hostess: Maureen Fugate
Displayer: Agnes Avolicino

WATERGATE CAKE

1 box white cake mix
1 box instant Pistachio pudding
1 cup cooking oil
3 eggs
1 cup soda water
1/2 cup nuts

Mix the first five ingredients with electric mixer at medium speed
for 2 minutes. Fold in nuts. Pour in greased and floured tube
pan. Bake 45-55 minutes at 350 degrees.

FROSTING:
1 box pistachio pudding, instant
1 envelope Dream Whip
1 1/4 cups cold water

Mix according to directions on Dream Whip box.

Hostess: Vickie Ambrose
Displayer: Rita Brown

WATERGATE CAKE

1 box Duncan Hines Deluxe II cake mix
1 box pistachio instant pudding
3 eggs
1/2 cup chopped nuts
1 cup wesson oil
1 cup club soda

In large mixing bowl put cake and pudding mix, combine. Add other
ingredients. Beat 4 minutes. Grease and flour bundt pan. Bake
45 minutes-1 hour. Cool and ice.

ICING:
2 packages Dream Whip
1 1/4 cups milk
Beat til stiff. Then add:
1 box pistachio pudding mix (instant)
Garnish with: coconut, chopped nuts, and cherries

Displayer: Linda Abel

Watergate Cake recipes also sent in by:

Hostesses: Judy Griffin, Kathy Parbel, Lillie Mae Keener,
            and Metta Rae Biehler
Displayers: Linda Case, Judy Braun, Sylvie Petry, and Cher Adams

17

JELLO-PUDDING CAKE

1 box yellow cake mix
1 small package strawberry jello
1 10 ounce strawberry soft drink
1 medium container Cool Whip
2 cups cold milk
1 large box vanilla pudding, instant

Bake cake in one layer in oblong pan. Let cool and pierce with
fork. Mix jello with 1 cup hot water, and strawberry pop. Pour
over cake. Mix Cool Whip, 2 cups milk, and vanilla pudding
together and pour over cake. Let stand in ice box for about
2 hours.

Hostess: Sylvia Verdin
Displayer: Pam Ortego

VANILLA WAFER CAKE

1 box vanilla wafers (12 oz)
6 eggs
1 cup chopped nuts (walnuts)
1 teaspoon vanilla
1 package angel coconut (7 ounce)
1 1/4 cups sugar
1 stick margarine
1 cup milk

Crush vanilla wafers into fine crumbs. Add eggs and vanilla.
Beat in sugar until smooth. Add walnuts and coconut. Bake at
350 degrees for 45 minutes. Serve with whipped cream or plain.

Hostess: Jackie Hacketts
Displayer: Mary Stockard

****

God knows YOU by name....
God never mistakes you in the crowd.
When a person fully realizes how much he or she matters to God -
then he doesn't have to go out and prove to the world how much
he matters.
From "Be Somebody" by Mary Crowley.
****

PINEAPPLE - COCONUT CAKE

1 box of Duncan Hines Pineapple Supreme Cake Mix
1 box Pineapple Instant Pudding Mix
4 eggs
1/2 cup Wesson oil
1 10 ounce bottle 7-Up

Mix cake, pudding mix, add eggs, oil and 7-Up. Mix well.
Bake in three 9" layer pans or four 8" pans. Bake at 325
degrees 20-25 minutes. Ice while warm.

ICING:

2 tablespoons flour
1 1/2 cup sugar
1 stick oleo
large can crushed pineapple
2 eggs, well beaten
1 can coconut

Melt oleo, add sugar, flour and pineapple. Add eggs, cook til
thick. Add coconut. Put between layers and on top of cake
while still hot.

Hostess: Dollie Clary
Displayer: Margee Duke

COCONUT CAKE

2 packages frozen coconut
8 ounces sour cream
2 cups sugar

Mix well and set in refrigerator over night.
Make butter cake in 3 pans and ice them with the icing. Wrap
in foil or cover and let set 3 days, if possible.

Hostess: Nellie Smith
Displayer: Sandy Webb

****

WORRY......

is a mis-use of the imagination.
is assuming responsibility that God never intended you to have.
never robs tomorrow of its sorrow.
only saps today of its strength.
From "Be Somebody" by Mary Crowley
****

FAMILY FAVORITES

FRESH APPLE CAKE

2 cups sugar
2 eggs
1 1/2 cups oil
2 teaspoons vanilla
3 cups chopped and peeled apples
3 cups flour
1 teaspoon cinnamon
1 teaspoon soda
1/2 teaspoon salt

Blend sugar, eggs, vanilla, and oil. Sift dry ingredients together and blend with sugar mixture. Add chopped apples. Pour into greased, floured pan and bake 1 hour or until done at 350 degrees. The cake mixture will be very thick, almost like paste, however, the result is a very moist, delicious cake. You may add a whipped cream topping if desired.

Hostess: Judy Keller
Displayer: Nancy Horst

DUMP CAKE

1 number 2 can crushed pineapple
1 can instant cherry pie filling
1 box yellow cake mix
1 cup chopped pecans
1 stick margarine

Spread the pineapple, juice included, in a 13 x 9" pan. Next spoon the cherry filling on top and sprinkle the dry cake mix over this. Spread the pecans over all and dot top with margarine. Do NOT stir any of the ingredients. Bake at 350 degrees for 1 hour.

Hostesses:Joy Skinner and Susan Bahner
Displayers: Eleanor Sheehe and Linda Gordon

DELICIOUS DUMP CAKE

1 can cherry pie filling
1 can crushed pineapple
1 two layer white cake mix
1 stick margarine

Mix pie filling and pineapple together and pour in a buttered 9 x 12" pan. Sprinkle with cake mix. Dab margarine over top. Bake at 350 degrees until golden brown. Serve warm with whipped topping.

Hostess: Bea Fiala
Displayer: Frances Burger

RAW APPLE CAKE

1/2 cup butter
1 cup sugar
2 cups chopped apples
2 cups flour
1/2 teaspoon salt
1 teaspoon cinnamon
1/4 teaspoon nutmeg
1 cup raisins
1 cup nuts
1 teaspoon soda
1 tablespoon hot water
1 egg

Cream butter and sugar, add the egg, then the apples. Dissolve
the soda in hot water and add to apples. Sift flour with salt,
nutmeg and cinnamon. Mix the raisins and nuts in the flour mixture and add to apple mixture. Stir well and bake in a 9 x 12"
pan at 350 degrees, til done.

Hostess: Velma Kugler
Displayer: Carolyn Olson

APPLE CAKE

1 cup cooking oil
2 cups sugar
3 eggs
2 cups self-rising flour
3 cups chopped fresh apples
1 teaspoon vanilla
1 cup pecans or black walnuts
1/2 cup raisins (optional)
1 teaspoon cinnamon
1 teaspoon nutmeg

Combine oil, sugar and eggs. Beat well. Add flour, beat
throughly, and add remaining ingredients. Stir to blend
well (be sure to flour nuts.) Pour into greased 11 x 7 x2 or
8 x 8x2 pan. Bake at 350 degrees for 40-45 minutes

ICING OR TOPPING:

1 cup sugar
1 tablespoon white syrup
1 teaspoon vanilla
1 stick margarine
1/2 cup buttermilk
1/2 teaspoon soda

Cook over medium heat to soft ball, and add vanilla last.
Remove from heat and beat until slightly thickened. Pour
over cake.

Hostess: Linda Guill

22

MARSHA'S PARTY APPLE CAKE

2 eggs
2 cups sugar
2 teaspoons baking soda
1/8 teaspoon vanilla
2 teaspoons cinnamon
1 teaspoon vanilla
4 cups diced apples
2 cups flour
1/2 cup cooking oil
1 cup chopped walnuts

Beat eggs, add sugar and cream well. Add vanilla. Sift together flour, soda, salt, and cinnamon. Add alternately with oil. Stir in apples and nuts. Pour mixture in 15 x 9 x 21 1/2 pan, which has been greased. Bake at 350 degrees for 1 hour. Cool and frost.

CREAM CHEESE FROSTING
1 1/2 cups powdered sugar
6 ounces cream cheese
3 tablespoons butter
1/2 teaspoon vanilla
pinch of salt
chopped nuts

Mix cream cheese and butter till it blends easily. Sift in powdered sugar; add vanilla and salt. Blend, spread on cake. Top with nuts, if desired.

Hostess: Marsha Sisneros
Displayer: Glenda Engman

INDIAN APPLE CAKE

1 cup shortening
1 1/2 cup brown sugar
2 eggs
2 cups flour
1 teaspoon baking soda
1 teaspoon baking powder
2 teaspoons cinnamon
2 medium apples, diced (reserve 2-3 tablespoons for topping)
1 cup buttermilk

Mix shortening and sugar, add eggs, sift in dry ingredients; add 1 cup buttermilk, then add apples. Place in 9 x 13 greased pan. Place topping on and bake 40-45 minutes at 350 degrees.
TOPPING:
1/2 cup brown sugar
1/2 cup chopped nuts
1/2 teaspoon cinnamon and reserved apples
Hostess: Colleen Tolle
Displayer: Connie Sordahl

FRESH APPLE CAKE

4 cups chopped apples
2 1/2 cups sugar
1/2 cups water (mix well together - liquid for cake)

1 cup melted butter
2 eggs
3 cups flour (mix)
Pour all together and mix

1 teaspoon soda
1/2 teaspoon salt
4 teaspoons cinnamon
2 teaspoons nutmeg
4 teaspoons allspice
2 cups chopped nuts (pecans) more if desired
2 cups raisins (light raisins)
Blend well.
Bake 300 degrees for 1 1/2 hours or until done. Most of the time
it takes 2 hours.

CARAMEL FROSTING:

2 cups light brown sugar
1 stick of butter
2/3 cup of milk or cream

Bring to boil for 1 minute, stir in
3 cups powdered sugar or enough to thicken.
People use this cake also at Christmas instead of fruit cakes,
it stays moist and is better 2 or 3 days later.

Hostess: Sharon Cobb
Displayer: Cora Holland

APPLE NUT CAKE

2 cups sugar
2 eggs
1/2 cup Mazola oil
2 cups flour
2 teaspoons soda
1/4 teaspoon salt
1 teaspoon vanilla
2 teaspoons cinnamon
3 cups chopped apples (Jonathan)
1 cup nuts
Bake 45 minutes at 350 degrees in a 9 x 13" pan, greased.
ICING:
1 1/2 cups powdered sugar
6 ounces cream cheese
2 tablespoons butter
salt
vanilla
Do Not Cover Cake.
Hostess: Genevieve Bowers
Displayer: Bonnie Laux

FRESH APPLE CAKE

1 1/4 cups oil
2 cups sugar
2 eggs
1 teaspoon vanilla flavoring
1/2 teaspoon black walnut flavoring
4-5 cups chopped apples
1 cup chopped walnuts
3 cups flour
1 teaspoon soda
1 teaspoon salt
1 1/2 teaspoon cinnamon

Mix together the oil, sugar, eggs and flavorings. Add the
chopped apples and chopped nuts. Stir in the flour, soda,
salt and cinnamon. Spread in ungreased 9 x 13" pan. Bake
for 1 hour and 15 minutes at 300 degrees.

TOPPING:
1 cup sugar
1/2 cup buttermilk
1/2 teaspoon soda
1 teaspoon dark corn syrup
1 stick margarine
1 teaspoon vanilla flavoring
Dash of salt

Combine all ingredients and cook for 10 minutes, stirring
occasionally. Pour over warm cake.

Hostess: Melody Nuesch
Displayer: Margaret Nuesch

APPLE CHIP CAKE

3 eggs
1 3/4 cups sugar
3/4 cup oil
1 cup nuts, Pecans or English walnuts
Mix first three ingredients well, then add nuts, then add:
2 cups flour
1 teaspoon soda
1 teaspoon cinnamon
1 teaspoon salt
1 teaspoon vanilla
2 cups chopped or grated apples

Bake in a 9 x 10" pan at 375 degrees until done, 25 minutes.
Top with whipped cream or ice cream. This is delicious without
a topping.

Hostess: Sandy Mattern
Displayer: Wanda A. Fowles

Apple Cake recipes also sent in by Donna Schneider, Sue Chandler,
and Ann Sorrell. Displayer: Jeneva W. Connor.

BEEFSTEAK CAKE*

THREE WHITE LAYERS:
2 cups sugar
1 cup butter (2 sticks)
Cream together.

3 cups plain flour
1 teaspoon baking powder
Sift together.
1 cup milk
1 teaspoon vanilla flavoring
6 beaten egg whites

Add flour mixture to sugar mixture, alternating with milk. Add
vanilla then fold in egg whites. Bake in three 9" round pans
at 350 degrees 25-30 minutes, or until done.

THREE DARK LAYERS:
2 cups sugar
1 cup butter
Cream together.
3 cups flour
1 teaspoon baking powder
1 teaspoon cinnamon
1 teaspoon allspice
1 teaspoon nutmeg
Sift together.
1 cup milk
1 box raisins
6 beaten egg yolks

Add flour mixture to sugar mixture, alternating with milk.
Add raisins, fold in egg yolks. Bake in three 9" round pans
at 350 degrees, 25-30 minutes or until done.

LAYER FILLING:
2 cups sugar
1 cup flour
Mix together and add:
3 cups boiling water
Boil til thick as starch and add:
2 grated coconuts
Flavor with vanilla as desired.

SEVEN MINUTE FROSTING:
2 unbeaten egg whites
1 1/2 cups sugar
5 tablespoons water
1 1/2 teaspoon corn syrup
Combine in top of double boiler. Beat until thoroughly mixed.
Place over boiling water, beating constantly. Cook 7 minutes or
until frosting will stand in peaks. Remove from heat. Add:
1 teaspoon vanilla
and beat until thick enough to spread.
*This recipe has been handed down 4 generations of Fay's family.
Her great-grandmother once declared it was "good as any beefsteak"
and the name just hung on.
Hostess: Fay Bownan
Displayer: Mardean DeShazo

CINNAMON TWIST POUND CAKE

2 1/2 cups flour
2 cups sugar
1/2 teaspoon soda
1/2 teaspoon salt
1 teaspoon vanilla
1 cup soft margarine (2 cubes)
3 eggs

Combine all the ingredients in a large bowl. Blend 3 minutes at
medium speed. Pour half the batter into a greased and floured
bundt ban. Put Twist topping (sprinkled) over the batter and add
remaining batter. Bake at 325 degrees for 55-65 minutes. After
cooling one hour, pour over glaze and sprinkle with nuts.

TWIST TOPPING:
2 teaspoons cinnamon
4 tablespoons brown sugar
1/2 cup nuts
GLAZE:
1 cup powdered sugar
1 tablespoon lemon juice

Hostess: Carol Ruiz
Displayer: June Lackey

****

Peoples minds are changed through observation, not through
arguement.   Will Rogers
****

CHOCOLATE CRAZY CAKE

2 cups sugar
3 cups flour
1/3 cup cocoa
1 teaspoon salt
2 teaspoons baking soda
Mix together and add:
1 teaspoon vanilla
2 tablespoons vinegar
3/4 cup oil
2 cups cold water
Mix but do not beat. Bake in 350 degree oven for 35 minutes.
Use a 9 x 13" pan.

Hostess: Bonnie Dehne
Displayer: Marge Fritsche

LOW CALORIE CHEESECAKE

2 envelopes unflavored gelatin
3/4 cup sugar
1/4 teaspoon salt
2 medium eggs seperated
1 cup skim milk
1 teaspoon grated lemon rind
3 cups small curd cottage cheese
1 tablespoon lemon juice
1 teaspoon vanilla
1/2 cup ice cold water
1/2 cup nonfat dry milk
1/3 cup graham cracker crumbs
1/8 teaspoon cinnamon
1/8 teaspoon nutmeg

Mix gelatin, sugar and salt in top of double boiler. Beat egg yolks
and skim milk; add to gelatin mixture. Cook, stirring constantly,
until gelatin is thoroughly dissolved. Remove from heat; add lemon
rind. Cool. Sieve cottage cheese; stir into gelatin mixture. Add
lemon juice and vanilla. Chill, stirring occasionally, until mixture
mounds slightly when dropped from spoon. Beat egg whites stiffly;
fold into gelatin mixture. Beat water and dry milk until stiff and
mixture stands in peaks; fold into gelatin mixture. Turn into 8"
pan. Spread top with mixture of graham cracker crumbs, cinnamon,
and nutmeg. Chill until firm. Yield: 6 servings.

Mrs. Francis O'Neal
Pilot Club Cookbook

****

MIXING MAGIC

There are two commonly used methods for making cakes; the Creaming
method and the Quick method.

CREAMING METHOD: In this method the shortening, sugar, eggs, and
salt are creamed or blended together until light and smooth. Then
the dry ingredients and liquid are added alternately and blended
until smooth. Most of the old-time favorate cake recipes are made
by this method.

QUICK METHOD: The shortening, dry ingredients and part of the
liquid are mixed for two minutes, then the eggs and remaining
liquid are added and mixed for two more minutes. This is a
modern method and takes advantage of today's improved products.

The special properties of a top quality vegetable shortening
make it possible to bake excellent cakes by either method.

CHRISTMAS APPLESAUCE CAKE

1 1/2 cups sugar
1 teaspoon cinnamon
1/2 teaspoon nutmeg
1/2 teaspoon clove
2 cups plain flour
2 teaspoons soda
Pinch salt
3 eggs
1 1/2 cups applesauce
1/2 cup dates
1/2 cup chopped nuts
1/2 cup butter
Cream butter and sugar, then add eggs one at a time. Sift dry
ingredients together, reserving a little flour to put over dates
and nuts. Add applesauce, nuts, dates and last, the dry ingredients to the sugar mixture. Bake in 2 layers, 30 minutes at 375
degrees. Spread fruit filling between layers after layers have
cooled.

FRUIT FILLING:
1/4 cup water
1 tablespoon sugar
2 tablespoons flour
2 tablespoons butter
3 tablespoons dates
2 tablespoons chopped nuts
3 tablespoons raisins
Mix all ingredients, cook until thick.

CARAMEL ICING:
1 cup brown sugar
1 cup white sugar
3/4 cup evaporated milk
1/2 stick butter

Combine sugar and milk. Cook to soft ball stage. Remove
from heat and add butter. Let stand till cool and then beat
to spreading consistency. Note: This cake may be filled,
frosted, and frozen weeks ahead.

Hostess: Ruth Roberts
Displayer: Loretta Humphries

****

Real joy comes not from ease or riches or from the praise
of men, but from doing something worthwhile. Sir Winfred Grenfell.

****

29

STRAWBERRY JELLO CAKE

1 cup minature marshmellows
2 10 ounce frozen sliced strawberries in syrup
1 3 ounce package strawberry jello
2 1/4 cups flour
1 1/2 cups sugar
1/2 cup shortening
3 teaspoons baking powder
1/2 teaspoon salt
1 cup milk
1 teaspoon vanilla
3 eggs

Grease a 9 x 13 pan, sprinkle marshmellow over bottom of pan.
Set aside. Combine strawberries and syrup with dry jello. Mix
and set aside. Combine remaining ingredients, beat until moistened
Beat for 5 minutes. Pour over Marshmellows. Then spoon berry
mixture over batter and bake in 350 degree oven for 45-50 minutes.

Hostess: Doris Dyer
Displayer: Sarah Cumens

KENTUCKY STACK CAKE

3/4 cup shortening or butter
1 cup sugar
1 cup molasses
1 cup buttermilk
4 cups all purpose flour
3 eggs
1 teaspoon soda
1/2 teaspoon salt
2 teaspoons baking powder
1/2 teaspoon of any spices, use at least 2-3 kinds, cinnamon,
   colves, alspice, nutmeg or any other you like.
lemon
vanilla
3 cups thick applesauce for filling, make the sauce from dried
    apples if you have them (sweetened and spiced)
Cream shortening and sugar, blend well and blend in molasses and
stir real good. Add eggs 1 at a time, stiring well after each.
Add milk alternately with sifted dry ingredients. The mixture
will be stiff. Divide into six balls. Place each one in 8"
cake pan, pat out to fill pan (I flour my hands to do this.)
Bake at 350 degrees for 18 minutes, when cool stack layers with
applesauce. Can be iced with favorite icing.

Displayer: Mae Mitchell

****
Our opinions become fixed at the point we stop thinking.
Joseph Ernest Renan.
****

ANGEL FOOD SURPRISE

1 Angel food cake and pan
1 large package Jello (any flavor)
2 cups drained fruit (reserve 2 cups juice for later)
1 package Dream Whip

First dissolve Jello in a bowl with 2 cups hot water. Add
fruit and remaining juice with part water to make 2 cups. Pour
into angel food cake pan, place angel food cake upside down in
Jello mixture. Cake will float,put heavy mugs on cake to hold
in down into pan. Let set in refrigerator untill firm. Remove
cake from tin onto plate and frost with Dream Whip. Variations:
Strawberry Jello and Strawberries. Orange Jello and Crushed
Pineapple. Black Cherry with cherries. Fruit Cocktail can
also be used.

Hostess: Martha Bendall
Displayer: Suzanne Briggs

FRUITED INTERIOR CAKE

1 large size sponge or angel food cake
1 large size can of fruit cocktail (drained)
1 large bowl of Cool Whip (or equivalent)

Fruit cocktail should be cold before using. Drain off juice and
mix in large bowl with Cool Whip. Slice cake in half (round)
to make 2 equal layers. Spread fruited mixture over bottom layer
about 1/4" thick and add top layer. Fill the "interior" of cake
with mixture and spread over the top of cake making a lush topping.
Keep refrigerated until ready to serve. Makes 12 servings for
"Home Interior Show" guests.

Hostess: Carolyn Drawdy
Displayer: Doris Weaver

****

Let me be a little kinder, let me be a little blinder
To the faults of those about me; let me praise a little more.
Let me be, when I am weary, just a little bit more cheery;
Let me serve a little better those that I am striving for;
Let me be a little braver, when temptation bids me waver;
Let me strive a little harder to be all that I should be;
Let me be a little meeker with the brother that is weaker;
Let me think more of my neighbor and a little less of me.

****

STRAWBERRY DELIGHT

1 small box frozen strawberries
1 large box white cake mix
1 large box white frosting mix

Thaw strawberries, drain off liquid and save. Mix cake according
to directions on box, stir in strawberries. Pour into pans and
bake according to directions on box. Mix frosting according to
directions on box, substituting liquid from strawberries for
water. Frost cake when cool and garnish with strawberries if
desired.

Hostess: Linda Maroney
Displayer: Mica Lego

STRAWBERRY ANGLEFOOD CAKE

2 cups crushed fresh strawberries
1 large angelfood cake from bakery
1 large Cool Whip topping
1 package Knox gelatin
1 tablespoon cold water
1/2 cup boiling water
1 cup sugar

Crush strawberries; add sugar. Dissolve Knox gelatin with cold
water and add boiling water to gelatin. Mix with strawberries
and let thicken in refrigerator about 30 minutes. While mixture
is setting, cube angelcake into 1 inch cubes and set aside.
Blend 1/2 the cool whip with thickened strawberries. Line
9 x 9" pan with waxed paper. Put layer of cake cubes and
then one of strawberries, alternating each, but ending with
cake on top. Put waxed paper on top of cake layer. Then
place another pan of about the same size on top of waxed paper
and weight it down with something heavy (a full milk carton or
the equivalent.) This blends the layers together. Refrigerate
for 2 hours, then pull off top waxed paper and turn out on a
serving plate. Pull off the other waxed paper and frost with
the remaining cool whip. Cut in squares and serve.

Hostess: Rolanda Allgood
Displayer: Claudia Rooker

****

Man's mind stretched by a new idea never goes back to its
original deminsions. Oliver Wendell Holmes.

****

JEWISH APPLE CAKE

In one bowl combine:
3 cups flour
2 1/2 cups sugar
1 cup cooking oil
4 eggs
1/2 teaspoon salt
1/3 cup orange juice
2 1/2 teaspoons vanilla
3 teaspoons baking powder

In another bowl combine:
6 apples, chopped
2 teaspoons cinnamon
3 tablespoons sugar
(If you add more apples, add more sugar and cinnamon)

Use greased and floured tube pan. Layer batter, then apples, etc. Bake 1 1/2 hours to 2 hours, until done, in preheated 350 degree oven.

Displayer: Linda S. Abel

APPLESAUCE BUNDT CAKE

1 package yellow cake mix
1 package instant vanilla pudding mix
4 eggs
1 teaspoon vanilla
3/4 cup cooking oil
3/4 cup water
1/3 cup applesauce
Combine above ingredients. Beat with electric mixer for 9 minutes.

SUGAR MIXTURE: ICING:
1/2 cup chopped nuts   Powdered sugar
1 teaspoon cinnamon
1/4 cup sugar
Combine above ingredients.
Preheat oven to 350 degrees. Grease and flour 9" bundt pan. In bottom of pan spread 1/3 of the batter then sprinkle 1/2 sugar mixture on top. Add another 1/3 of batter and add remaining sugar mixture. Add remaining 1/3 batter. Bake for 50 minutes. Let cake cool for 15 minutes and remove from pan. Drizzle with powdered sugar icing.

Hostess: Billie Leader
Displayer: Marilyn Kathol

BANANA SPLIT CAKE

2 cups crumbled graham cracker crumbs
1 stick melted butter
Mix above ingredients and smash in bottom of pan, bake at 350
degrees for 5 minutes, cool throughly.
2 sticks margarine
2 eggs
1 box powdered sugar
Whip above ingredients until fluffy. Spread over other mix.
7 bananas
1 large can crushed pineapple, drained
1 medium carton Cool Whip
Slice bananas lenthwise, Lay bananas on crust mixture and put
pineapple on bananas. Top with Cool Whip. Use 9 x 12" pan.

Displayer: Esther Graham

BANANA SPLIT CAKE

1 stick of margarine (melted)
2 cups of graham crackers (crushed)
Place into bottom of 9 x 13" pan
2 eggs
2 sticks margarine (melted)
2 cups of powdered sugar
Beat the above 3 ingredients for 15 minutes. Spread over the
graham cracker crumbs.
3-5 bananas
1 can (20 ounces) crushed pineapple (well drained)
2 cups of whipped cream
1/2 cup maraschino cherries
3/4 cup chopped nuts

Slice bananas and put over top of sugar mixture. Put pineapple
over bananas. Put whipped cream over the pineapple. Place
cherries and nuts over the whipped cream.

Hostess: Elaine Schwarting
Displayer: Margaret L Muesch

****

Nothing is more efficient than honesty; those who break the
law or abuse the basic moral code in the name of profit, are
doing more to make "profit" a dirty word than all of the critics
of the free-enterprise system put together. William Simon.

****

BANANA BREAD

1 cup sugar
1/2 cup margarine
2 eggs beaten
2 cups flour
1/2 teaspoon salt
1 teaspoon soda
3 bananas mashed
1/2 cup chopped nuts

Beat eggs well. Cream sugar and margarine. Add to eggs and stir.
Sift flour, salt, and soda. Add to creamed mixture. Beat in
bananas, stir in chopped nuts. Bake in large loaf pan at 350
degrees for 40-45 minutes.

Hostess: Margaret Ironthunder
Displayer: Marilyn Kathol

BANANA NUT BREAD

1 3/4 cups flour, sifted
1 1/4 teaspoon baking powder
1/2 teaspoon soda
1/3 cup shortening
2/3 cup sugar
2 eggs
1 cup mashed bananas
1/2 cup chopped walnuts
3/4 teaspoon salt

Sift flour, baking powder, soda, salt, cream shortening, and
sugar thoroughly. Add eggs one at a time; beat well. Add dry
ingredients alternately with mashed bananas. Stir just enough
to blend. Do not beat. Add nuts with last addition of flour.
Put batter into an oiled loaf pan. Bake at 350 degrees, 1 hour.

Hostess Carol Horine

****

"Fret not thyself because of evildoers, neither be thou
envious against the workers of iniquity.
For they shall soon be cut down like the grass, and wither
as the green herb.
Trust in the Lord, and do good; so shalt thou dwell in the
land, and verily thou shalt be fed.
Delight thyself also in the Lord; and he shall give thee the
desires of thine heart.
Commit thy way unto the Lord; trust also in him; and he shall
bring it to pass"   Psalm 37:1,5.

 Mary Crowley's pattern for living. Taken from "Be Somebody"

****

PINEAPPLE CAKE AND TOPPING

1 teaspoon vanilla
2 cups flour
2 teaspoons baking soda
2 eggs
2 cups sugar
1/2 cup water
1 #2 can crushed pineapple and juice

Mix first 6 ingredients well. Fold in pineapple and juice.
Grease and flour pan. Bake at 350 degrees, 25-30 minutes.

TOPPING:
1 stick butter
1 package 8 ounce cream cheese
1 cup powdered sugar
1 teaspoon vanilla

Cream well. Spoon over cake right out of oven.

Hostess: Bea Kirchinger
Displayer: Ruth Young

PINEAPPLE SURPRISE

1 box Washington Cake Mix
2 packages instant vanilla pudding
Mix each according to package directions
8 ounce package cream cheese, softened
1 large can crushed pineapple, drained
1 large box Dream Whip, mix according to directions
Slivered almonds

Put thin layer of cake mix in 13 x 9 x 2" pan (you might not use
it all) Bake and cool. Cream together pudding and cream cheese.
Refrigerate 1 hour. Layer onto cooled cake, pudding mixture, then
pineapple, then dream whip. Top with nuts and refrigerate til used.

Hostess: Linda Abel

****
True strength does not depend on the size of one's biceps. It
is related to a sense of purpose, the ability to think, and
analyze, and the proper respect for human response.
****

CARROT CAKE

2 cups sugar
1 1/2 cup oil
4 eggs
2 cups flour
2 teaspoons soda
1 teaspoon salt
2 teaspoons cinnamon
3 cups finely grated carrots
1/2 cup shredded coconut
3/4 cup chopped nuts

Mix sugar, oil and eggs until thoroughly blended. Sift togehter flour, soda, salt and cinnamon. Add to first mixture and beat till smooth. Stir in carrots, coconut and nuts. Pour into greased 13 x 9 1/2 x 2" pan. Bake at 325 for 55 minutes.

FROSTING:
1 3 ounce package of cream cheese
1 3/4 cups sifted powdered sugar
1/4 cup butter
1 teaspoon vanilla
Combine ingredients, mix until smooth.

Hostess: Gayle McMasters

PINEAPPLE UPSIDE DOWN CAKE

1/3 cup butter
1/2 cup brown sugar (packed)
8 pineapple rings
8 maraschino cherries
1/3 cup pecan halves
2 eggs
2/3 cup sugar
6 tablespoon pineapple juice
1 teaspoon vanilla
1 cup sifted enriched flour
1/3 teaspoon baking powder
1/4 teaspoon salt

Melt butter in a heavy 10 inch skillet. Evenly spread the brown sugar over the butter and arrange pineapple over the brown sugar butter mixture. Center each pineapple ring with a maraschino cherry and arrange pecan halves between the rings. Beat eggs until thick and lemon colored. Beat in sugar gradually, then beat in pineapple juice and vanilla. Sift together and beat in flour, baking powder, and salt. Pour batter over pineapple rings in skillet. Bake in moderate oven for 45 minutes at 350 degrees. Immediately turn upside down on serving plate.

Hostess: Jean Wilson
Displayer: Rama Howard

BROWN SUGAR POUND CAKE

3 sticks butter
1 pound light brown sugar
1/2 cup white sugar
5 eggs
2 teaspoons vanilla
3 cups flour
1/2 teaspoon baking powder
1 cup milk

Cream butter and sugars thoroughly. Add eggs 1 at a time, beating
at medium speed. Add flavoring. Sift dry ingredients together;
add to creamed mixture alternately with milk. Mix well. Place
in large tube pan. Bake at 325 degrees 1 hour and 30 minutes.

Hostess: Mrs. Rosa Garner
Displayer: Rita Brown

COLD OVEN POUND CAKE

1/2 cup crisco
1 stick margarine
3 cups plain flour
3 cups sugar
1/2 teaspoon baking powder
5 eggs
1 cup milk
1 teaspoon vanilla
1 teaspoon butternut flavoring
Sift flour and baking powder well. Cream sugar and crisco well.
Add melted margarine (let cool) Add 1 egg at a time, beat after
each. Add milk, flour and flavoring alternately, beat 10 minutes.
Pour into greased and floured bunt or tube pan. Put in cold oven
and turn heat to 350 degrees and bake 1 hour and 15 minutes.

Hostess: Mary Ruth Cox
Displayer: Loretta Humphries

****
The Lord is my Shepherd - Perfect Salvation.
I shall not want - Perfect Satisfaction.
He maketh me to lie in green pastures - Perfect Rest.
He leadeth me beside still waters - Perfect Refreshment.
He restoreth my soul - Perfect Restoration.
He leadeth me in the paths of righteousness - Perfect Guidance.
I will fear no evil - Perfect Protection.
Thou art with me - Perfect Company.
Thy rod and Thy staff - Perfect Comfort
Thou preparest a table - Perfect Provision.
Thou anointest my head - Perfect Consecration.
My cup runneth over - Perfect Joy.
Surely, surely - Perfect Confidence.
Goodness and mercy shall follow me - Perfect Care.
I will dwell in the House of the Lord forever - Perfect Destiny.

38

POUND CAKE

3 sticks butter
1 pound box powdered sugar
1 pound box Swan Down Cake Flour
6 eggs
1 1/2 teaspoon butter flavor

Preheat oven to 350 degrees. Cream butter until creamy. Add
sugar and flavor. Add eggs one at a time. Beat until smooth
and creamy. Pour batter in a greased and floured bundt pan.
Bake for 1 1/2 hours.

Hostess: C. L. Daniels
Displayer: Izella Allen

POLISH POUND CAKE

2 sticks butter or oleo
1/2 cup crisco
3 cups white sugar
2 tablespoons of flavoring (vanilla, butternut, or nutmeg)
5 large eggs
3 cups flour
1/2 teaspoon salt
1 cup chopped nuts
1 10 ounce jar of maraschino cherries, drained and cut up
1 small can carnation milk

Beat butter and crisco until fluffy, add sugar, 1 cup at a time
and beat well. Add flavoring and salt, eggs one at a time. beat
after each egg. Add flour and milk, alternating with flour ending.
Fold in nuts and cherries. Grease and flour angel food cake pan
Put in cold oven, turn heat to 300 degrees. Bake 2 1/2 hours.
Do NOT open oven before 2 hours.

Hostess: Peggy Marosy
Polish Pound Cake recipe also sent in by Vicki Ambrose, displayer:
Rita Brown.

****

You cannot push anyone up the ladder unless he is willing
to climb himself.   Andrew Carnegie.

****

APRICOT NECTAR CAKE

3/4 cup apricot nectar
3/4 cup oil
yellow cake mix
4 eggs
1 package lemon jello
1 teaspoon vanilla
1 teaspoon lemon extract

Mix well and bake in angel food pan for 35 minutes at 350 degrees.

ICING:
1/4 cup lemon juice
1 cup powdered sugar
Mix well and pour over cake that has been pierced so that icing may be absorbed.

Hostess: Maida Godwin
Manager: Marty Rickman

CRUMB CAKE

2 cups sugar
2 cups flour
2 cubes (1 cup) butter or margarine
Save 1 cup for crumbs. Add:
3 eggs
1 cup nuts
1 cup buttermilk
1/2 teaspoon salt
1 teaspoon vanilla
1 teaspoon soda

Beat and pour in 13x 9" pan. Cover with crumbs. Bake 40 minutes at 350 degrees.

Hostess: Mollie Hauf
Displayer: Ellen Heinze

****

Take time to think...it is the price of success.
Take time to read...it is the fountain of wisdom.
Take time to be friendly... it is the road to happiness.
Take time to laugh...it is the music of the soul.
Take time to give...it is too short a day to be selfish.
Take time to play...it is the secret to eternal youth.
Take time to love..and be loved..it is a God given privilege.
Take time to pray...it is because of God that you are here.

★★★★★★★★★★★★★★★★★

OATMEAL CAKE

1 1/4 cups boiling water
1 stick butter
1 cup quick oats, instant
Mix and heat until butter melts

1 cup brown sugar
1 cup white sugar
2 eggs
1 1/2 cups flour
1 teaspoon soda
1 teaspoon baking powder
1/2 teaspoon salt
1 teaspoon cinnamon
1 teaspoon vanilla

Bake at 350 degrees for 30-35 minutes in a 13 x 9 x 2" pan.

ICING:
1 cup brown sugar
1/2 cup canned milk
4 tablespoons butter
1 cup coconut
Mix and spread on hot cake. Broil until bubbly.
Hostess: Joyce Challis
Displayer: Bernie Lorraine

THREE LAYER CAKE

1 cup flour
1/2 cup margarine
1/2 cup nuts
Press into 9 x 13" pan. Bake 15 minutes at 350 degrees. Cool.
1 8 ounce package cream cheese
1 cup powdered sugar
1 cup Pet Whip
Cream together, and place on top of first layer.
2 packages Lemon Instant Pudding
3 cups milk
Combine and beat until thick. Place on top of second layer.
Top the last layer with Pet Whip. Make the day before and
refrigerate.

Hostess: Arlou Ripplemeyer

****
One of the best things about being a woman is I don't have to go
out into the world and prove I'm a man....I speak from a full cup..
I am deeply glad I am a woman. I do not feel complimented when
men say I think like a man.....I don't think like a man........
I think like me.   Mary C. Crowley. from "Be Somebody"

****

ZUCCHINI CAKE

1/2 cup margarine
1/2 cup oil
1/3 cup sugar
Cream together above ingredients.

ADD:
2 eggs
1 teaspoon vanilla
1/2 cup sour milk
4 tablespoons cocoa
2 1/2 cups unsifted flour
1/2 teaspoon baking powder
1 teaspoon soda
1 teaspoon salt
2 cups grated zucchini, stirred in last.

Pour mixture into 9 x 13" greased pan. Sprinkle 1/2 cup chocolate chips on top and bake at 325 degrees for approximately 50 minutes.

Hostess: Joyce Koertje
Displayer: Marilyn Kathol

ZUCCHINI CAKE

3 cups flour
3 cups granulated sugar
1 teaspoon salt
1 1/2 teaspoon soda
1 teaspoon baking powder
2 1/2 teaspoons cinnamon
1 teaspoon vanilla flavoring
4 eggs
1 1/2 cups cooking oil
3 cups of grated squash

Mix together in a bowl, thoroughly. Add 1 cup chopped nuts. Stir and pour into a greased and floured 13 x 9" pan, or three 9" round pans, or four 8 x 8" pans. Bake at 325 degrees, approximately 35 minutes according to pan size used.

FROSTING:
1 8 ounce package Philadelphia cream cheese (room temperature)
1 stick of oleo (room temperature)
1 pound powdered sugar
1-2 teaspoons vanilla
Beat together til fluffy and spread over cooled cake.

Hostess: Mary Stearley
Displayer: Carol Post

RED VELVET CAKE

1/2 cup butter
2 eggs
2 teaspoons cocoa
1 1/2 cups sugar
2 ounces red food coloring
2 cups flour
1 cup buttermilk
1 1/2 teaspoons baking soda
1 tablespoon vinegar
1 teaspoon vanilla
1 teaspoon salt

Cream butter and sugar. Add eggs. Make paste with coloring
and cocoa. Add to cream mixture. Mix salt, vanilla and
buttermilk and with flour. Mix soda and vinegar, Add last,
folding in. Do not beat after vinegar and soda added. Bake
at 350 degrees for 30 minutes.

Hostess: Dolly Fields
Displayer: Donna Broodt

RED CAKE

4 large bottles red food coloring
3 Tablespoons cocoa
Mix together and set aside.
1/2 cup crisco
1 1/2 cups sugar
Cream together with mixer. Then add:
2 eggs   and the coloring paste. Add
1 cup buttermilk alternately with
2 1/4 cups cake flour (sifted three times) Add
1 teaspoon salt
1 teaspoon vanilla
Remove from mixer and add
1 Tablespoon vinegar
1 teaspoon soda
Stir by hand. Bake 30-35 minutes in two layer pans (small) at 350
degrees.

FROSTING FOR RED CAKE:
1 stick butter
8 tablespoons crisco
Cream together. Add:
1 cup granulated sugar
3 tablespoons flour one at a time
2/3 cup milk (tepid temperature)
1 teaspoon vanilla
Beat 15 minutes at high speed. Spread on cake.

Hostess: Sherry Muhlbach
Displayer: Cheri Scranton

COCA-COLA CAKE

2 cups sugar
2 cups flour
1 cup coca-cola
3 tablespoons cocoa
2 sticks butter
1/2 cup buttermilk in which
1 teaspoon baking soda has been disolved
2 beaten eggs
1 1/2 cups minature marshmellows

Sift together sugar and flour. Bring butter, cocoa, and coca-cola to a boil. Pour into flour mixture, stir in marshmellows buttermilk and eggs. Pour in 9 x 13" pan. Bake at 350 degrees for 35 minutes.

COCA-COLA TOPPING:
6 tablespoons coca-cola
3 tablespoons cocoa
1 stick butter
1 box sifted confectioners sugar
1 cup nuts
1 teaspoon vanilla

Bring to boil butter, cocoa, and coca-cola. Add other ingredients. Top cake while hot.

Hostess: Sharon Ann Spivev
Displayer: Teresa Graham

COKE CAKE

2 cups sugar
2 cups flour
1 teaspoon soda
1/2 pound margarine
1 cup coke
3 tablespoons cocoa
1/2 cup buttermilk
1 1/2 cup minature marshmellows
2 beaten eggs
1 teaspoon vanilla

Combine flour, sugar, soda in bowl. Heat butter, cocoa and coke to boiling. Pour over flour and sugar mixture. Add buttermilk, marshmellows, eggs and vanilla. Mix well. Bake 35 minutes at 350 degrees.

ICING:
1 stick margarine
6 tablespoons cocoa
6 tablespoons coke
1 box confectioners sugar
1 cup pecans
Combine first 3 ingredients and bring to a boil. Pour into sugar. Beat, add nuts, spread over warm cake.
Hostess: Beverly Crane   Displayer: Ruth Young

CRAZY CAKE

1 1/2 cups flour
1 cup white sugar
1 teaspoon soda
1/2 teaspoon salt
2 tablespoons cocoa

Use square or large round layer cake pan. Do not grease.
Put above ingredients into sifter and sift once. Return to
sifter and sift into cake pan. Make three depressions in
dry ingredients. Put one of the following ingredients in each
depression:

1 teaspoon vanilla
1 tablespoon vinegar
6 tablespoons salad oil or melted shortening

1 cup cold water poured over all. Mix well stir with fork.
Bake until done in medium oven, 350 degrees. Approximately
30 minutes. Cool in pan.

Hostess: Toni McCracken
Dodie Carpenter

COKE CAKE

2 cups sugar
1 1/2 cup minature marshmellows
2 cups flour, unsifted
2 sticks or 1 cup butter or margarine
1 cup coke
3 tablespoons cocoa
2 eggs beaten
1/2 cup bettermilk
1 teaspoon soda
1 teaspoon vanilla

In a bowl add flour and sugar. Let coke, cocoa, and margarine
come to a boil in boiler. Pour over flour,mix thoroughly, add
eggs and buttermilk, soda and vanilla. Beat well. Bake in
13 x 9" pan at 350 degrees for 30 minutes or until done.

COKE ICING:
1/2 cup margarine
3 tablespoons cocoa
6 tablespoons coke
Heat until boiling, pour into sugar, add nuts, pour onto hot cake
1 box confectioners sugar
1 cup nuts

Hostess: Trecy Nanney
Displayer: Carol Anderson

HOT WATER CHOCOLATE CAKE

1 1/2 cups flour
1 1/2 cups sugar
1 teaspoon salt
4 Tablespoons cocoa
1 stick butter
1 1/2 teaspoons baking powder
1 teaspoon baking soda
1 1/2 cups water
1 egg
2 teaspoons vanilla

Mix flour and sugar and salt and cocoa and butter together.
Add 1 cup hot water, beat until smooth. Mix soda and baking
powder with 1/2 cup hot water. Add to mixture egg and vanilla.
Beat, this makes a thin batter. Bake at 350 degrees for 20-30
minutes.

BOILED ICING FOR HOT WATER CAKE:
1 cup sugar
1/4 cup cocoa
1/4 cup oleo
1/4 cup milnot (or evaporated milk)
2 teaspoons vanilla (reserved to last)
Cook 1 minute after it reaches a boil then add vanilla. Beat
for a short time.

Hostess: Betty Shaw
Displayer: Earlene Young

BROWNIE MARSHMALLOW CAKE

1 cup pecans
2 cups sugar
2 sticks oleo
4 eggs (one at a time)
1 1/2 teaspoon butter flavoring
1 teaspoon vanilla
1 1/2 cups flour
2/3 cup cocoa
1 5 1/2 ounce package marshmallows
Bake at 350 degrees for 30 minutes, in greased oblong pan, 9 x 13".
When cake is done take out of oven and put marshmallows on hot cake.
Return to oven to melt marshmallows. When melted, take out of oven
and pour icing over the whole cake.

ICING:
1/2 box powdered sugar
1/2 cup cocoa
1/2 stick hot melted oleo
1/2 cup evaporated milk
1 teaspoon vanilla
1 teaspoon butter flavoring
Beat until creamy, spread on cake.
Hostess: Jean M. Koncar
Displayer: Jackie Everitt

46

MISSISSIPPI MUD CAKE

2 cups sugar
1 cup soft margarine
4 eggs
1 1/2 cups plain flour
1/3 cup cocoa
2 teaspoons vanilla
1/4 teaspoon salt
1 cup chopped nuts
1 bag small marshmallows

Mix sugar, margarine, and eggs; then blend in other ingredients
except marshmallows. Grease and flour oblong pan and cook 30
minutes on 300 degrees. Remove and spread marshmallows on top.
Return to oven for 10 minutes or until marshmallows melt.
(Watch closely)

ICING:
1 stick margarine
1/3 cup cocoa
1 box confectioners sugar
1/2 cup evaporated milk
1 teaspoon vanilla
dash salt
1 cup chopped nuts
Mix and spread on cake when cool.

Hostess: Billie Ramsey

CRAZY CHOCOLATE CAKE

3 cups unsifted flour
1/3 cup cocoa
1 teaspoon salt
2 cups sugar
2 teaspoons soda
Sift the above ingredients into a 9 x 13" cake pan, then add:
2 tablespoons vinegar
2/3 cup or 12 tablespoons oil
2 teaspoons vanilla
2 cups cold water
Stir with fork to blend. Do not beat. When well mixed, bake
at 350 degrees for 25-35 minutes. Cool in pan. If mixed in a
bowl this recipe will make 2-9" cakes, 3-8" cakes, or 2 1/2
dozen cupcakes.

Hostess: Pam Layer
Displayer: Grace Simpson

CHOCOLATE CHIP CAKE

1 stick margarine
1 cup sugar
2 eggs
1 cup sour cream
1 teaspoon vanilla
2 cups flour
1 1/2 teaspoon baking powder
1 teaspoon baking soda
1/4 teaspoon salt
Cinnamon mixture, 1/2 cup sugar and 1 teaspoon cinnamon
large package chocolate chips

Cream margarine, sugar, and eggs together. Add sour cream, vanilla, flour, baking powder, baking soda, salt. Grease and flour 13 x 9" pan. Pour half of batter into pan and spread out. Sprinkle half the cinnamon mixture over batter and half the chocolate chips. Spread rest of batter over. Sprinkle remaining cinnamon mix. Lightly press chocolate chips into batter. Bake at 350 degrees for 30 minutes.

Hostess: Peggy Marosy

DEVIL'S FOOD CAKE

1/2 cup butter
4 ounces bitter chocolate
2 eggs
1 1/2 cups milk
2 teaspoons baking powder
1 cup nuts
2 teaspoons vanilla
2 cups sugar
2 cups flour

Cream butter and one cup of sugar. Melt chocolate. Beat eggs and add to butter mixture. Add second cup of sugar. Beat mixture well. Add melted chocolate. Mix dry ingredients and add to butter mixture, alternately with milk. Add vanilla and nuts. Bake in loaf pan at 350 degrees for 50 minutes. Frost with choice of frosting. This recipe was passed along from a cookbook over 50 years old, with a clipping from the Kansas City Star, "About Town" column, not dated. The story goes that a young Kansas woman, visiting in New York couldn't forget the flavor of the Devil's food cake served by a top notch hotel, so she wrote, asking the hotel for the recipe....they sent it, along with a bill for $100.00. She must have thought it worth it because she paid the bill, and here is the recipe.

Hostess: Mildred Yahr
Displayer: Sharon Wiendandt

CHOCOLATE OATMEAL CAKE

1 1/2 cups boiling water
1 cup quick oatmeal
1 cup margarine
1 cup brown sugar
1 cup granulated sugar
2 eggs
1 teaspoon soda
1 teaspoon cream of tartar
1/2 cup bitter cocoa
1 1/3 cups flour

Pour water over oats and margarine, let stand 15 minutes. Stir and add both sugars and eggs that have been slightly beaten. Blend. Sift soda, cocoa, cream of tartar and flour together and add to batter. Stir until well blended. Put into greased and floured 9 x 13" pan and bake at 350 degrees for 30-40 minutes.

FUDGY FROSTING:
1/2 cup sugar
2 tablespoons brown sugar
1 cup coconut
1/4 cup evaporated milk
6 tablespoons margarine
1 cup chopped nuts
6 ounce package chocolate chips

Put all ingredients in double boiler and heat until melted. Spread over warm cake and return to oven and bake until frosting becomes bubbly. Cool 2 hours before serving.

Hostess: Barbara Stecker
Displayer: JoAnn Engels

SURPRISE CAKE

2 cups sugar
2 cups flour
2 teaspoons baking soda
2 teaspoons instant chocolate
2 eggs
1 large can fruit cocktail
Mix dry ingredients. Add eggs and fruit cocktail. Bake at 325 degrees for 50-60 minutes.

FROSTING:
1/2 block margarine
1 cup sugar
1 cup coconut
1 cup canned milk
1 heaping teaspoon chocolate
Mix all together and boil about 8 minutes, or until thick.

Hostess: Patricia Lormand

WHITE CHOCOLATE CAKE

1/4 pound white chocolate
1 cup butter
4 egg yolks
1 teaspoon soda
4 egg whites
1 cup coconut
1/2 cup water
2 cups sugar
2 1/2 cups cake flour
1 cup buttermilk
1 cup pecans
1 teaspoon vanilla

Melt chocolate in hot water and cool. Cream butter and sugar,
Add egg yolks one at a time, beat well after each addition.
Add chocolate mixture and vanilla. Sift flour and soda together
and add alternately with buttermilk. Don't overbeat. Fold in
4 beaten egg whites. Gently stir in nuts and coconut. Bake
in 3 layers at 350 degrees for 25-30 minutes. Let cool.

ICING:
2/3 cup evaporated milk
4 tablespoons butter
1 teaspoon vanilla
1 cup sugar
1 cup coconut
3 egg yolks
1 cup pecans

Bring to boil milk, sugar and butter. Beat egg yolks well and
add to mixture. Add vanilla. Cook over low heat until thick.
Remove from heat, add nuts and coconut. Beat until spreading
consistency.

Hostess: Geneva Stroup
Displayer: Shirley Meador

EASY CHOCOLATE CAKE

3 cups flour
2 cups sugar
2 teaspoons baking soda
1 cup salad oil
2 teaspoons vinegar
1 teaspoon salt
6 tablespoons cocoa
2 teaspoons vanilla
2 cups cold water

Mix well with a fork. Pour in baking pan and bake at 350 degrees
for 40 minutes. Can be mixed in greased pan and then baked, or
this recipe will make 24-28 cupcakes.

Hostess: Sandy Wicht
Displayer: Frances Burger

WHITE CHOCOLATE SHEATH CAKE

1 stick butter or margarine
4 tablespoons (1 square) White Chocolate
1/2 cup shortening
1 cup water
Bring to a rolling boil in a sauce pan.

2 cups white sugar
2 cups all purpose flour
1 teaspoon cinnamon
1/2 teaspoon salt
Combine chocolate mixture and dry ingredients in a large
mixing bowl. Mix well and add:

1 cup buttermilk
2 eggs
1 teaspoon soda
1 teaspoon vanilla
Mix well again and pour into jelly roll pan. Bake in hot
oven (400 degrees) for 20 minutes.

ICING:
1 stick butter
4 tablespoons cocoa (white)
6 tablespoons milk
1 pound powdered sugar
1 teaspoon vanilla
1 cup chopped pecans
Bring butter, cocoa, and milk to a boil, add other ingredients.
Spread on cake as it comes from oven. Iced cake freezes great.

Hostess: Janice Blackburn
Displayer: Brenda Sipes

****

ENTHUSIASM!!

That certain something that makes us great- that pulls us
out of the mediocre and commonplace - that builds into us
Power. It glows and shines - it lights up our faces -
ENTHUSIASM, the keynote that makes us sing and makes men
sing with us.

ENTHUSIASM - the maker of friends - the maker of smiles -
the producer of confidence. It cries to the world, "I've
got what it takes." It tells all men that our job is a swell
job - that the house we work for just suits us - the goods
we have are the best.

ENTHUSIASM - the inspiration that makes us "Wake Up and Live."
It puts spring in our step - spring in our hearts - a twinkle
in our eyes and gives us confidence in ourselves and our
fellow men.

ENTHUSIASM - It changes a pessimist to an optimist, a loafer
to a go-getter.

ENTHUSIASM - If we have it, we should thank God for it. If we
don't have it, then we should get down on our knees and pray for it.

WHITE CHOCOLATE CAKE

1/4 pound white chocolate
1/2 cup boiling water
1 cup butter
2 cups sugar
4 egg yolks
2 1/2 cups flour
1 teaspoon soda
1/2 teaspoon salt
1 cup buttermilk
4 egg whites (beaten stiff)
1 cup pecans
1 cup coconut

Melt chocolate in boiling water. Mix butter, sugar, egg yolks,
flour, soda, salt, buttermilk together, fold in egg whites
then pecans and coconut. Bake 30 minutes at 325 degrees in
three 9" pans.

ICING:
1 1/4 cups Pet Milk
1 cup sugar
1 stick butter
3 egg yolks
1 cup pecans
1 cup coconut
Cook until thick. Pour over cake and between layers.

Hostess: Faye Hoke
Displayer: Marie Keel

CHOCOLATE MARBLE CAKE

2 1/2 cups cake flour (sifted)
1 1/2 teaspoons baking powder
1/2 teaspoon soda
1 teaspoon salt
1 2/3 cups sugar

Sift together, then measure into mixing bowl:
3/4 cup shortening
1 square melted chocolate
2 tablespoons hot water
1/4 teaspoon soda
1 tablespoon sugar
Sift dry ingredients into shortening bowl. Add:
1 cup sour or buttermilk   Beat 2 minutes and add:
1 teaspoon vanilla and
3 eggs   and beat one minute at low speed. Add chocolate
mix to 1/4 of batter mixing only to blend. Bake at 350 degrees
for 35-40 minutes.

Hostess: Polly Anna Core
Displayer: Marty Rickman

MISSISSIPPI MUD CAKE

2 sticks margarine
2 cups sugar
1/3 cups cocoa
4 eggs
1 cup chopped nuts
1 cup coconut
1 cup flour
miniature marshmellows
1 stick margarine
1/3 cup cocoa
1/3 cup milk
1 teaspoon vanilla
1 box powdered sugar (1 pound)

Mix the two sticks of margarine with the sugar and cocoa and
cream well. Beat the eggs one at a time, beat them well, then
add to the sugar and margarine mixture. Add chopped nuts, coconut,
flour and mix well again. Pour into greased and floured 9 x 13"
pan. Bake in 350 degree oven for 30 minutes, or until done.
Take from oven, cover with minature marshmellows and put it back
into oven until marshmellows are brown and puffy.

ICING:
Put in saucepan 1 stick margarine, cocoa, milk, stir and let it
BOIL. Then add vanilla and 1 pound of powdered sugar and mix.
Then pour the hot icing over warm cake. Serve warm with vanilla
ice cream.

Hostess: Andrea McCoy
Displayer: Agenes Avolicino

CHOCOLATE BAR CAKE

2 cups flour
2 cups sugar
1/2 cup cocoa
Sift in a bowl and add:
1 cup buttermilk with
1 teaspoon soda added to the buttermilk
1 cup cooking oil
1 teaspoon vanilla
Mix well to dry ingredients. Then add:
1 cup boiling water
Batter is thin. Pour in large cookie sheet and bake 20 minutes
at 350 degrees. Frost while warm with chocolate frosting.
CHOCOLATE FROSTING:
1/2 cup butter or margarine
4 Tablespoons cocoa
6 Tablespoons cream or milk -Bring to boil, pour into:
5 cups powdered sugar
Mix well and add vanilla and 1/2 cup chopped nuts.
Hostess: Frances Holdbrook
Displayer: Dodie Carpenter

TEXAS SHEET CAKE OR BROWNIES

2 cups sugar
1/2 teaspoon salt
1 cup water
1/2 cup sour cream
1 teaspoon soda
2 cups flour
2 cubes butter or margarine (1 cup)
4 tablespoons cocoa
2 eggs

In large bowl put sugar, flour and salt. In heavy pan
bring butter, water, and cocoa to a boil. As it
boils immediately add dry ingredients. Add sour cream.
Add eggs and soda. Mix until well blended after each addition.
Batter will be thin. Bake in greased cookie sheet with high
sides at 370 degrees 20-25 minutes. May use two 9 x 13" pans.
Prepare frosting while cake is baking.

BUTTER NUT FROSTING:
1 cup nuts
1 box powdered sugar
6 tablespoons canned milk
1 cup butter or margarine
1 teaspoon vanilla
4 tablespoons cocoa
Boil milk butter, cocoa in heavy pan until bubbly. Stir in
sugar and vanilla until smooth. Add nuts. Spread over hot
brownies and restrain everyone from eating until warm at
least. Serves 24-48 2" squares.

Hostess: Wilma Taylor
Displayer: Linda Gordon

****

A SURE WAY TO A HAPPY DAY

Happiness is something we create in our mind,
It's not something you search for and so seldon find -
It's just waking up and beginning the day
By counting our blessings and kneeling to pray -
It's giving up thoughts that breed discontent
And accepting what comes as a "gift heaven-sent" -
It's giving up wishing for things we have not
And making the best of whatever we've got -
It's knowing that life is determined for us,
And pursuing our tasks without fret, fume, or fuss -
For it's by completing what God gives us to do
That we find real contentment and happiness, too.
                              Helen Steiner Rice.

CHOCOLATE SHEET CAKE

2 cups sugar
2 cups flour
pinch salt
Mix in large bowl and set aside
1/2 cup oleo margarine
1/2 cup Crisco oil
1/4 cup cocoa
1 cup water
Combine and bring to a boil. Add to flour mixture and stir. Add:
2 eggs
1/2 cup buttermilk
1 teaspoon baking soda
1 teaspoon vanilla

Pour into greased and floured sheet cake pan. Frost while cake
is still very hot.

FROSTING:
1 cup sugar
dash salt
1/4 cup canned milk
1/4 cup oleo margarine

Bring to a boil and add:
1/2 cup chocolate chips

Hostess: Suzanne Leavens
Displayer: Linda Case

CHOCOLATE ZUCCINE CAKE

1/2 cup butter or margarine
1/2 cup oil
1 3/4 cups sugar
2 eggs
1 teaspoon vanilla
1/2 cup canned milk or sour milk if preferred
2 1/2 cups flour
4 tablespoons cocoa
1/2 teaspoon soda
1/2 teaspoon cinnamon
1/2 teaspoon cloves
1/2 teaspoon salt
2 cups semi-sweet chocolate pieces
1/4 cup chopped nuts
2 cups shredded Zuccine or carrots if preferred

Cream margarine, oil, and sugar together. Add eggs, vanilla, and
milk and blend. Sift flour, cocoa, soda, cinnamon, cloves, and
salt. Blend with creamed mixture. Stir in zuccine. Spoon into
greased and floured baking pan (loaf) Sprinkle chocolate pieces
and nuts on top. Bake 40-45 minutes at 325 degrees.

Hostess: Nellie Wray
Displayer: Jackie Fetterhoff

55

CARROT PINEAPPLE CAKE

3 cups sifted cake flour
2 cups sugar
2 teaspoons cinnamon
1 1/2 teaspoon soda
1 1/2 teaspoon salt
1 teaspoon baking powder
1 8 ounce can crushed pineapple
3 eggs, beaten
3/4 cups cooking oil
3/4 cup buttermilk
2 teaspoons vanilla
1 1/2 cups chopped walnuts
2 cups raw carrots, grated and loosely packed
3 1/2 ounces shredded coconut

Mix together all dry ingredients. Drain pineapple; reserve syrup.
Add pineapple syrup to dry mixture, add eggs, cooking oil,
buttermilk, and vanilla; beat 3 minutes. Stir in pineapple, nuts,
carrots and coconut. Bake in greased and floured 12 cup bundt
pan at 325 degrees for about 1 1/2 hours or until cake tests done.
Cool in pan 10-15 minutes, turn out on wire rack or serving plate.
top with Buttermilk Glaze.

BUTTERMILK GLAZE:
1/2 teaspoon baking soda
1 teaspoon white corn syrup
1 cube butter (1/2 cup)
1 cup sugar
1/2 cup buttermilk
1/2 teaspoon vanilla

Mix first 5 ingredients in saucepan. Bring to a boil and boil
for 5 minutes. Remove from heat and add vanilla. Prick cake
all over with fork and pour glaze over hot cake. Cover cake
completely.

Hostess: Pat Bettenhausen
Displayer: Claudia Rooker

****

There is no such thing as moral neutrality. Those who do
not stand up forthrightly in behalf of their convictions, by
their inaction are supporting the opposite view. On any scale
whatever a person perceives right and wrong, silence turns out
to be a vote for wrong.   John A Howard.

****

Carrot Cake Recipes sent in by:
Hostesses: Maralee Lemke, GerogAnn Dyer, Rose Hoing, Ferta Duke,
          Kathy Chavez and Elaine Kaufman
Displayers: Bernie Lorraine, Jackie Fetterhoff, Darlene Menneke,
           Margee Duke, Gloria Aldinger, and Dodie Carpenter

NO ICING CHOCOLATE CHIP CAKE

1 cup raisins
1 cup + 3 tablespoons hot water
1 teaspoon soda
1 cup white sugar
1 cup shortening
2 eggs
2 cups flour
1/2 teaspoon salt
1 tablespoon cocoa
1 teaspoon vanilla
1/2 cup chopped nuts
1 cup chocolate chips

Preheat oven to 350 degrees. Pour hot water over raisins. Remove
enough water to dissolve soda and return to raisins. Cream sugar
and shortening. Add beaten eggs, flour, salt, cocoa, and vanilla.
Beat well. Add 1/2 cup of chocolate chips, raisins, and water mix
and stir. Pour into greased and floured 9 x 13" pan. Sprinkle
remaining chips and nuts on top. Bake for 40 minutes.

Hostess: Vicki Freeman
Displayer: Cindy Capers

FUDGE MARBLE POUND CAKE

1 package Fudge Marble Cake Mix
1/2 cup Crisco Oil (use Crisco as some other oils may cause cake to fall
4 eggs
1 package instant vanilla pudding mix (4 serving size)
1 cup water

Preheat oven to 350 degrees. Blend all the ingredients except the
small packet in a large bowl, then beat at medium speed for 2 minutes.
Pour 3/4 of the batter into a greased and floured bundt pan. Blend
contents of small packet into remaining batter. Spoon dark batter
here and there over light batter. Pull knife through batter in
wide curves several times. Bake at 350 degrees for about 45-55
minutes until center springs back when touched lightly. Cool right
side up for about 25 minutes, then remove from pan. If desired,
dust top of cooled cake with confectioners sugar or drizzle with
chocolate glaze.

Hostess: Deloris Heminger
Displayer: Connie Becker

****

Always be enthusiastic...Imperfections are lost in the glory of
enthusiam.

****

CHOCOLATE POUND CAKE

1 cup butter or margarine (cold)
1/2 cup shortening (cold)
3 cups sugar
5 eggs (cold)
1 1/2 cups sifted cake flour
1 1/2 cups regular flour
1 teaspoon baking powder
1/2 teaspoon salt
1/2 cup cocoa
1 cup sweet milk
1 teaspoon vanilla

Cream butter, shortening,eggs, and sugar together. Sift
dry ingredients together, then add all other ingredients.
Bake 1 1/2 hours at 325 degrees or until done. Do not
overcook. May be cooked in tube pan or loaf pans. Freezes well.

Hostess: Sondra Simmons
Displayer:Linda Coffee, and Pat Anderson, Manager.

SOUR CREAM GERMAN CHOCOLATE CAKE

2/3 cups sugar
1/2 cup milk
1 slightly beaten egg
3 1 ounce squares unsweetened chocolate

1/2 cup shortening
1 cup sugar
1 teaspoon vanilla

2 eggs

2 cups flour
1 teaspoon soda
1/2 teaspoon salt
1 cup sour cream

Combine first four ingredients in saucepan and cook. Stir
over medium heat until chocolate melts and mixture comes just
to boiling. Cream together shortening, sugar, until fluffy.
Add vanilla. Add eggs 1 at a time, beating well after each.
Sift dry ingredients and add to creamed mixture alternately
with sour cream. Beat until smooth after each addition.
Blend in cooled chocolate mixture. Bake in two greased
and floured 9" round pans at 350 degrees for 25-30 minutes.
Cool ten minutes before removing from pans. Cool and frost
with chocolate frosting and garnish with chocolate curls.

Hostess. Gladys Zuehlke
Displayer: Judy Braun

****

58

RUSSIAN DRESSING
Serve on Angel Food Cake

4 egg yolks
1 cup sugar
1/3 cup orange juice or one orange
2 teaspoons grated orange rind
1/2 pint whipped cream
1/2 cup walnuts cut fine - added just before serving

Beat egg yolks until light and lemon colored. Blend in
orange juice, sugar and grated rind. Cook in double
boiler stirring constantly, until thick (about 20 minutes.)
Fold in stiffly beaten whipped cream. Fold in nuts just
before serving.

Hostess: Stella Sterling
Displayer: Dodie Carpenter

GRASSHOPPER ICING

1 envelope unflavored gelatin
1/4 cup water
1/2 cup creame de mint
1/3 cup white creame de coca
1 large container Cool Whip

Soften gelatin in water. Heat creame de mint with creame de
cocoa, add to softened gelatin and stir until dissolved. Let
cool. Mix in Cool Whip, whip together. Keep refrigerated until
served. Ice any chocolate cake with this light green icing.

Hostess: Carolyn Banning
Displayer: Charlyn K. Travers

****

MEMORY SYSTEM

Forget each kindness that you do as soon as you have done it;
Forget the praise that falls to you as soon as you have found it;
Forget the slander that you hear before you can repeat it;
Forget each slight each spite, each sneer, wherever you may meet it.

Remember every kindness done to you whatever its measure;
Remember praise by others won and pass it on with pleasure;
Remember every promise made and keep it to the letter;
Remember those who lend you aid and be a grateful debtor.
Remember good, remember truth, Remember Heaven's above you,
And you will find, through age and youth, that many hearts will
love you.

****

ITALIAN CREAM CAKE

1 stick butter
1/2 cup vegetable shortening
2 cups sugar
5 egg yolks
2 cups self rising flour
1 teaspoon soda
1 cup butter milk
1 teaspoon vanilla
1 small can coconut
1 cup chopped nuts
5 egg whites

Cream butter and shortening, add sugar and beat until smooth.
Add egg yolks and beat well. Combine flour and soda and add
mixture alternately with buttermilk. Stir in vanilla and
add coconut and nuts. Fold in egg whites, pour in greased
pans. Bake at 350 degrees for 25 minutes.

CREAM CHEESE FROSTING:
1 package cream cheese softened
1 box powdered sugar
1 teaspoon vanilla
nuts and coconut to suit taste
pet cream

Hostess: Charlotte Matthews
Displayer: Maxine Rodgers

MATHILDA'S ONE-PAN CAKE

1 box yellow cake mix
2 eggs
water
1 large package strawberry gelatin
1 large package vanilla instant pudding
1 carton whipped topping (8 ounce size)

First grease generously a long sheet cake pan. Preheat oven at
350 degrees. Prepare cake mix according to package directions
adding two eggs and water. Bake for 40 minutes. Remove from
oven immediately, prick cake with fork all over to make little
holes. Mix jello with 2 cups hot water and pour over cake so
jello will go into the holes and saturate the cake. Allow the
cake to cool. Prepare pudding according to directions and spread
over cake. Top with whipped topping. Place in refrigerator to
cool, and keep refrigerated.

Hostess: Patricia R. Lormand

Vegetables

HOT BEAN SALAD

2 cans butter beans
1 can kidney beans
1 can limabeans
1 large can pork and beans
1 large onion, cubed and browned
1/2 pound bacon, cubed and browned
3/4 cup brown sugar
1/4 cup vinegar
1/3 cup catsup
1/4 teaspoon dry mustard

Combine and mix beans. Make sauce of other ingredients and simmer
15 minutes, pour over beans. Bake one hour at 350 degrees.

Hostess: Erlene Hauser
Displayer: Diane Johnson

BROCCOLI CASSEROLE

2 10 ounce packages chopped broccoli
2 1/2 to 3 cups cooked rice
2 cans cream of chicken soup
1 large jar of cheese whiz
1 teaspoon Worcestershire sauce

Cook broccoli, add rest of ingredients except 1 can of soup.
Pour it over top and bake 30 minutes at 350 degrees.

Hostess: Billie Ramsey

CAULIFLOWER SALAD

Combine raw cauliflower with any or all of the following
diced vegatables - radishes, onions, tomatoes, celery,
peppers, cucumbers, and carrots. Combine the following
dressing and add to salad.
Mayonnaise
Lemon Juice
Powdered Sugar (enough to give it a sweet taste)

****

Houses are made of wood and stone. But only LOVE
can make a home.
                              From "Be Somebody"
****

61

ANTIPASTO NAPOLI

2 cups tomato wedges
2 cups fresh mushroom slices
8 ounce polish sausage, cut into strips
1 cup (8 1/2 ounce jar) artichoke hearts, drained and quartered
1 cup fresh zucchini slices
1 cup bottled Italian dressing
2 quarts torn assorted salad greens
Grated parmesan cheese is optional

Combine tomatoes, mushrooms, sausage, artichoke hearts and
aucchini. Add dressing, cover and marinate in refrigerator
2 hours. Drain reserving marinate. Toss vegetables with
assorted greens. Serve with reserved marinate. Sprinkle
with parmesan to taste. Serves 4-6.

Hostess: Nancy Perotti

FIESTA-RONI SALAD

1 package Chicken Rice-a-roni
2 tablespoons wine vinegar
2 tablespoons lemon juice
1 tablespoon sugar
1/2 teaspoon garlic salt
1 cup diced tomato
1/2 cup diced celery
1/4 cup sliced scallion
1 cup diced green chile (mild)
3 ripe avocados, diced
1/4 cup chopped ripe olives (pitted)

Prepare rice-aroni per package instructions. Cool. Combine
rest of ingredients and add to rice-a-roni. Lay on bed of lettuce
in large bowl or individual salad bowls and chill.

Hostess: Virginia Turner
Displayer: Dorothy L. Quinn

CARROTS SUPREME

2 pounds carrots
1/4 cup vinegar
1 cup sugar
1 can tomato soup
1 stick margarine
1 bell pepper and 1 onion
Slice and cook carrots until tender. Combine other 4 ingredients
and bring to boil; pour over cooked carrots and add
bell pepper and onion. Serve warm. This is better the next day.

Displayer: Billie Ramsey

ASPARAGUS-PEA CASSEROLE

1 stick oleo
6 slices bread, cut into fingers without crust
2 cans drained asparagus
2 cans mushroom soup
2 cans english peas
1 can water-chestnuts
1/2 cup celery, chopped

Melt oleo in a 9 x 13 pan. Soak bread in oleo and remove.
Lay drained asparagus in dish. Mix soup, peas, water-chestnuts,
and celery and pour over the asparagus. Top with bread fingers.
Bake at 325 degrees for 20 minutes or until brown on top.

Hostess: Jean Wilcox
Displayer: Nancy Thompson

SMOKED CHEESE CARROTS

3 cups cooked carrots, mashed
2 tablespoons chopped onion
16 crushed soda crackers
1 cup milk
1 roll smoky cheese

Mix all together, dot with butter, bake 35 minutes at 350 degrees.

Hostess: Sharon Louig

KENTUCKY FRIED CORN

6 strips bacon, 1 inch cubes
4 ears corn, sweet or horse, scraped from cob
2 small cucumbers thinly sliced
1 medium onion, minced or in rings
1 large egg
Salt, pepper, and sugar to taste

Lightly fry bacon, mix other ingredients thoroughly,pour into
bacon grease. Fry slowly so as not to brown too quickly.
about 25 minutes. Note: Pimento strips and green sweet
pepper can also be used if desired. Yield, 4-6 servings.

Hostess: Mae Mitchell
Displayer: Sue Cornelius

****

One person with a belief is equal to nienty-nine with only interest.
                    From "Be Somebody" by Mary Crowley.
                ****

CHOWDER PARMESAN

2 cups diced potatoes
1 cup carrot slice
1/2 cup celery slices
1/4 cup chopped onion
1 1/2 teaspoon salt
1/4 teaspoon pepper
Add above to 2 cups boiling water. Simmer until tender.
Make white sauce of:
1/4 cup butter
1/4 cup flour
2 cups milk
Stir into cooked vegetables. Add 1/2 cup Parmesan Cheese.
Variations: Add 1 can creamed corn or 2 cans shrimp, or clams.
Yield, 6-8 servings.

Hostess: Joanne Roe
Displayer: Carol Craig

STUFFED HARD ROLLS

1 pound grated cheddar cheese
1/2 cup chopped green pepper
1/4 cup sliced green onions
2 chopped hard-boiled eggs
1/2 pint sliced stuffed olives, green
1 (8ounce) can tomato sauce
3/4 cup oil

Slice hard rolls in half, scoop out centers. Spoon mixture into
rolls. Wrap individually in foil. Bake at 350 degrees for 20-
25 minutes. Yield, about 12.

Hostess: Joanne Roe
Displayer: Carol Craig

****

I passed a gleaming mirror ashining in the sun.
'Twas but a wayside puddle for dainty feet to shun
But that small sheet of water was deep as clouds were high
For in its glinting surface was seen God's vast blue sky.

I would that I could feel assured that people passing me
Could overlook my littleness and something greater see.
That my small life with all its faults could show God's loving grace
And to the passer by reflect the beauty of His face.

****

64

MARINATED CARROTS

5 cups cooked sliced carrots
1 cup sliced red onion
1 sliced green pepper
1 10 3/4 ounce can tomato soup
1/2 cup salad oil
1 cup sugar
3/4 cup vinegar
1 teaspoon mustard
1 teaspoon Worcestershire sauce
1 teaspoon salt
1 teaspoon pepper

Cook the sliced carrots, then mix with sliced pepper and onion.
Mix the seasonings together. Pour over the vegetables. Cover
and let sit 24 hours in refrigerator. Drain all the sauce off
before serving.

Hostess: Roberta Husband
Displayer: Nancy Thomas

CARROT PENNIES

2 cans sliced carrots, drained
1 green pepper, sliced and divided
1 medium onion, sliced and divided
1 small jar pimentoes
Mix together and chill

1 can tomato soup
1/2 cup salad oil
1 cup sugar
3/4 cup cider vinegar
1 teaspoon prepared mustard
2 teaspoons worcestershire sauce
1/4 teaspoon black pepper
Mix and pour over vegetables in mix. Refrigerate lightly.
Will keep for weeks. Serve as salad.

Hostess: Martha Moore

****

HAPPY is the person:
Who possesses unbounded enthusiasm for life
Who practices unlimited forgiveness toward others
Who expresses unending gratitude toward God
Who wages uncompromising war on injustice.
From "Be Somebody"
****

65

SQUASH CASSEROLE

3 packages frozen yellow squash, cooked
1 can cream of chicken soup
1/2 pint sour cream
1/2 cup grated carrot
1/2 cup grated cheese
1 small jar chopped pimentos, optional
1 small onion diced

TOPPING:
1 package Pepperidge Farm Stuffing, Herb Seasoning
1 stick margarine, melted
1 dash poultry seasoning

Layer 1/2 stuffing mixture in 9 x 12" dish, add squash mixture.
Add remaining stuffing mixture on top. Bake 30 minutes at 350
degrees.

Hostess: Adelene Stevens
Displayer: Julie Stevens

ZUCHINNI SQUASH DISH

2 pounds squash
1 cup butter or oleo
1 large onion
1 box cheese crutons
8 ounces sour cream
1 can creamed chicken soup
1 small jar pimentos
Parsley and seasoning of your choice

Cut up squash and onion. Boil until tender. Pour off liquid
and let cool. Mix in sour cream, chicken soup, and pimentos.
Melt butter and pour over croutons. Let set. Put 1/2 of the
croutons in a baking dish. Pour in squash mixture. Put
remaining croutons on top. Bake at 350 degrees until brown.
A great dish to freeze.

Hostess: Mrs. Mildred Marsh
Displayer: Dodie Carpenter

****

The first four words in our Bible "In the beginning God" may
be taken as the Christian's life motto. In everything we should
begin with Him - in companionships, in marriage, in business
partnerships and every day and always, we should begin with God,
turning to Him in all circumstances and on all occasions, doing
nothing without first referring to Him.

****

PEPPY POTATOES

1 package seasoned coating mix for chicken
1/4 teaspoon salt
4 unpeeled potatoes cut in 1 inch wedges
melted butter

Pour coating mix and salt in plastic or paper bag. Dip
potatoes in melted butter, shake in bag. Place potatoes
on well greased baking sheet. Bake at 325 degrees for 55
minutes.

Hostesses: Bonnie and Shelley Dunn with Karen Miller
Displayer: Karen Miller

EASY BAKED BEANS

4 slices bacon
2 tablespoons bacon drippings
1/2 cup chopped onion
2 1 pound cans pork and beans in tomato sauce
2 tablespoons brown sugar
1 tablespoon Worcestershire sauce
1 teaspoon prepared mustard

Cook bacon til crisp, then crumble. Cook onion in bacon drippings
til tender; add crumbled bacon, pork and beans, brown sugar,
Worchestershire sauce, and mustard. Mix well. Bake uncovered
in a 1 1/2 quart casserole at 325 degrees for 1 1/2 to 1 3/4
hours. Serves 6.

Hostess: Carol Childress
Displayer: Eleanor Sheehe

MOM'S BEANS

2 pounds Navy beans
2 cups sugar
1 1/2 tablespoon salt
3/4 tablespoon pepper
1/2 pound lard, cut in pieces
2 tablespoons Karo syrup (dark or light)

Cook beans on top of stove in water covering beans 1 inch
for 2 hours. Put in oven dish, add and mix other ingredients.
Bake at 350 degrees for 4 hours.

Hostess: Kitty Masengarb
Displayer: Darlene Menneke

SUPER POTATO CASSEROLE

5 large potatoes
4 tablespoons green pepper, chopped
1 cup grated cheese
1 teaspoon salt
1/4 cup milk
1 1/2 tablespoons chopped pimento
6 tablespoons chopped onions
1/2 teaspoon pepper
1/2 stick butter

Cook potoates with jackets, and peel while still warm, then let cool and cube them. Mix in green pepper, cheese, salt, milk pimento, onion and pepper and mix well. Melt butter and pour over, then sprinkle with parsley. Bake in pre-heated oven at 400 degrees for 45 minutes. This can be prepared a day ahead of time, removing from refrigerator at least 3 hours before putting in oven. Leave butter and parsley off until then.

Hostess: Mildred Yahr
Displayer: Sharon Wienandt

HOT GERMAN POTATO SALAD

9 slices bacon
1 cup sliced onions
2 tablespoons flour
2 tablespoons sugar
2 teaspoons salt
1/2 teaspoon celery seed
dash pepper
1 cup water
1/3 cup vinegar
9 medium potatoes, about (boiled with skins on, peeled and sliced.)

Fry bacon in a large skillet until crisp. Remove and drain. Cool onions in bacon drippings until golden brown. Blend in flour, sugar, salt, celery seed, pepper. Cook over low heat, stirring til bubbly. Remove from heat and add water and vinegar. Boil and stir for 1 minute. Pour warm sauce over sliced potatoes. Crumble bacon and stir in just before serving. This goes great with a fresh roasted ham.

Hostess: Marilyn Lambie

****

The value of all human endeavor must be graded on this:
Is it good for the children?
Does it build people into better human beings?
                              From "Be Somebody"
                    ****

POTATOE DUMPLINGS

9 large potatoes, grated & drained
8-9 slices bread, soaked with water and squeezed out
3 large onions grated
1 1/2 tablespoons salt
5 teaspoons baking powder

Mix together and add flour to stiffen. Drop by spoonful into boiling water. Boil at least 20 minutes. Good with pork roast and gravy.

Hostess: Barb Ahlers
Displayer: Connie Sordahl

SHAKE 'N BAKE POTATOES

6 medium potatoes, peeled and quartered
1 envelope original flavor Shake 'n Bake
Milk
Dip potatoes in milk and coat with Shank 'n Bake. Salt to taste. Bake on cookie sheet that has 1/8" cooking oil. Bake at 400 degrees for 30 minutes. Turn two or three times. Serve with sour cream.

Hostess: Cheryl Purington
Displayer: Dodie Carpenter

AU GRATIN POTATOES

8 large potatoes, cook unpeeled, then peel and cube
1/4 cup butter
1/4 cup finely chopped onion
1/4 cup flour
4 cups milk
1 teaspoon salt
1/4 teaspoon hot pepper sauce
1/4 teaspoon marjoram
1/2 pound Cheddar cheese, shredded
Paprika and parsley for garnish

Saute onion in butter, blend in flour then remove from heat. Stir in milk, return to heat to thicken. Stir in salt, pepper sauce, marjoram and cheese. Add potatoes to sauce. Bake in casserole for 25 minutes at 350 degrees. Garnish with paprika and parsley.

Hostess: Joanne Roe
Displayer: Carol Craig

SWEET POTATO CASSEROLE

3 cups mashed sweet potatoes
pinch of salt
3/4 cup white sugar
2 eggs beaten
1 teaspoon vanilla
1/2 teaspoon almond extract
1/2 cup milk
1/2 cup margarine (1 stick)
grated orange peel
4 tablespoons cooking wine

Mix and put in greased dish. Bake at 350 degrees for 30-35
minutes.

TOPPING:
1 cup brown sugar
1 cup chopped nuts (walnuts or pecans)
1 cup plain flour
1/3 cup butter

Cut butter into flour, add sugar and nuts, spread on top of
mixture and bake until it looks good.

Hostess: Shirly Dixon
Displayer: Loretta Humphries

SWEET POTATOES AND COCONUT

4 cups sweet potatoes, cooked
4 eggs
1/4 cup flour
1 cup coconut
2 teaspoons vanilla
2 cups sugar
1 cup milk
1 stick butter, melted

Blend and bake in moderate oven until firm. Use as a
vegetable or dessert.

Hostess: Mrs.Rosa Garner
Displayer: Rita Brown

****

It takes a clever man to turn cynic, and a wise man to
be clever enough not to.   Fannie Hurst.

****

A leaf of lettuce dropped into the pot absorbs the grease from the top of the soup. Remove the lettuce and throw it away as soon as it has served its purpose.

To prevent splashing when frying meat, sprinkle a little salt into the pan before putting the fat in.

Small amounts of leftover corn may be added to pancake batter for variety.

To make bread crumbs, use fine cutter of the food grinder and tie a large paper bag over the spout to prevent flying crumbs.

When bread is baking, a small dish of water in the oven will help to keep the crust from getting hard.

Rinse a pan in cold water before scalding milk to prevent sticking.

When you are creaming butter and sugar together, it's a good idea to rinse the bowl with boiling water first. They'll cream faster.

To melt chocolate, grease pan in which it is to be melted.

Dip the spoon in hot water to measure shortening, butter, etc., the fat will slip out more easily.

When you buy cellophane-wrapped cupcakes and notice that the cellophane is somewhat stuck to the frosting, hold the package under the cold-water tap for a moment before you unwrap it. The cellophane will then come off clean.

When you are doing any sort of baking, you get better results if you remember to preheat your cooky sheet, muffin tins, or cake pans.

Chill cheese to grate it more easily.

The odor from baking or boiling salmon may be eliminated by squeezing lemon juice on both sides of each salmon steak or on the cut surface of the salmon and letting it stand in the refrigerator for one hour or longer before cooking.

Use the type can opener that leaves a smooth edge and remove both ends from a flat can (the size can that tuna is usually packed in) and you have a perfect mold for poaching eggs.

Use the divider from an ice tray to cut biscuits in a hurry. Shape dough to conform with size of divider and cut. After baking biscuits will separate at dividing lines.

A clean clothespin provides a cool handle to steady the cake tin when removing a hot cake.

Try using a thread instead of a knife when a cake is to be cut while it is hot.

SALADS

Salads are ideal accompaniments for rich dishes, they provide a welcome astringency of flavor and their brilliant colors enliven any menu. In all salads, texture is important — cooked vegetables should be firm, not mushy, and crisp vegetables should be really crisp. Wash and chill fresh vegetables in the refrigerator or if necessary soak them in ice water for a short time.

Remember to taste a salad for seasoning when it is complete — often a dressing that is perfectly seasoned on its own will taste bland when mixed with vegetables. Many of the following salads are also suitable as appetizers.

GRACE'S SPECIALTY SALAD DRESSING

1/2 cup vinegar
3/4 cup oil
1 cup sugar
1 teaspoon dry mustard
1 teaspoon celery seed
dash of salt
2-3 teaspoons dry onion flakes

Mix vinegar, oil, and sugar in sauce pan, heat until sugar is melted.
Then add mustard, celery seed, and salt, put in blender and
blend until thickened. Then add onion flakes. Chill at least two
hours before serving over your favorite salad greens.

Hostess: Grace Manley
Displayer: Charlyn K. Travers

ITALIAN SALAD DRESSING

1 cup oil
1 cup vinegar
1 cup sugar
2 teaspoons salt
1 teaspoon pepper
2 teaspoons garlic powder
1 teaspoon celery seed
1 teaspoon oregano

Mix in blender.

Hostess: Connie Ramsey
Displayer: Janet Sroka

BAR-B-Q SAUCE

1 cup ketchup
1/2 cup brown sugar
3 teaspoons liquid smoke
1 tablespoon prepared mustard
1 teaspoon worcestershire
1 small onion diced very fine

Mix together in a small sauce pan and bring to a boil. Spoon this
over your favorite meat that has been cooking in the oven. Then
simmer for 1/2 hour at 200 degrees.

Hostess: Geneva Walker
Displayer: Darlene Simpson

JANIE'S "AIN'T THIS SUMPIN'" SALAD

1 package strawberry jello
Tomato soup diluted to make 2 cups
Heat soup and add to jello, stir well and add
1/2 cup chopped celery
1 small jar stuffed olives, cut up
1 teaspoon lemon juice

Place in mold, chill until set.

Hostess: Janie Pollock
Displayer: Eleanor Sheehe

STRAWBERRY FLUFF

1 small box strawberry jello
1 small carton cottage cheese
1 #2 can pineapple, drained
1 large container Cool Whip

Sprinkle jello over cottage cheese to dissolve. Fold drained
pineapple and Cool Whip into cottage cheese mixture. Refrigerate.
Serve as salad or dessert.

Hostess: Jayle Riecken
Displayer: Ruth Young

SYLVIA'S FAVORITE SALAD

1 can condensed milk
1 9 ounce container Cool Whip
1 small can crushed pineapple, drained
1 can coconut
1/3 cup lemon juice
1/2 cup chopped pecans
1/2 cup maraschino cherries

Mix above ingredients very thoroughly and chill.

Hostess: Sylvia Kerr
Displayer: Barbara Key

****

The work of the world does not wait to be done by perfect people.

****

BLUEBERRY SALAD OR DESSERT

1 can blueberries
1 small can crushed pineapple
2 packages blueberry jello (may use blackberry jello)
2 cups boiling water
1 cup juice drained from pineapple and blueberries
Dissolve jello in hot water. Add fruit and cup of juice. Let congeal.

TOPPING:
1 cup sour cream   1/2 cup chopped nuts for topping
1 8 ounce package cream cheese
1/2 cup sugar
1 1/2 teaspoons vanilla
Blend together and spread on top of jello a few hours before
serving. Sprinkle chopped nuts on top. Serves 10-12.

Hostess: Rosalie Rumph

CUCUMBER AND PINEAPPLE SALAD

1 tablespoon gelatin
4 tablespoons cold water
3/4 cup boiling water
1/2 cup mayonnaise
1/2 cup whipped cream
2/3 cup cold water
6 tablespoons lemon juice
3/4 cup sugar
pineapple
cucumbers

Mix gelatin with 4 tablespoons cold water and let soften. Add
softened gelatin to boiling water. Add cold water,
lemon juice, sugar and stir until sugar dissolves. Add equal
parts of diced cucumber and pineapple. When partially set, fold
in 1/2 cup each of mayonnaise and whipped cream. Chill. Cut into
squares for serving.

Hostess: Barbara McDonald

CRANBERRY SALAD

1 package 1 pound ground cranberries
2 cups crushed pineapple
1 cup sugar
2 packages raspberry jello
1 cup chopped nuts
Combine sugar, cranberries and pineapple, let stand. Make
jello, let partially set and then add cranberry/pineapple
mixture and nuts. Mix well and let set.

Hostess: Ethel Anderson
Displayer: Carla Jones, Manager

FROZEN FRUIT SALAD

2   3 ounce packages philadelphia cream cheese
2 tablespoons salad dressing
1/2 cup of drained crushed pineapple
2 cups of diced ripe banana
1/2 cup of chopped maraschine cherries
1/2 cup chopped pecans
1/2 cup diced marshmallows
1   cup whipping cream
1/2 teaspoon salt
1 tablespoon lemon juice

Mash cheese with fork, add salt, salad dressing, lemon juice,
and mix well. Fold in pineapple, cherries, nuts, bananas, and
marshmallows. Whip cream until thick and add to cheese and
fruit mixture, turn into freeze tray and freeze until firm.

Hostess: Nona Balke
Displayer: K. Selby

FROZEN SALAD DESSERT

1   #1 14 ounce can Thank You cherry pie filling
1   #1 12 ounce can crushed pineapple, drained
1 can Eagle Brand Milk (sweetened)
10 ounce container Cool Whip

Fold pie filling and pineapple together. Gently stir in milk
then fold in cool until well blended. Put in 9 x 13" pan.
Sprinkle with chopped nuts. Cover with foil, then freeze.
Keeps forever in freezer. Also good with peaches or blueberries.

Hostess: Julia Mrvan
Displayer: Helen Barnett

FIVE CUP SALAD

1 cup sour cream
1 cup pineapple tid bits
1 cup orange tid bits
1 cup cocoanut
1 cup minature marshmellows

Mix all together and let set 24 hours. Then serve.

Hostess: June Flye
Displayer: Jean Brown

LEMON LIME SALAD

1/4 pound small marshmallows
1 package lemon gelatin
1 package lime gelatin
1 cup hot water
1 cup pineapple juice
1 #2 can crushed pineapple, drained, use juice
1 3 ounce package cream cheese, crumble or cut into small pieces
1/2 pint cream whipped, or 1 can evaporated milk, chilled and whipped

Dissolve gelatin in hot water and pineapple juice and stir
until dissolved. Cool until slightly thickened. Fold in
pineapple, cheese and whipped cream. Pour into 8 x 8 x2"
pan or larger. Chill until firm. Serve in lettuce or cut
into squares in serving dish. Makes 12 servings.

Hostess: Marie Green
Displayer: Linda Gordon

CREAM CHEESE SALAD

1 package gelatin, lime, lemon, or pineapple
1 cup boiling water
1 small can crushed pineapple and juice
1/2 cup nutmeats, chopped fine
1 cup cream, whipped
1/2 cup celery cut fine
1 3 ounce package cream cheese
1 cup minature marshmallows
some grated American cheese

Dissolve gelatin in water. When syrupy, add pineapple, nut
meats, celery, marshmallows and grated cheese. Mix thoroughly.
Whip the cream and cream cheese together and add to other ingredients.
Pour in mold and chill till firm.

Hostess: Mary Weir
Displayer: Linda K. Case

FRUIT SALAD

2 11 ounce cans mandarin oranges, drained
1 large can crushed pineapple (packed in it's own juice) drained
1 12 ounce carton cottage cheese
1 6 ounce package orange jello, dry
1 9 ounce carton Cool Whip

Mix well drained oranges and pineapple together. Add remaining
ingredients one at a time, mixing well after each. Good with ham.

Hostess: Martha Lowery

COOL WHIP SALAD

1 large Cool Whip
1 package peach Jello
1 cup cottage cheese
1 cup pecans
1 cup pineapple

Mix Cool Whip and Jello together. Add other ingredients.
Chill one hour.

Hostess: Linda Wallingsford
Displayer: Patricia McClure

DESSERT SALAD

1 large box jello, any flavor but raspberry is good
1 large can crushed pineapple, well drained
1/2 cup finely chopped nuts
Mix together and chill, after preparing jello as directed on box.

1 package Dream Whip, prepared as directed
1 8 ounce package cream cheese, softened
Whip together and pour over jello mixture

1 cup pineapple juice
1 teaspoon lemon juice
3/4 cup sugar
2 tablespoons flour
2 eggs, well beaten
Cook over moderate heat til it thickens. Cool and spread
over Dream Whip mixture.

Garnish several ways: Sprinkle top with nuts; or add more Dream
Whip to top. Serve with fancy cookies. Excellent for pot lucks
in a large casserole dish. Serve in individual dishes. Will
keep in refrigerator for several days.

Hostess: Betty Moore
Displayer: Nancy Evans

****

Every human being has human dignity, and we must not injure it.

Every person is important - to God there is no such thing as
an "unwanted child."
                              From "Be Somebody" by Mary Crowley
                    ****

PISTACHIO SALAD

1 package instant pistachio pudding
1 large tub Cool Whip
1 can crushed pineapple, do not drain
1 cup minature marshmallows
1 small jar maraschino cherries

Mix together and refrigerate.

Hostess: Beverly Kuck
Displayer: Dodie Carpenter

DREAMY BANANA SALAD

1 can crushed pineapple
1 pint heavy whipped cream
1 box vanilla wafers
3-4 bananas

Whip cream. Put layer of vanilla wafers in bottom of
rather large shallow dish. Add layer of crushed pineapple
with juice, layer of sliced banana, layer of whipped cream.
Start again with layer of vanilla wafers, pineapple, bananas,
and cream. Approximately 3 layers, I top the cream off with
some design made with vanilla wafers. Refrigerate, and serve.

Hostess: Kathi Batson

LEMON JELLO SALAD

1 family size lemon jello
2 1/2 cans crushed pineapple (drained but reserve juice)
3 bananas
Mix together and pour into a cake pan. Cover with minature
marshmellows.
4 tablespoons flour
1 cup sugar
2 beaten eggs
2 cups pineapple juice (may add water to make 2 cups)
1 medium size Cool Whip
chopped walnuts for garnish
Mix flour with sugar, add eggs and pineapple juice, boil until
thick. Cool. Mix Cool Whip into flour mixture, pour over jello
set. Sprinkle chopped walnuts on top. Refrigerate.

Hostess: Linda Napier
Displayer: Marilyn Kathol

PISTACHIO DESSERT-SALAD

1 pound can crushed pineapple and juice
1 package Pistachio instant pudding
1 medium size Cool Whip
1 cup minature marshmallows
1 cup chopped nuts

Stir dry ingredients into pineapple and juice. Mix in other ingredients. Pour into mold and chill. Can be used either for light dessert or a salad. Serves 10.

Hostess: Bonnie Dunn
Displayer: Karen Miller

WATERGATE SALAD

1 large can crushed pineapple
1 small box instant pistachio pudding
1 cup minature marshmallows
1 cup chopped nuts
1 large Cool Whip
coconut - optional

Combine and chill.

Hostess: Vercie Cole
Displayer: Gesele Ross

WATERGATE SALAD

9 ounce size carton Cool Whip
1 can (15 1/4 ounces) crushed pineapple, don't drain
1/2 - 3/4 cup chopped nuts
1 box dry instant pistachio pudding mix

Fold each of the above ingredients into the Cool Whip. Cool to enhance the flavor. Maraschino cherries placed on the top add a festive touch at Christmas.

Hostess: Dixie Thorne
Displayer: June Lackey

****

There are two ways of attaining an important end - force and perserverance. Force falls to the lot of only a few, but austere and sustained perservance can be practiced by the most insignificant. It's silent power grows irresistable with time.

****

PARTY DESSERT SALAD

1 3 ounce package cherry gelatin
1 cup hot water
1/2 cup pineapple juice
1 1/3 cups drained crushed pineapple
1/2 cup cottage cheese
1/2 cup whipping cream, whipped
1/2 cup chopped maraschino cherries
1/2 cup chopped almonds

Dissolve gelatin in hot water. Add pineapple juice and chill
until slightly thickened. Fold in crushed pineapple, cottage
cheese, and blend well. Fold cherries, almonds and whipped
cream into the gelatin mixture. Chill until firm.

Hostess: Erlene Hauser
Displayer: Diane Johnson

A MULTITUDE OF SINS

1 large package lime jello
2 cups miniature marshmellows
1 cup grated cheese
1 1/2 cups diced celery
1 No. 2 can crushed pineapple
1/2 cup chopped walnuts
2 tablespoons lemon juice
1/2 pint whipping cream
1/3 cup mayonnaise

Dissolve gelatin and marshmellows in 2 cups boiling water.
Chill until it thickens. Add cheese, celery, pineapple,
nuts and lemon juice. Combine whipped cream and mayonnaise
and fold into first mixture. Chill for 12 hours before serving.

Hostess: Rosie Blackford
Displayer: Dodie, Carpenter

****

The best things in life must come by efforts from within.....
and not by gifts from without.

****

81

ORANGE SALAD

3 ounces orange gelatin
small can crushed pineapple
1 cup cheese
1/2 cup nuts
small cool whip

Mix hot water with gelatin. Add pineapple, let thicken. Add other ingredients. Chill until ready to serve.

Hostess: Marie Keel

HEAVENLY ORANGE FLUFF SALAD

2 small packages orange gelatin
2 cups hot water
1 small can undiluted frozen orange juice
1 large can crushed pineapple
2 cans Mandrin oranges

TOPPING:
1 cup cold milk
1 small package lemon instant pudding
1   4 1/2 ounce Cool Whip (fold into pudding)

Mix gelatin and water in cake pan, size 11 3/4 x 7 1/2 x 1 3/4.
Add frozen orange juice and mix in. Drain pineapple and oranges.
Add to the gelatin mixture. Put in refrigerator until set. Make topping and pour on top. Cut into squares and serve.

Hostess: Barbara Murphy
Displayer: Sandra McClure

JELLO SURPRISE

1 large package jello prepared according to instructions. Let set over night. Just before serving, prepare 2 packages of Dream Whip. Stir into Jello along with your favorite fruit (drained if in juice) and 1-2 cups minature marshmallows.
Shirley's favorite fruit is bananas.

Hostess: Shirley Borses
Displayer: Darlene Simpson

****

If your dollar won't do as much as it once did...consider...
Are you doing as much as you once did for a dollar?

****

82

COOKIES

Without the Lord's gift of the Date Palm, the peoples
of Biblical times might not have survived. Indeed,
they called it the Tree of Life, for it provided them
with food; it's fiber was used for making rope and
of course it provided shade from the sun. They even
made wine from the fruits and brewed a kind of coffee
from the roasted pits. You might make this lovely
confection for any occasion, but it would be very
nice for Palm Sunday visitors.

DATE BARS WITH APRICOTS

1 1/2 cups all purpose flour
1 tsps. baking powder
1/4 tsps. salt
3 eggs
1 cup honey
1 cup finely chopped apricots, dried
1 1/4 cup chopped pitted dates, 8 oz.
1 cup chopped nuts, walnuts, pecans, or almonds
Confectioner's sugar
1 tsps. vanilla extract

WITH LOVE:
In a bowl, beat the eggs until light. Beat in the
honey and vanilla until well blended. Sift the flour,
salt and baking powder together and stir into the
egg-honey mixture. Now stir in the fruit and the
nut meats. Preheat the oven to 350-F and spread the
mixture evenly on a greased 13 X 9 X 2 inch baking
pan. Bake for 45 minutes and let cool in the pan.
Cut into bars about 1 X 3 inches (makes about 38)
and roll in confectioners sugar. Arrange in stacks
on your prettiest plate.

> AND THE LAND SHALL YIELD HER FRUIT,
> AND YE SHALL EAT YOUR FILL, AND DWELL
> THEREIN IN SAFETY.
>
> LEVITICUS 25:19

PUMPKIN COOKIES

3 cups sugar
5 cups flour
3 teaspoons baking soda
3 teaspoons cinnamon
1 1/2 cups shortening
3 teaspoons vanilla
3 tablespoons baking powder
3 cups pumpkin (from can)

Mix together then add:

1 cup chopped nuts
1 cup raisins

Drop by spoonful on ungreased cookie sheet. Bake at 325 degrees for
15 minutes. Yield approximately 6 dozen.

Hostess: Dorothy Bailey
Displayer: Marilyn Lambie

EASY TARTS

Vanilla Wafers
4 tablespoons butter
8 ounces cream cheese
2 teaspoons lemon juice
1 teaspoon vanilla
1/3 cup sugar
1 egg
Cherry pie filling
Put a vanilla wafer in the bottom of each cupcake paper and put
a dab of butter on top. Mix together cream cheese, lemon juice,
vanilla, sugar and egg until it is smooth. Spoon this mixture into
cupcake paper on top of the vanilla wafer and butter until it is
about half full. Bake at 375 degrees for 15 minutes. Remove from
oven and place 1 tablespoon of canned cherry pie filling on top.

Hostess: Edith Jericke
Displayer: Karen Greenwood

****

THIS IS THE
VERSE ON
THE CHAPEL
AT OUR
HOME.

"Thus saith the Lord,
Let not the wise man glory in his wisdom,
Neither let the mighty man glory in his might,
Let not the rich man glory in his riches;
But let him that glorieth glory in this,
That he understandeth and knoweth me,
That I am the Lord which exercise
Lovingkindness, judgement, and righteousness in the earth:
For in these things I delight, saith the Lord."
Jeremiah 9:23,24

****

84

BANANA OATMEAL COOKIES

1 1/2 cups flour
1 cup white sugar
1 teaspoon salt
1/2 teaspoon baking soda
1/4 teaspoon nutmeg
3/4 teaspoon cinnamon
1 1/4 cups soft oil or shortening
1 egg
3 large bananas, mashed (or 4 small ones)
1/2 cup walnuts
1 3/4 cups uncooked oatmeal

Mix all ingredients together, drop by spoonsfull on ungreased
cookie sheet. Bake at 350 degrees until golden. Makes a nice
moist cookie.

Hostess: Deanna Burr
Displayer: Sandra Hayes

SEVEN LAYER BARS

1/4 cup butter
1 cup graham cracker crumbs
1 cup shredded coconut
1 6 ounce package semisweet chocolate bits
1 6 ounce package butterscotch bits
1 can sweetened condensed milk
1 cup chopped walnuts

Preheat oven to 350 degrees. Melt butter in 13 x 9 x 2" pan.
Sprinkle cracker crumbs evenly over butter, press down. Sprinkle
with coconut, sprinkle chocolate bits, then butterscotch bits.
Pour milk evenly over all. Sprinkle on nuts, press lightly.
Bake 30 minutes. Cool and cut into 1/2" bars, makes 48.

Hostess: Darlene Quinlan
Displayer: Barbara Spilsbury

****

A famous Chinese proverb: "If you are planning for one year, sow
grain; ten years, plant trees; but when planning for one hundred
years, grow men."

****

WHOOPEE PIES

1/2 cup Spry
1 cup sugar
2 egg yolks
5 tablespoons cocoa
2 cups flour
1 teaspoon baking powder
1 teaspoon soda
1 teaspoon salt
1 teaspoon vanilla
1 cup milk

Cream Spry and sugar together. Add other ingredients. Drop from
spoon on ungreased sheet by spoonsful. Bake 10-15 minutes at
375 degrees.

FILLING:
1/2 cup Spry (shortening)
2 cups confectioners sugar
2 egg whites
pinch of salt
1 teaspoon vanilla

Hostess: Jennie Pelotte
Displayer: Jean Brown

HAIRY RANGER COOKIES

1 cup butter - it has to be real butter
1 1/2 cups sugar
1 cup brown sugar, packed in
2 eggs
1 cup flour
1 teaspoon baking soda
1/2 teaspoon baking powder
1/2 teaspoon salt
1 1/2 teaspoons vanilla
2 cups oatmeal - the regular, not the 1 minute kind
2 cups corn flakes
1/2 cup shredded coconut
1 cup raisins or dates
1/2 cup nuts
Cream the butter, then add both sugars and cream some more, then cream
in the eggs and vanilla. In a separate mixing bowl, thoroughly mix the
flour, baking powder and salt. Then add this and beat into creamed mix.
Mix remaining ingredients in a dish pan. Gently stir the beaten mix into
this stuff. It will be very thick and hard to stir, but try not to
crush the cornflakes. Pat it into flat baking pans, about 1 inch thick.
You don't have to do a beautiful job of it, since it spreads out while
baking. Bake at 325 degrees about 30 minutes, until medium brown on top.
Watch it carefully. The raisins on bottom tend to burn. When you remove it from oven, let cool a while, then run a knife around edges and
turn out onto a plate. Pick out the black raisins, they'll give a burned
taste. You can vary the big ingredients, like using more or less nuts
and coconut or rasins or dates or currents or whatever.
Hostess: Patty White
Displayer: Lou Ridinger

WALNUT BARS

1 pound light brown sugar
4 eggs
1 1/4 cup flour
1 1/2 cups walnuts
1/2 teaspoon baking powder

Preheat oven to 350 degrees. Beat eggs til light. Add remaining
ingredients. Spread in greased and floured 9 x 13" pan. Bake 25-
30 minutes. DO NOT OVER BAKE. Cut into bars while warm. Roll in
powdered sugar. Makes approximately 18 bars.

Hostess: Ada Dalley
Displayer: Margaret Hamler

PECAN TARTS

1 cup flour
1 stick butter
1-3 ounce package cream cheese

Mix together to make pastry. Chill-form little tarts (tart pan.)

FILLING
1 large egg, beaten
1 cup brown sugar
2 tablespoons butter, melted
1 cup pecans, chopped
Mix and fill tarts. Bake at 350 degrees for 20 minutes.

CHRUNCHY BARS

1 package Crescent Rolls
1 can sweetened condensed milk
1 package coconut pecan frosting mix
1/4 cup melted butter or margarine

Press rolls to cover 9 x 13" pan, (do not leave any open holes) and
come up on the sides about 1/2". Pour milk to cover dough. Sprinkle
frosting mix evenly over milk, then drizzle melted butter over the top.
Bake in 400 degree over 12-15 minutes. Cool at room temperature. Cut
into squares.

Hostess: Marian Rasmussen
Displayer: Agnes Avolicino

****
Decorating your home is a little like falling in love, it's full of
excitement, anticipation, and delight. And while, on one hand, it sets
you to daydreaming, on the other, it makes you more aware of everything around you. Helping you to create a warm and beautiful
environment is what we believe in.
****

BROWNIES

3/4 cup shortening
4 oz. (or 8 tablespoons) cocoa
Melt together and cool above ingredients.
1 cup brown sugar firmly packed
1 cup granulated sugar
3 eggs
1 teaspoon vanilla
1 1/4 cup flour
1 teaspoon baking powder
1/2 teaspoon salt
1/2 cup nuts
Marshmellow creme
Mix all ingredients together and pour onto cookie sheet. Bake at 350
degrees for 15 minutes. Upon removing brownies from oven spread
marshmellow creme on top. Cool and ice with frosting.

Hostess Luella Smith
Displayer: Marilyn Kathol

EASY BROWNIES

2 sticks melted butter or margarine
3/4 cup cocoa
2 cups sugar
4 eggs
1 1/2 cups flour
1/2 teaspoon soda
1/2 teaspoon salt
2 teaspoons vanilla
1/2 cup chopped nuts

Measure and sift together into bowl dry ingredients. Add melted
shortening, eggs, and vanilla - beat until smooth. Fold in nuts.
Pour into greased and floured 10 1/2" x 15 1/2" pan and bake for
20 minutes in 350 degree oven. Cool for 5 minutes and frost.

Hostess: Georgia Schmeckpeper
Displayer: Marilyn Kathol

****
I met God in the morning, when my day was at it's best,
And His presence came like sunrise, like a glory in my breast.

All day long the presence lingered, all day long He stayed with me..
And we sailed in perfect calmness, o'er a very troubled sea.

Other ships were blown and battered, other ships were sore distressed,
But the wind that seemed to blow them...brought to us..a peace and rest.

Then I thought of other mornings, with a keen remorse of mind,
When I too, had loosed the moorings, with His presence left behind.
So I think I know the secret..learned from many a troubled way;
You must seek Him in the morning, if you want Him through the day.
****

QUICK CHOCOLATE COOKIES

1/4 cup butter
2 cups sugar
1/4 cup Hershey's Cocoa
1/2 cup evaporated milk
Bring mixture to boil for one minute. Remove from heat. Add:
3 cups Mother's Oats
1 teaspoon vanilla
1/2 cup peanut butter
Mix well. Drop by teaspoonsful onto waxed paper. Let cool & serve.

Hostess: Polly Gregor
Displayer: Sandi McClure

CONGO BARS

1 Box brown sugar
3 eggs
2/3 cup oil
2 3/4 cups flour
2 1/2 teaspoons baking powder
1 teaspoon baking soda
1/2 teaspoon salt
1 cup chopped nuts
1 6 ounce package chocolate chips
1 6 ounce package butterscotch chips
1 teaspoon vanilla

Mix sugar, eggs, and oil together. Sift together and add to first
mix, the flour, baking powder, soda, and salt. Then add nuts, chocolate chips, butterscotch chips, and vanilla and mix well. Spread
on ungreased cookie sheet. Bake 375 degrees for 15 minutes. DO NOT
OVER BAKE.

Hostess: Sophie Zagar
Displayer: Marilyn Lambie

****
When you work for the thing you believe in you are rich, though the
way is rough. When you are working only for money, you can never
make quite enough.   From "Be Somebody" by Mary Crowley
                              ****

89

LEMON COOLERS

1 package Lemon Cake Mix*
1 large container Cool Whip
1 egg
 1/2 cup powdered sugar

Preheat oven to 350 degrees. Ingredients do not need to be room
temperature. Mix first three ingredients in large bowl by hand.
Drop mixture by teaspoon into powdered sugar to coat. Place onto
greased cookie sheet. Bake for 10-15 minutes. Let cool on sheet
for 5 minutes before removing. Aproximately 4 dozen.
* Spice or applesauce cake mix may be used. Omit 1/2 cup powdered
sugar and use 1/2 cup sugar and cinnamon mixture. Chocolate Mix is
used with powdered sugar.

Hostess: Katie Stuedemann
Dispalyer: Margaret Hamler

TOPPED COOKIES

2 cups sifted flour
1/2 teaspoon soda
1/4 teaspoon salt
1 egg
1 cup brown sugar
1/2 cup butter
1 teaspoon vanilla

Combine flour, soda, salt. Gradually add butter and sugar in
mixing bowl, creaming until light and fluffy. Add egg and vanilla.
Beat well. Shape into one inch balls and place 2 inches apart on
ungreased cookie sheet. Make a depression in the center of each
with thumb and place one teaspoon topping in each depression.

TOPPING
Combine one cup chopped walnuts, 1/2 cup firmly packed brown sugar
and 1/4 cup dairy sour cream.
Bake at 350 degrees for 12-14 minutes.

Hostess: Nancy Scott
Displayer: Linda Case

****
To believe only in possibilities is not faith, but mere philosophy.
If anything can be done..experience and skill can do it.
If a thing cannot be done, only faith can do it.
Faith is fear that has said its prayers.
Faith is not contrary to reason, but rather. reason grown courageous.
    Elton Trueblood (I think) from "Be Somebody" by Mary Crowley.

****

90

DELICIOUS PEANUT BUTTER BALLS
(Taste just like peanut butter cups)

1 18 ounce jar crunchy peanut butter
4 cups powdered sugar
1 cup margarine (room temperature)
8 oz. milk chocolate bar
1/2 bar paraffin

Mix peanut butter, sugar, and margarine and form into one inch balls.
Place on a big cookie sheet and chill for a few minutes.
Melt chocolate and paraffin in a double boiler. Dip each peanut
butter ball into chocolate. Keep chocolate at low temperature while
dipping. These freeze beautifully and taste great right out of the
freezer.

Hostess: Linda Read
Displayer: Linda Case

FIVE LAYER COOKIES

1 stick butter, melted add to:
1 1/4 cups crushed Graham Crackers and pat down in bottom of 9x13 pan.
1/2 can coconut sprinkled over crumbs, then
6 ounce bag of chocolate chips over coconut, then
6 ounce bag butterscotch chips sprinkled over chocolate.
1 can Eagle Brand milk poured over chips.
Sprinkle chopped pecans over all.
Bake 35-40 minutes at 350 degrees.

Displayer: Sharon Anderson

MAYONNAISE COOKIES

3/4 cup mayonnaise
1 cup sugar
3 teaspoons cocoa
Cream above together. Then add:
1 cup chopped raisins or dates
1 cup nuts
1 teaspoon soda
1 cup boiling water
Mix well then add:
2 cups flour
1/2 teaspoon salt
1 teaspoon vanilla.
Bake in an 8 x 8 x 2 inch pan or make drop cookies. Bake at 325 degrees
for 12-15 minutes.

Hostess:Nettie Brown
Displayer: Linda Case

MARSHMELLOW COOKIES

2 cups sugar
1/2 cup cream

Cook on medium heat to soft ball stage. Remove from heat and add:

1 jar of marshmellow creme
1/4 pound margarine
2 cups graham cracker crumbs (reserve)

Stir until melted. Add crumbs. Drop at once on waxed paper.

Hostess: Kathy Darlene Carver
Displayer: Teresa Graham

POTATO CHIP COOKIES

2 cups brown sugar
1 cup shortening
2 eggs
2 cups flour
1 teaspoon baking soda
1 teaspoon pure vanilla
1 cup crushed potato chips
1 cup chopped nuts

Cream together sugar, shortening and eggs. Stir in flour, baking soda and vanilla. Mix well. Add chips and nuts: mix well to distribute evenly. Drop by teaspoonsfull onto ungreased cookie sheet. Bake in 350 degree oven for 10-12 minutes.

Hostess: Glorie Mello
Displayer: Linda Millikan

OLD FASHIONED SUGAR COOKIES

2 cups flour
1/2 teaspoon soda
1/2 teaspoon salt
1/2 cup shortening
1 cup sugar
1 egg yolk
1/2 cup buttermilk
1 teaspoon vanilla
1 egg white
Mix first 3 ingredients. Mix shortening, sugar and egg yolk, add flour alternately with buttermilk, then add vanilla & egg whites. Drop by spoonful and flatten.

Hostess: Marvis Johnson
Displayer: Karen Pratt

BROWNIES

2 tablespoon cocoa
1 cup sugar
3/4 cup self-rising flour
1 stick melted butter
2 eggs
1/2 teaspoons vanilla
pinch salt
1/2 cup pecans
Bake at 350 degrees for 20 minutes.

ICING
1 stick butter
3 tablespoons cocoa
6 tablespoons milk
pinch of salt

Bring to boil; remove and add:
1 box confectioners sugar
1/2 teaspoon vanilla.
Pour over brownies when removed from oven.

Hostess: Faye Hoke
Displayer: Marie Keel

BROWNIES

1 pound can Hershey syrup
1/2 cup butter - soft
1 cup sugar
1 cup flour
1 dash salt
4 eggs
1/2 cup nuts (walnuts)

Mix in large bowl butter and sugar. Add other ingredients and beat
with mixer, then add nuts. Use 9 x 13" pan. Bake 350 degrees for
20 minutes.

FROSTING:
1/2 cup butter   1/2 cup chocolate chips
1 1/2 cups sugar
1/3 cup milk.
Use medium size pan. Boil for one minute. Take off heat and add
chocolate chips. Stir often and frost while brownies are still warm.

Hostess: Darlene Menneke

****

QUICK BROWNIES

1 cup sugar
4 tablespoons cocoa
5 tablespoons Crisco Oil
3/4 cup plain flour
pinch of salt
1/3 cup milk
2 eggs
1 teaspoon vanilla

Put all ingredients into medium tupperware mixing bowl and mix well.
Pour into greased and floured 9 x 13" pan and bake at 350 degrees for
20 minutes.

FROSTING

2 cups powdered sugar   1/2 cup pecans (optional)
1/2 stick melted oleo or margarine
2 tablespoons cocoa
3 or 4 tablespoons evaporated milk (canned)
1 teaspoon vanilla

Put all ingredients into bowl and mix until smooth, then add pecans,
if desired, and spread on brownies while hot.

Hostess:Janice McCalip
Displayer: Dodie Carpenter

BUTTERSCOTCH BROWNIES

1/2 cup butter
2 cups brown sugar
2 eggs
1 teaspoon vanilla
2 cups flour
2 teaspoons baking powder
1/4 teaspoon salt
1 cup coconut
1 cup walnuts

Melt butter; remove and stir in brown sugar. Add eggs, one at a
time until smooth. Stir in vanilla; add all the other ingredients.
Stir well. Bake in greased cookie sheet at 350 degrees for 25 min.

Hostess: Connie Reimers
Displayer: Connie Becker

****
Mothers as well as fools, sometimes walk where angels fear to tread.
****

HERSHEY BROWNIES

1/2 cup shortening
1 cup sugar
Cream above with mixer, add and beat well:
4 eggs - then add:
1 cup flour
1/2 teaspoon baking powder
1 1 pound can Hersheys syrup
3/4 cup nuts
Dash of salt
1/2 teaspoon vanilla
Mix well and pour into greased large pan. Bake at 350 degrees, 20-25 min.

FROSTING:
6 tablespoons butter
6 tablespoons milk
1 1/2 cups sugar
Cook only until dossolved. Add reamining ingredients and beat
until smooth:
1 cup chocolate chips
1/2 bag miniature marshmallows
nuts if desired

Hostess: Gwen Pigott
Displayer: Judy Braun

CHOCOLATE MARSHMELLOW COOKIES

1 3/4 cups flour
1/2 teaspoon salt
1/2 teaspoon soda
1/2 cup cocoa
1/2 cup shortening
1 cup sugar
1 egg
1 teaspoon vanilla
1/4 cup milk
1/2 cup chopped fine nuts
Package large marshmallows
Sift dry ingredients together. Beat well by hand the shortening,
sugar, egg vanilla, milk, then add to the dry ingredients. Add
the nuts. Preheat oven to 350 degrees. Drop mix by spoonsful onto
greased cookie sheet. After baking 8 minutes, remove from oven and
press 1/2 a large marshmellow into each cookie. Return to oven and
bake 2 minutes longer. Cool and frost with your favorite Chocolate
frosting. Makes approximately 3 dozen.

Displayer: Margaret Hamler

CHOCOLATE CHIP COOKIES

1/2 cup butter
1/2 cup sugar
1/4 cup brown sugar
1 beaten egg
1 cup plus 2 tablespoons flour
1/2 teaspoon baking soda
1/2 teaspoon salt
1/4 teaspoon hot water
1 6 ounce package chocolate chops
1/2 teaspoon vanilla

Cream butter and sugars. Add egg and beat well. Sift dry
ingredients and add to creamed mixture, add hot water, mix well,
add chocolate chips and vanilla. Drop by rounded teaspoonfull on
ungreased cookie sheet and bake in preheated oven at 350 degrees 10
to 12 minutes. Yield: 3 1/2 dozen.

Hostess: Karen Rohrbaugh
Displayer: Linda Keller

M & M COOKIES

1 cup margarine
1 cup brown sugar
1/2 cup sugar
2 teaspoons vanilla
2 eggs
2 1/4 cups flour
1 teaspoon baking soda
1/2 teaspoon salt
M & M's

Blend shortening and two sugars. Beat in vanilla and eggs. Mix
soda and salt and 1/4 cup flour, beat in. Add rest of flour and
mix well. Drop by teaspoons (scant) on cookie sheet. Decorate
each with 3,4, or 5 candies. Bake 8-10 minutes at 375 degrees.

Hostess Dolores Arsenault
Displayer: Jean Brown

****
Stress is really an integral part of life. We set our whole pattern
of life by our stress end-point. If we hit it exactly, we live
dynamic, purposeful, useful, happy lives. If we go over, we break.
If we stay too far under, we vegetate.   H. M. Marvin, M.D.
****

CHOCOLATE SQUARES

2 cups sugar
2 cups flour
1/2 teaspoon salt
1 stick oleo
1/2 cup salad oil
1/4 cup cocoa
1 cup water
2 eggs
1 teaspoon vanilla
1/2 cup sour milk
(1 teaspoon vinegar and 1 teaspoon soda dissolved in milk)

Mix sugar, flour and salt together in bowl. Mix oleo, oil, cocoa
and water in pan and bring to a boil, pour hot mixture over dry
stuff and stir. Add remaining ingredients and beat well. Pour
in a greased and floured pan 12 x 18". Bake at 350 degrees for
30 minutes.

Hostess: JoAnn Weber
Displayer: Carla Jones, Mgr.

CHOCOLATE BUTTERSWEETS

1/2 cup butter or oleo
1/2 cup powdered sugar
1/4 teaspoon salt
1 teaspoon vanilla
1 to 1 1/4 cups flour
Mix well and make into small balls, the size of a walnut, and put on
a cookie sheet and press thumb in center for the topping. Bake at 350
degrees for 10 to 12 minutes. Fill while still warm.

CREAMY NUT FILLING
Soften 3 ounce package of cream cheese. Blend in 1 cup powdered
sugar and 1 teaspoon vanilla. Add 2 tablespoons flour. Cream well.
Stir in 1/2 cup nuts and put on cookie while still warm.

CHOCOLATE ICING
Melt 1/2 cup Nestles Semi-Sweet Chocolate Chips and 2 tablespoons
butter with 2 tablespoons water over low heat stirring occasionally.
Add 1/2 cup sifted powdered sugar and beat smooth. Put chocolate
icing over the cream filling.

Hostess: Helen Marie Rossi
Displayer: Helen Barnett

****
If you don't think every day is great....try missing a few.
****

97

MISTI'S SUGAR COOKIES

3/4 cup shortening (no butter)
2 1/4 to 2 1/2 cups flour
1 teaspoon baking powder
1 cup sugar
2 eggs
1 teaspoon vanilla
1 teaspoon salt
food coloring if desired

Mix shortening, sugar, eggs, flavoring and food coloring until fluffy.
Mix flour, baking powder and salt together in a seperate bowl. Combine
the two mixtures and chill for one hour. Heat oven to 400 degrees and
roll dough 1/8 inch thick on a lightly floured board. Cut with a
cookie cutter and place on an ungreased baking sheet. Bake just until
the cookies are set (about 6 minutes) Makes about 3 dozen. Cool
cookies and ice them with mixture below.

ICING:
Milk
Powdered sugar
Pinch of salt
1/2 teaspoon of flavoring
Beat well together.

Hostess: Julie Wallis
Displayer: Marty Rickman

RYAN'S SNICKERDOODLES

1 cup shortening (part butter)
1 cup sugar
2 eggs
2 1/2 cups flour
1 teaspoon baking soda
1/2 teaspoon salt

Mix together 2 teaspoons sugar
2 teaspoons cinnamon.

Heat oven to 400 degrees. Mix shortening , sugar, and eggs until
fluffy. In a seperate bowl mix flour, soda and salt throughly and
add to shortening mixture. Make sure the dough is not too dry. It
should just barely form into nearly golf ball sized balls. Roll in
sugar/cinnamon mixture. Place on an ungreased cookie sheet and
bake just until the cookies are set (about 10 minutes) Yield 2 dozen.

Hostess: Julie Wallis
Displayer: Marty Rickman

APPLE BARS

1 cup sugar
1 cup water
2 tablespoons cornstarch
1 teaspoon vanilla

Bring to a boil and cook about 5 minutes, then cool.

1 1/2 cups oatmeal
1 cup brown sugar
2 cups sifted flour
3/4 cup soft shortening
salt
4 -5 apples
Mix above well with fork, except apples.
Grease large cake pan 9 x 13". Cover bottom and sides with dry
mixture, oatmeal. Reserve some for top. Cover crumbed pan with
apples, sliced thin. Pour cooked filling over apples. Sprinkle
rest of crumbs over filling. Bake in 375 degree oven for 45 min.
to 1 hour.

Hostess: Bettie Leustek
Displayer: Priscilla Stalker

MICHIGAN APPLE COOKIES

1/2 cup butter or oleo
1 1/3 cup brown sugar
1 egg
1/4 cup apple juice (use baby's cans for economy)
2 cups flour
1/2 teaspoon salt
1/2 teaspoon cloves
1 teaspoon cinnamon
1 teaspoon soda
1 cup peeled and chopped apples
1 cup rasins
1 cup chopped nuts

Cream together the first 4 ingredients. Combine all day ingredients
and add to cream mixture. Stir in apples, rasins, and nuts. Drop
on cookie sheet, bake 13 minutes ant 350 degrees.

GLAZE:
1/2 cup powdered sugar
1 tablespoon butter
2 tablespoons apple juice or water
Spread a little glaze on each cookie while still warm.

Displayer: Doris Roper

YUM YUM COOKIES

1 cup shortening
1 1/2 cup sugar
3 eggs
3 cups self rising flour (if plain, add 1 tsp. soda, & 1/4 tsp. salt)
1 teaspoon ground cinnamon
1 tablespoon water
1 8 ounce package chopped dates
1 cup nuts

Blend shortening with sugar until light and fluffy. Add eggs one at a time, beating well after each addition. Combine dry ingredients and add to sugar mixture. Add water to dates and add with nuts to flour mixture. Drop by teaspoons onto greased cookie sheet. Yield 6 dozen. Bake at 375 degrees for 12 to 15 minutes.

Hostess: Barbara McDonald

REFRIGERATOR DATE COOKIES

1 cup shortening
2 cups brown sugar
2 eggs
1 cup nuts, ground
1 cup dates, ground
3 1/2 cups cake flour
1 teaspoon salt
1 teaspoon soda

Cream shortening and sifted sugar thoroughly. Add eggs 1 at a time and beat well after each addition. Add nuts and dates which have been put through food chopper. Sift dry ingredients together, add to creamed mixture and mix well. Shape in rolls 2 inches in diameter. Wrap in waxed paper and store in refrigerator until firm. Slice thin and bake 8 minutes at 400 degrees. Makes 11 to 12 dozen cookies.

Hostess: Evelyn Lord
Displayer: Dodie Carpenter

DATE BARS

1 cup flour
1/2 teaspoon salt
1 teaspoon baking powder
1 cup sugar
1 teaspoon cinnamon

1 egg
2/3 cups milk
1 1/4 cups chopped dates
1 cup chopped nuts

Sift dry ingredients. Add nuts and dates. Beat egg add milk and mix well. Add gradually to dry mixture and combine. Pour into 9" x 13" shallow pan. Bake 350 degrees for 25 to 30 minutes. Cut into squares.

Hostess: JoAnn Weber
Displayer: Carla Jones

ORANGE DROP COOKIES

1 1/2 cups packed brown sugar
1 cup margarine
2 eggs
1 tablespoon grated orange peel
1 teaspoon vanilla
3 cups flour - sifted
1/2 teaspoon salt
2 teaspoons baking powder
1 teaspoon baking soda
3/4 cup buttermilk

Cream brown sugar and margarine. Add eggs, orange peel and vanilla. Beat until fluffy. Add flour, soda and baking powder and salt, alternating with buttermilk. Drop by teaspoonsfull on ungreased sheet. Bake at 350 degrees for 10-12 minutes. Frost while still warm.

FROSTING:
1 tablespoon orange peel
3 tablespoon orange juice
3 tablespoon margarine
Add enough powdered sugar to make a good frosting consistancy.

Hostess: Debbie Wark
Displayer: Linda Case

FROSTY STRAWBERRY SQUARES

1 cup flour
1/4 cup brown sugar
1/2 cup chopped wlanuts
1/2 cup butter or oleo melted

Stir together first 4 ingredients; spread evenly in shallow baking pan. Bake at 350 degrees for 20 minutes stirring occasionally. Sprinkle 2/3 of these crumbs in 13 x 9 x 2 pan.

2 egg whites
2/3 cup sugar
1 package Dream Whip
1 10 ounce package frozen strawberries, partially thawed

Combine egg whites, sugar, berries in a large bowl; with electric mixer beat at high speed to stiff peaks (about 10 minutes) Fold in whipped cream. Spoon over crumbs; top with remaining crumbs. Freeze 6 hours or overnight. Cut in squares and trim with whole strawberries.

Hostess: JoAnn Weber
Displayer: Carla Jones

BISCOCHITOS
(COOKIES)

1 cup sugar
3 eggs
2 teaspoons vanilla
2 teaspoons anise seed
1 cup shorening
4 cups flour
3 teaspoons baking powder

Mix thoroughly sugar, eggs, vanilla, anise seed. Add shortening
and stir. Sift flour and baking powder and blend into mixture.
Roll out about 1/8" thick, cut with cookie cutter and place on a
slightly greased baking sheet. Bake at 400 degrees 6-8 minutes.

Hostess: Aurora De La O
Displayer: Diana M. Herrera

MERINGUE SURPRISES

2 egg whites
1 teaspoon vanilla
1/8 teaspoon salt
1/2 cup sugar
1 6 ounce package chocolate chips

Combine egg whites, vanilla and salt. Beat until stiff. Beat in
sugar gradually until stiff and satiny. At Christmas, divide mixture into 2 parts and add red and green food coloring. Fold half
of chocolate chips into each mixture. Drop by teaspoonfull onto
greased cookie sheet. Bake 30 minutes at 300 degrees.

Hostess: Norma Juriek
Displayer: Margie Duke

HOLIDAY FRUIT DROPS

1 cup shortening
2 cups brown sugar
2 eggs
1/2 cup buttermilk
3 1/2 cups flour
1 teaspoon soda
1 teaspoon salt
1 1/2 cup broken pecans
2 cups candied cherries, chopped
2 cups cut up dates

Mix shortening, sugar, and eggs well. Stir in buttermilk, add dry
ingredients. Stir, add pecans, cherries, and dates. Chill one hour.
Drop rounded teaspoonsful of dough on greased cookie sheet. Place
pecan halves on top of each cookie. Bake 8-10 minutes at 400 degrees.
Hostess: Florence Pruiett
Displayer: Fodie Smith

CHERRY BARS

1 cup butter or margarine
1 3/4 cups sugar
1/2 teaspoon salt
1 teaspoon vanilla
1 teaspoon almond flavoring
4 eggs
3 cups flour
1 teaspoon baking powder
1 can cherry pie filling

Mix sugar, butter, eggs and flavorings. Add dry ingredients. Add
a little milk if the dough is stiff. Put about 1/2 of this in
brownie size pan and cover with pie filling and dab rest of dough on.
Drizzle with icing.

Hostess: Ginny Kommer
Displayer: Judy Braun

CREAM WAFERS

1 cup soft butter
1/3 cup whipping cream
2 cups flour
Mix and chill 1 hour. Roll 1/8 inch thick. Cut into small shapes
1 1/2 inches in diameter. Transfer onto plate with 1/2 cup sugar
on it. Coat both sides with sugar. Place on ungreased baking
sheet. IMPORTANT: Prick 4 times with fork. Bake at 375 degrees
for 7-9 minutes.

CREAMY BUTTER FILLING:

1/4 cup soft butter
3/4 cup Powdered sugar
1 egg yolk
1 teaspoon vanilla
color (optional)
Mix together and place filling between two wafers.

Hostess: Judy Sandberg
Displayer: Bernie Lorraine

****
The greatest discovery of my generation is that people can alter
their lives by altering their attitudes of mind. William James
of Harvard.
****

DESSERTS

Honey was the only sweetener known in Biblical times, until the Queen of Sheba brought sugar cane to Solomon, seeking his wisdom in exchange for her many gifts. Nutritionally, honey is much better for you than the refined sugar of today and sugar cannot duplicate it's delicate sweetness which enhances the flavor of any fresh fruit.

HONEYED APPLES

4 cooking apples
1 cup water
1 cup honey
1 stick cinnamon
Sour cream
Nutmeg

Core and slice the apples into eights. In a saucepan place the cinnamon stick, honey and water and bring to a boil. Lower the flame and add some of the apple slices a little at a time. Do not crowd too many in the pan or they will not cook evenly. Cook slowly until they are tender, turning several times and transfer to individual desert dishes. When all the slices have been cooked, bring the syrup in the pan to a boil again for a minute, then let it cool slightly. Remove the cinnamon stick and pour the syrup over the apple slices, some in each dish. This is delicious served while still warm, topped by a dollop of cold sour cream and dusted with a little fresh grated nutmeg. It is also a wonderful side dish served plain with pork.

AS THE APPLE TREE AMONG THE TREES OF
THE WOOD, SO IS MY BELOVED AMONG THE
SONS. I SAT DOWN UNDER HIS SHADOW
WITH GREAT DELIGHT, AND HIS FRUIT
WAS SWEET TO MY TASTE.
SONG OF SOLOMON 2:3

FRUIT CREAM PIE

1 large package instant pudding and pie filling
1 small tub Cool Whip
1 8 ounce package frozen berries (thawed and drained)
1 8 or 9" pre-cooked pie shell

Make up pudding as instructed on the box, except slight the
liquid a little. Chill until partially set. Fold in Cool
Whip and berries. Pour into pie shell and chill.

Hostess: Nancy Haldarman
Displayer: Tonya Pember

PRIZE WINNING CUSTARD PIE

5 whole eggs, or 6 small ones
1 cup sugar
2 cups warm sweet milk
2 tablespoons melted butter
1 teaspoon vanilla

Beat eggs till foamy, then add sugar and beat till foamy
again. Add milk, butter, vanilla and salt. Pour into
unbaked pie shell. Bake at 400 degrees until foamy top
starts to brown. Turn oven down to 350 degrees. Let bake till
about 1 1/2 inches of outside of custard is firm. Take out
before center is firm. May be baked as a custard (without
crust) in pan with one inch water.

Hostess: Pollyanna Core
Displayer: Marty Rickman, Manager

BREAD PUDDING

1 loaf bread
1/2 block butter
4 eggs (beat whites separately)
1 teaspoon vanilla
2 cans carnation
1 cup sugar
1 small box raisins

Boil milk; add sugar, eggs, butter and pour over softened bread
wet with water, add vanilla and raisins. Bake in pre-heated
oven at 350 degrees for 40-45 minutes.

Hostess: Patricia Lormand

****

The best place to spend your vacation this summer is somewhere
near your budget.

****

HOME MADE BANANA PUDDING

1 cup sugar
2 tablespoons flour
3 eggs
1 small can Pet evaporated milk
1 cup water
1 teaspoon vanilla
1/2 stick butter
pinch of salt
1 box vanilla wafers
3 medium bananas

Mix sugar, flour, eggs, evaporated milk, water, vanilla, butter
and salt in a double boiler, and cook over medium heat; bring to
a boil stirring often. Continue cooking until it thickens, like
pudding. Lay vanilla wafers in bottom of medium casserole dish,
crumble 2 or 3 handsful of wafers and add to pudding mixture after
removing from the heat. Slice bananas and arrange them on top
of wafers in the bowl. Pour pudding on top of wafers and bananas.
Chill till thickened, or eat it warm.
NOTE: This basic pudding receipe can be used as the base for any
of these pies:
      Coconut - add coconut
      Cocoa - add cocoa
      Pumpkin - add pumpkin

Hostess: Cynthia Shumway
Displayer: Helene Thompson, Manager

CORNSTARCH PUDDING

1/4 cup cornstarch
1/3 cup sugar
1/8 teaspoon salt
2 3/4 cups milk
2 tablespoons margarine
1 teaspoon vanilla

Mix in small saucepan. Stir in milk slowly, keeping mixture smooth.
Cook over medium heat, stirring til it comes to a boil. Boil
gently for 1 minute, take off heat. Stir margarine and vanilla
into hot pudding. Pour into serving dishes. Cool and chill.
Makes eight 1/2 cup servings. For chocolate pudding, add
3 tablespoons cocoa, and increase sugar to 2/3 cup. Mix extra
ingredients with cornstarch poured as directed above.

****

Any housewife, no matter how large her family, can always
get some time alone by doing the dishes.

****

RICE PUDDING

1 quart milk
1/2 cup sugar
1/2 teaspoon nutmeg
1/2 cup raw rice
1/2 teaspoon salt
1/2 cup raisins

Combine all and pour into buttered pan (Cake pan is good.) Bake at 350 degrees for 2 hours, stirring occasionally in the first hour.

Hostess: Mildred Yahn
Displayer: Sharon L. Wiendandt

CORN MEAL PIE

1 cup brown sugar
2 tablespoons corn meal
1/2 tablespoon vanilla
1 tablespoon water
2 eggs
1 cup white sugar
2 tablespoons butter
Unbaked pie shell
Mix all ingredients together. Then pour into an unbaked pie shell. Bake at 400 degrees for 45 minutes.

Displayer: Linda Stabler

PEACH COBBLER

1 large can of sliced peaches. Pour with juice in cake pan
1 Butter Brickle cake mix, sprinkeled over peaches
1 cup coconut over cake mix
1 cup walnut meats over coconut
1/4 pound of butter, melted and poured over entire mixture

Bake at 350 degrees for 40 minutes. Can be turned upside down, serve with cool whip or ice cream.

Hostess: Karen Olson
Displayer: Judy Braun

****

Duty makes us do things well...but love makes us do them beautifully.
                                        Phillip Brooks
****

PUMPKIN CHIFFON PIE

2 envelopes unflavored gelatin
1/4 cup cold water (combine to soften gelatin)
2 eggs separated
1 1/2 cup pumpkin pie filling
1 cup milk
3/4 cup brown sugar
2 teaspoons pumpkin pie spice
1/2 teaspoon salt
8 ounce container Cool Whip
Graham Cracker crust
Beat egg yolks together and add pumpkin, milk, 1/2 cup only of
brown sugar, spices, salt. Cook over low heat until thick,
stirring constantly. Pour in gelatin water mixture and put
in refrigerator to cool. Now beat egg whites to peak and add
remainder brown sugar til stiff. Fold in cooled mixture and
Cool Whip. Pour into graham cracker crust. This pie will
keep in refrigerator for 2 weeks.

Hostess: Lynn Gordon
Displayer: Bonnie Laux

DAIQUIRI PIE

1 package (4 serving size) lemon pie filling
1 3 ounce package lime jello
1/3 cup sugar
2 1/2 cups water
2 eggs, slightly beaten
1/2 cup Bacardi light rum
2 cups non-dairy whipped cream (thawed)
1 9" crumb crust

Mix pudding, jello and sugar in saucepan. Stir in 1/2 cup water
and eggs; blend well. Add remaining water. Stir over medium
heat until mixture comes to full boil. Remove from heat, stir
in rum. Chill about 1 1/2 hours. To hasten chilling place
bowl of filling mixture in larger bowl of ice water; stir until
mixture is cold. Blend topping into chilled mixture. Spoon
into crust. Chill until firm. Garnish with additional whipped
cream or graham cracker crumbs.

Hostess: Sherrie Kautz
Displayer: Dodie Carpenter

****

LOVE transforms --
     Ambition into aspiration
     Greed into gratitude,
     Selfishness into service
     Getting into giving,
     Demands into dedication.
                                   From "Be Somebody"
          ****

MILLION DOLLAR PIE

2 Graham cracker crusts
1 can Eagle Brand Milk
1/4 cup lemon juice
1 small can angel flake coconut
1 large can crushed pineapple, drained
1 cup pecans, chipped
1 large Cool Whip, 13 ounces

Cream milk and lemon juice with beaters. Add coconut, pineapple and pecans. Fold in Cool Whip. Put in crusts. Makes two pies.

Displayer: Esther Graham

CHERRY CHEESECAKE PIE

2 cups graham cracker crumbs (about 14 double crackers)
1/2 cup (1 stick) butter, melted
1 cup (1/2 pint) whipping cream
1/2 cup fresh lemon juice
1 8 ounce package cream cheese
1 can condensed milk (not evaporated)
1 envelope plain gelatin
1/4 cup cold water
1 teaspoon pure vanilla extract
1 can cherry pie filling (ready for use)

Combine graham cracker crumbs and butter.   Line 9 inch deep dish pie plate with graham cracker mixture. Stir lemon juice into cream, let stand 10 minutes. Mash cream cheese thoroughly. Gradually beat in condensed milk. Mixture should be smooth. Add gelatin to water; let stand 5 minutes, then dissolve over hot water. Whip lemon-cream mixture just until it begins to stiffen. Pour in cream cheese mixture and continue beating until well blended. Stir in gelatin and vanilla. Pour into pie crust; chill until firm, 1 1/2 hours. Top with cherry pie filling and chill a while longer. 8-10 servings.

Hostess: Debbie Scott
Displayer: Claudia Rooker

CHERRY TOPPED CHEESE PIE

1 8 ounce package cream cheese
1/2 cup sugar
2 cups Cool Whip
1 9" graham cracker crust
1 cup cherry pie filling

Beat softened cream cheese and sugar together until creamy. Blend in thawed Cool Whip. Pour into unbaked crust. Top with cherry filling. Chill at least 3 hours before serving.

Hostess: Pat Steinberg
Displayer: Earlene Young

STRAWBERRY GLACE PIE

1 piecrust shell, or 1 graham cracker shell
1 quart fresh strawberries, cut up 1 cup berries
1 cup sugar
3 tablespoons cornstarch
1 cup water
1cup whipping cream, whipped and sweetened
Red food coloring

Mix 1 cup sugar and cornstarch in 2 quart saucepan. Stir in water gradually until smooth. Add cut-up berries. Cook and stir over medium heat until thick and clear. Stir in a few drops red food coloring. Cool. Stir in remaining berries, saving 1/4 cup for garnish. Pour into piecrust shell. Chill until firm, about 3 hours. Top with whipped cream, and garnish with berries. Serves 6.

PINK LEMONADE PIE

1 small can frozen pink lemonade
1 can Eagle Brand milk
8 ounces Cool Whip
Food coloring as desired

Mix the above ingredients together and pour into a graham cracker crust and freeze. Thaw 10 minutes before serving. This makes a beautiful and easy to make dessert.

Hostess: Anita Davidson
Displayer: Pat Lipscomb

****

FAITH

Faith is needed all the way,
Faith to toil and faith to pray,
Faith to learn and faith to teach,
Faith to practice, faith to preach,
Faith to start each day anew,
Faith to do our duty, too;
Faith to help the weak along.
Faith to hear, in patience, wrong;
Faith to smile, though sad within,
Faith to conquer every sin,
Faith to ask Him for His care
While we earthly trials bear;
Faith to smother every sigh,
Faith to live and faith to die.

STRAWBERRY PIE

Baked pie shell
1 quart halved strawberries
2/3 cup water
1 cup sugar
3 tablespoons cornstarch
1/3 cup water
Whipped cream
Mix 1 cup of halved strawberries and 2/3 cup water, simmer on stove.
Blend in sugar, cornstarch, and 1/3 cup water. Cook til thick
and clear. Let cool. Fill baked pie shell with remaining
halved strawberries. Cover with cooled glazed mixture and
add whipped cream on top. Granish with strawberries on top.
Chill 2-3 hours before serving.

Hostess: Judi Houdek
Displayer: Marilyn Kathol

IMPOSSIBLE PIE

1 stick margarine
2 cups milk
2 teaspoons vanilla extract
1 cup sugar
4 eggs
1/2 cup flour
1/4 teaspoon salt
1 cup shredded coconut

Place all ingredients in a blender and combine thoroughly.
Grease and flour a 10" pie pan. Pour mixture into pan and
bake in a pre-heated oven at 350 degrees for 30-40 minutes,
or until set. "Pie" will make its own crust as it cooks.
Serve at room temperature.

Hostess: Mrs. Rosa Garner
Displayer: Rita Brown

IMPOSSIBLE COCONUT PIE

4 eggs
3 tablespoons butter
1/2 cup sugar
1/2 cup Bisquick
1 can coconut
2 cups milk
1 teaspoon vanilla

Put all in blender, blend on mix for 15 seconds. Bake in well
greased 9" pan, 40 minutes at 350 degrees.

Hostess: Bee Fraley
Displayer: Edel Anders

RHUBARB COBBLER

BASE:
1 cup sugar
1/3 cup pancake mix
9 cups rhubarb (cut in 1/2 inch pieces)
Combine sugar, pancake mix and add rhubarb, toss lightly.
Place in 13 x 9 x 2" pan.

TOPPING:
3/4 cup pancake mix
2/3 cup sugar
1 egg beaten
1/4 cup melted oleo or butter
Combine pancake mix and sugar. Stir in egg until mixture
resembles coarse crumbs. Sprinkle evenly over rhubarb base.
Drizzle with melted oleo. Bake at 375 degrees for 35-40 minutes.

Hostess: JoAnn Weber
Displayer: Carla Jones, Manager

APPLE-BERRY PIE

5-7 medium tart apples
1 can blueberry pie filling (cherry or blackberry if desired)
3/4 -1 cup sugar
2 tablespoons flour
1 1/2 teaspoon cinnamon
1/4 teaspoon nutmeg (Optional)
dash of salt
3 tablespoons butter or margarine

Pare apples and slice thin; in a large bowl put in apples, sugar,
flour, cinnamon, nutmeg, and salt: mix this well. Line a 9" pie
plate with pastry pie crust, fill this with 1/2 apple mixture,
1/2 blueberry filling, and remaining apples, then blueberry.
Dot with butter add top pie crust. Seal sides. Make three
small cuts in top then sprinkle with sugar. Bake in a hot
oven at 400 degrees for 50 minutes or until crust is done.

CRUST RECIPE:
3 cups sifted flour (1 pound)
2 sticks soft margarine
2 eggs
1/4 cup sugar

Take flour and margarine and crumble together then make a well
in the center. Mix eggs and sugar together then add to flour
mixture. Should feel like cookie dough; take half the mixture
and roll out for your pie plate.

Hostess: Jan M. Klaerner
Displayer: Jackie Fetterhoff

WALNUT PIE

22 Ritz crackers, crushed
1 cup sugar
1 cup chopped walnuts
1 teaspoon baking powder
3 egg whites
Cool Whip (Reserve for serving)
Beat egg whites until stiff, then gently mix in rest of
ingredients. Generously butter a 9" pie pan and pour mixture
into it. Bake 30 minutes at 350 degrees. Cool completely and
serve topped with Cool Whip.

Hostess: Liz Vasquez
Displayer: Sharon Kossieck

DELUXE PECAN PIE

3 eggs
3/4 cup Karo dark syrup
1 cup sugar
2 tablespoons melted margarine (1/2 stick butter)
1 teaspoons vanilla
1 cup pecans
1 unbaked 9 inch pastry shell

Melt butter over low heat. Remove from heat and mix in sugar and
corn syrup. Blend in eggs and vanilla extract. Add pecans and
pour into pie shell. Bake at 350 degrees for 35-40 minutes or
until well done.

Hostess: Patricia R. Lormand

PECAN PIE

3 egg whites
1 cup sugar
20 Ritz Crackers
1 cup chopped pecans
1 1/2 teaspoons vanilla
Whipped cream for topping
Beat egg whites until stiff. Add sugar, fold in crushed
crackers and pecans. Add vanilla. Pour into greased 8 or 9"
pie pan. Bake at 350 degrees for 25 minutes. If using glass
pan, 325 degrees. Serve with whipped cream topping. Let cool
before adding topping.

Hostess: Jeanette Ferguson
Displayer: Theresa Rolewicz

PUMPKIN PECAN PIE

3 slightly beaten eggs
1 1/2 cups canned or mashed cooked pumpkin
1/2 cup granulated sugar
1/2 cup brown sugar
1/2 cup light corn syrup
1/2 cup milk
2 teaspoons flour
1 teaspoon vanilla
1 teaspoon pumpkin pie spice
1/4 teaspoon salt
1 unbaked 9 inch pie shell
1 cup chopped pecans
Whipped cream for topping
In small mixing bowl, combine eggs, pumpkin, sugar, syrup, milk,
flour, vanilla, spice and salt. Mix well. Pour into unbaked
pastry shell. Top with chopped pecans. Bake in moderate oven,
350 degrees for 40 minutes or until knife inserted half way
between center and edge comes out clean. Chill. Serve topped
with whipped cream. Makes one 9 inch pie.

Hostess: Pauline Mitchell
Displayer: Jeneva W. Connar

NO BAKE BROWNIES

1 cup evaporated milk
2 cups minature marshmallows
6 ounce package Toll House chocolate bits
1/2 cup sugar
1/4 teaspoon salt
1 tablespoon butter or margarine
1 teaspoon vanilla
1 cup chopped walnuts
2 packages Nabisco Graham Crackers

Cook first 5 ingredients until melted. Cook and stir to a full
all over boil, 5-6 minutes. Remove from heat, gradually stir in
remaining ingredients. Press into 9 inch buttered pan, chill 1 hour.

Hostess: Sue Noble
Displayer: Lucinda Dwyer

LOW CALORIE CHEESECAKE

2 envelopes unflavored gelatin
1 cup reconstituted nonfat dry milk
4 eggs, seperated
artificial sweetener equivalent to 1 1/4 cups sugar
1/4 teaspoon salt
1 teaspoon grated lemon rind
1 teaspoon grated orange rind
1 tablespoon lemon juice
1 1/2 teaspoons vanilla
1/2 teaspoon almond extract
3 cups creamed cottage cheese
1/2 teaspoon cream of tartar
1/3 cup graham cracker crumbs
1/8 teaspoon cinnamon
1/8 teaspoon nutmeg

Sprinkle gelatin over milk in top of double boiler; add yolks;
stir until completely blended. Place over hot water; stir constantly
for about 5 minutes until gelatin dissolves and mixture thickens
slightly. Remove from heat; stir in sweetener, salt, rinds, lemon
juice, vanilla and almond extract. Sieve or beat cottage cheese on
high speed of mixer 3-4 minutes or until smooth; stir into gelatin
mixture. Chill, stirring occasionally until mixture mounds slightly
when dropped from spoon. Beat egg whites and cream of tartar until
very stiff, fold into gelatin mixture. Combine cracker crumbs,
cinnamon and nutmeg. Sprinkle about half the crumb mixture over
the bottom of 8-9" springform pan. Pour gelatin mixture into pan,
sprinkle with remaining crumb mixture. Chill till firm. Loosen
from side of pan with sharp knife, release springform. Yield 12
servings.

Ruby M. Jameson
Pilot Club Cookbook

NO FAIL PIE CRUST

2 cups flour
1 cup Crisco
1/2 cup cold water
pinch of salt
2 tablespoons sugar

In medium tupperware mixing bowl, place flour, salt, sugar and crisco. Put seal on and shake very briskly. Then add water, replace seal and shake again. Dough will need very little if any handling.

Hostess: Janice McCalip
Displayer: Dodie Carpenter

MAGIC FRENCH FUDGE

3 packages (6 ounces each) semi-sweet chocolate chips
1 can Eagle Brand sweetened condensed milk
1 1/2 teaspoons vanilla
Pinch salt
1/2 cup chopped nuts, optional

In top of double boiler, melt chocloate and milk over low heat until chocolate is melted and mix is smooth add vanilla, salt and nuts. Stir until smooth. Turn into wax paper lined 8" square pan. Chill. Store in airtight container. Makes 2 pounds.

Hostess: Joyce Moss
Displayer: Lou Ridinger

CHOCOLATE CHEESE FUDGE

6 ounces cream cheese, softened
2 tablespoons milk
1 teaspoon vanilla extract
1/8 teaspoon salt
4 cups sifted confectioners sugar
4 ounces unsweetened chocolate, melted
1 cup chopped walnuts

1) Mix cheese, milk, extract & salt; add sugar gradually, & mix well
2) Add warm chocolate and mix throughly.
3) Add nuts and mix.
4) Press into a buttered 8" square pan
5) Chill until firm enough to cut (about 15 minutes)
Yield approximately 2 pounds.

Hostess: Pat Motyka
Displayer: Anne Neyhard

LILLIE'S BABAS

1 package yellow cake mix
3/4 cup sugar
3/4 cup water
3/4 cup orange juice
3 tablespoons orange peel cut into thin slivers (white part removed)
Whipped cream
Prepare the batter for cake mix according to package directions. Place well-greased paper hot-drink cups on a baking sheet and spoon in the batter filling the cups about half full. Bake in moderate oven (375 degrees) for 25 minutes or til done. Meanwhile make syrup. Combine sugar, water, orange juice, and orange peel. Cook mixture for 5 minutes. When cakes are done, cool a minute or two, then turn out of cups onto serving plate. Drizzle immediately with the hot orange syrup soaking the cakes well. Chill. Serve cold with whipped cream. Makes 9 or 10.

Hostess: Lillie Wheeler
Displayer: Jean Davidson

BLUEBERRY SALAD

2 packages red rasberry jello, 3 ounces
3 cups boiling water
1 package plain Knox gelatin
1 cup half and half
1 cup sugar
1 teaspoon vanilla
1 8 ounce package cream cheese
1/2 cup walnuts
1 can of blueberries in juice

FIRST LAYER:
Dissolve one package jello in 2 cups boiling water. Pour into
ring mold and let set really good.
SECOND LAYER:
Dissolve Knox gelatin in 1/2 cup cold water. Heat half and half
til just before boiling. Stir in sugar and Knox gelatin.
Add vanilla and blend in cream cheese and nuts. Chill till
partly set and pour on first layer.
THIRD LAYER:
Dissolve one package rasberry jello in 1 cup boiling water.
Add blueberries and juice. Chill and pour on second layer.
Refrigerate.

Hostess: Lee Obermeyer
Displayer: Marilyn Kathol

STRAWBERRY BABARIAN

1 3 ounce package wild strawberry flavor gelatin
1/4 cup sugar
1 cup boiling water
3/4 cup cold water
1 box of whipped topping
1 cup fresh strawberries, sliced

Dissolve gelatin and sugar in boiling water. Add cold water.
Chill until slightly thickened. Blend in 1 1/2 cups of the
whipped topping, chill until very thick. Fold in strawberries.
Push into 4 cup mold or individual molds, chill firm, unmold
in about 4 hours. Garnish with remaining whipped topping and
fresh strawberries if desired. Makes about 4 cups or 8 servings.

Hostess: Anna Marie Galvan
Displayer: Guillermina Nanes

****

What you are is God's gift to you...What you make of yourself...
that's your gift to God.

****

BONNIE'S YOGURT POPSICLES

1 3 ounce package jello, prepared and chilled
1 8 ounce carton yogurt
1 tablespoon honey

When jello has thickened, add yogurt and honey, pour into cups
and freeze.

Hostess: Bonnie Dunn
Displayer: Karen Miller

FRUIT PIZZA

3 dozen sugar cookies (home made or store bought)
8 ounces Philadelphia Cream Cheese
1/2 cup sugar
1 teaspoon vanilla
Strawberry glaze
Fresh fruit, Suggestions: Strawberries, peaches, cherries, bananas,
     or pineapple
Nuts, optional
Whipped cream, optional

Roll cookies out on a cookie sheet. Bake then let cool. Top with
a mixture of cheese, sugar, vanilla. Top with strawberry glaze and
any kind of fresh fruit. Then nuts and whipped cream if desired.

Hostess: Janet David
Displayer: Judy Timmons

MAKE YESTERDAY DESSERT

Pie crust, your choice to cover bottom of 9 x 13" pan, bake as necessary
1 8 ounce package cream cheese
1   container Cool Whip
1 cup powdered sugar
2 packages chocolate pudding, prepared according to directions
1/2 cup chopped nuts
Stir cream cheese, 1/2 Cool Whip, and powdered sugar together and
spread over the crust. Over that spread chocolate pudding,
cover with remainder Cool Whip. Sprinkle with nuts. Chill and
cut into 12 squares.

Hostess: Bonnie and Sheila Dunn
Displayer: Karen Miller

HOME MADE ICE CREAM

2 1/2 cups sugar
1 teaspoon vanilla
6 eggs
1 quart Half & Half
2 cups Cool Whip
2 1/2 cups fruit

Mix all together and pour into ice cream freezer.

Hostess: Marie Keel

ICE CREAM PIE

1/2 gallon vanilla ice cream (softened)
2 cups chocolate chips
7 ounce package of minature marshmellows
1 tall can of evaporated milk
2 graham cracker crusts

Mix chocolate chips, marshmellows, and milk in a double boiler,
Cook until melted. Cool thoroughly (1 hour in refrigerator)
In graham cracker crust layer 1/4 ice cream 1/4 sauce, 1/4
ice cream, 1/4 sauce. Repeat for second pie. Freeze over night.

Hostess: Nancy Frizzell
Displayer: Pat Anderson, Manager

ICE CREAM DESSERT

16 Graham Crackers
16 Soda Crackers
1/2 cup (1/4 stick) butter or margarine, melted
2 packages Vanilla Instant Pudding
1 Cup Milk
1 quart softened vanilla ice cream
9 ounce Cool Whip (or 8 ounces cream, whipped)
2 Butterfinger Candy Bars, crushed

Crush crackers. Mix with melted butter. Press into 9x13 pan or two
10" round cake pans. Mix Instant Vanilla Pudding with the milk and
combine with ice cream. Spread over crumb crust. Top with Cool Whip,
and sprinkle with crushed candy bars. Refrigerate 12 to 24 hours.
Freezes well.

Hostess: Shirley Birkeland
Displayer. Alice Erickson

****

LEMON DELIGHT

1 1/2 cups flour
1 1/2 sticks oleo
1/2 cup nuts, chopped
8 ounces Philedelphia Cream Cheese
1 cup powdered sugar
9 ounce carton Cool Whip
2 packages lemon instant pudding (chocolate or butterscotch may be used)
3 cups milk
chopped nuts

Blend flour, oleo and 1/2 cup nuts and press into 9 x 13" pan.
Bake at 350 degrees for 20 minutes. Cool. Mix cream cheese,
sugar and 1/2 of the Cool Whip, spread over baked crust. Mix
pudding with milk, pour over creamed cheese mixture. Spread rest
of Cool Whip over top and sprinkle with chopped nuts.

Hostess: Mrs. Kathy Moore
Displayer: Mary Alice Corman

FROZEN STRAWBERRY DESSERT

CRUST:
1 cup flour
1/4 cup brown sugar
1/2 cup melted butter or oleo
1/2 cup chopped walnuts
Spread in 13 x 9" pan. Bake 20 minutes at 350 degrees, stirring
often to crumble. Cool. Remove some to sprinkle on top of dessert.

FILLING:
2 egg whites   1 cup whipped cream, or
3/4 cup sugar   Cool Whip
10 ounces partially thawed strawberries
2 tablespoons lemon juice
Beat at low speed 2 minutes and then on high speed 10-12 minutes
until really firm. Fold in 1 cup whipped cream, or Cool Whip.
Spoon over crust, and sprinkle with reserved crust mixture.
Freeze 6 hours or overnight.

Hostess: Sandy Sears
Displayer: Karen Denger

****

When God measures men, He puts the tape around the heart -
not around the head.

****

121

RASPBERRY DESSERT

1 cup water
1/2 cup sugar
2 teaspoons lemon juice
2 10 ounce packages frozen raspberries in syrup
4 tablespoons cornstarch
1/4 cup cold water
50 large marshmellows
one cup milk
2 cups cream, whipped
1 1/4 cups graham cracker crumbs
1/4 cup chopped nuts
1/4 cup butter, melted

Heat raspberries with water, sugar and lemon juice. Dissolve
cornstarch in 1/4 cup cold water. Stir into raspberries and
cook until thickened and clear. Cool.
Melt marshmallows in milk in double boiler and cool. Whip cream
and fold into marshmallow mixture. Mix graham crackers, nuts
and butter in a 13 x 9 x 3" pan. Press firmly into bottom of
pan. Spread marshmallow cream mixture over crumbs. Spread
raspberry mixture over top. Refrigerate until firm.

Hostess: Sylvia Osterbauer
Displayer: Linda Case

RASPBERRY DESSERT

1 1/4 cups graham cracker crumbs
3/4 cup fine chopped nuts, pecans
5 tablespoons melted oleo
Whipped cream, reserved for topping
Combine and press in 9 x 12" pan. Bake 10 minutes at 300 degrees.

1 package Lemon Jello
1 cup boiling water
4 tablespoons lemon juice
Set aside after dissolved to cool. When it starts to set,
beat til fluffy. In another bowl, beat :
1 cup sugar   2 cups whipped cream
1 teaspoon vanilla
1 8 ounce package Philladelphia cream cheese
Beat into thickened jello. Fold in whipped cream. Pour on
crust and chill until set.
1 package Danish dessert (raspberry)
2 packages frozen raspberries, drained and thawed
Add enough water to raspberry juice to make 2 cups, add danish
dessert. Mix and bring to boil, stirring constantly. Boil 1
minute, cool. Add whole raspberries and pour over jello layer.
Chill. Top with whipped cream.

Hostess: Sue Dilts
Displayer: Iris Edkin

PUDDING DESSERT

1 cup soda crackers
2 cups graham crackers
1 stick oleo melted
1 box instant butterscotch pudding
1 box instant vanilla pudding
2 cups milk
4 cups vanilla ice cream
9 ounce Cool Whip topping
1 Butterfinger candy bar-crushed

Crush crackers together, mix in oleo and put 3/4 of crumbs in bottom of a 9 x 13" pan. Mix puddings and milk, add ice cream. Put in pan and add layer of cool whip. Cover with remaining crumbs and crushed Butterfinger. Keep in refrigerator.

Hostess: Janese Gengenbach
Displayer: Barb Miller

DREAM WHIP TORTE'

6 egg whites
3/4 teaspoon cream of tarter
2 cups sugar
2 teaspoons vanilla
2 cups unsalted cracker crumbs (broken not rolled)
1 cup nuts (walnuts) chopped
1 or 2 cans cherry or blueberry pie filling
2 packages Dream Whip
Beat whites with tarter, form soft peak. Add sugar slowley, beat til golssy, add vanilla. Mix crumb and nuts, add to egg mixture carefully, folding gently. Pour into greased 9 x 13" pan, bake at 350 degrees until golden brown, approximately 15-20 minutes. Remove and cool before removing from pan. Spread Dream Whip on cool torte, spread pie filling over Dream Whip. Chill and serve.

Hostess: Terri Cota
Displayer: Carol Anderson

BANANA SAILBOATS

1 package vanilla pudding, large size
Vanilla Wafer cookies
Bananas
Miniature Marshmallows

Prepare pudding according to package directions. Line individual serving dishes with vanilla wafers. Slice bananas over wafers. Spoon cooled pudding over this. Decorate with marshmallows and additional banana slices if desired.

Hostess: Deb Willis

PARTY DIET DELIGHT

2 large packages strawberry jello
2 large packages lime jello
2 large cans fruit cocktail
1 large container cool whip
1 small bottle cherries

Prepare jello early and have ready to serve. Just before party, in clear glasses or goblets, layer jello, starting with strawberry, fruit cocktail, and cool whip. Top with cherries. Yield 15 servings.

Hostess: Dorothy Gonzalez
Displayer: Doris Weaver

FROZEN LEMON DESSERT

6 eggs
1 cup sugar
3 tablespoons lemmon juice
1 pint whipping cream
1 1/2 cups graham crackers

Separate egg yolks from whites. Mix yolks with sugar and juice. Cook till thick (do not boil) Remove and cool. Beat whites. Whip cream till stiff. Gently stir lemon mixture into whites, pour this gently into cream. Sprinkle 1/2 crumbs on bottom of pan, then pour in dessert, then remainder of crumbs on top. Freeze for several hours before serving.

Hostess: Linda George
Displayer: Marian Casalan

****

THREE GATES

If you are tempted to reveal
A tale someone to you has told
About another, make it pass
Before you speak, three gates of gold,
Three narrow gates: "First is it true?"
Then, "Is it needful?" In your mind
Give trughful answer, and the next
Is last and narrowest, "Is it kind?"
And if to reach your lips at last
It passes through these gateways three,
Then you may tell, nor ever fear
What the result of speech may be.

True Living

PISTACHIO DESSERT

1 cup flour
2 teaspoons sugar
1/2 cup butter
1/4 cup chopped nuts
Mix and press into a greased 9 x 13" pan. Bake at 375 degrees
15 to 18 minutes. Cool.

1 8 ounce package Cream Cheese
2/3 cup powdered sugar
1 19 ounce Cool Whip
2 packages Royal Pistachio Pudding, instant
3 cups milk

Soften cream cheese and beat in powdered sugar. Use 1/2 of the
cool whip in cream cheese mixture. Save the rest for top of next
layer. Spread cream cheese/cool whip mixture over crust. Prepare
pudding with 3 cups milk, spread over cream cheese/cool whip mixture. Let stand for 30 minutes in refrigerator. Spread remaining
cool whip on top of pudding. Garnish with chopped nuts if desired.

Hostess: Ruth Ann Hockins
Displayer: Roberta Steel

WATERGATE DESSERT

1 package pistachio pudding mix, instant
1 9 ounce package non-dairy whipped topping
1 20 ounce can crushed pineapple (do not drain)
1/2 cup minaiture marshmellows
1/2 cup chopped nuts

Mix and chill. Pour into prepared crust. Do not prepare pudding,
just use the powder as it comes from the box.

CRUST:
1 cup flour
1/4 cup brown sugar
1/2 cup butter
3/4 cup chopped nuts

Press into bottom of 9 x 13" pan. Bake at 350 degrees for 15
minutes. Cool before pouring in above dessert mixture.

Hostess: Jill Roen
Displayer: Marlys R. Anderson

DELICIOUS INEXPENSIVE CARMELS

2 cups sugar
1/2 cup white corn syrup
1/2 cup milk
1 teaspoon vanilla
4 tablespoons butter
1 cup cream (canned milk works wonderfully)

Cook ingredients except vanilla to stiff ball stage or 246 degrees.
Remove from stove and add vanilla, pour into buttered pan. When
cool, cut into squares and wrap in waxed paper.

Hostess: Kathy Martinez
Displayer: Joan Niernberger

CARMEL/TURTLES

CARMEL:
1 cup oleo
1 can Eagle Brand Milk
1 pound brown sugar
1 cup light corn syrup
dash of salt
1 teaspoon vanilla

In heavy pan, melt oleo, add brown sugar and salt. Stir in
syrup gradually. Cook to 245 degrees or almost hard boil.
(I cook to 250 degrees.) Remove from heat, stir in vanilla.
Pour in buttered 9 x 13" pan. Will cover 20 medium apples and
make 8 x 8" pan.

FOR TURTLES:

Press pecans into each square of carmel and cover with the following:

1 package 12 ounce milk chocolate chips
1 package Bakers german sweet chocolate
1/3 bar paraffin
Melt and pour over carmel pecan patties.

Hostess: Irene Myers
Displayer: Darlene Menneke

****

The mother's heart is the child's schoolroom. Henry Ward Beecher.

****

GOATS MILK FUDGE
(WHITE FUDGE)

2 1/4 cups white sugar
1/2 cup sour cream
1/4 cup milk
2 tablespoons butter
1 tablespoon light corn syrup
1/4 teaspoon salt
1 tablespoon vanilla
1/3 cup candied cherry halves (optional)

In saucepan combine sugar, sour cream, milk and butter, corn
syrup, salt and stir over medium heat until sugar is dissolved
and mixture reaches a boil. Boil for 10 minutes, remove from heat
and let set for 1 hour until lukewarm. Add vanilla and beat with
mixer until mixture holds shape. Add cherries. Put in buttered
9 x 9" pan immediately. Makes 1 1/2 pounds.

Hostess: Kim DeRosa
Displayer: Karen Greenwood

FUDGE

4 cups sugar
1 tall can pet milk

Combine and cook together. After it starts boiling good, boil
9 minutes (no longer) stir continously. Turn fire off. Add:

1 7 ounce jar Kraft marshmallow cream
3 6 ounce packages chocolate chips
2 cubes margarine
3 cups nuts (or more)
2 teaspoons vanilla

Mix well. Pour into a large pan (18 x 11) cool, and cut into squares.

Hostess: Ethel Serpa
Displayer: Nancy Evans

****

In the affairs of life or business, it is not intellect that tells
so much as character - not brains so much as heart - not genius so
much as self-control, patience, and discipline, regulated by
judgement. Samuel Miles.

****

O'HENRY BARS

2/3 cup margarine
4 cups dry oatmeal (quick-cooking)
1 cup brown sugar
2 teaspoons vanilla
1/2 cup dark or light syrup

Melt margarine. Add remaining ingredients. Spread in greased
9 x 13" pan. Bake at 350 degrees for 12 minutes or until mixture
is bubbly. Remove from oven and cool for 10 minutes.

TOPPING:

1 cup semi-sweet chocolate chips
2/3 cup Skippy super chunk peanut butter

Melt chocolate chips and peanut butter in double boiler. Spread
this over first mixture. This may be put in the refrigerator to set.

Displayer: Ann Dee Hermann

TOFFEE

1 cup almonds, chopped
3/4 cup brown sugar
1/2 cup butter or margarine
1 bar (4 1/2 ounces) milk chocolate, broken into pieces

Butter square 9x9x2 pan. Spread almonds in pan. Heat sugar and
butter to boiling, stir constantly. Boil 7 minutes over medium
heat, stir constantly. Immediately spread mixture evenly over
nuts in pan. Sprinkle chocolate pieces over hot mixture, place
baking sheet over pan so contained heat will melt chocolate. Spread
melted chocolate over candy. While hot cut into 1 1/2" squares.
Chill until firm. This recipe burns easily on electric stoves, so
be careful.

Hostess: Nance Randall
Displayer: Dodie Carpenter

****

Sight is a faculty; seeing is an art. George Perkins Marsh.

****

HOLIDAY BON BON'S

1/2 pound shelled walnuts
1/2 pound pitted dates
1 egg white
2 tablespoons sugar

Grind nuts and dates fine; knead and shape into date shaped bon-bon's
Chill overnight. Beat egg white slightly, add sugar and food color if
desired. Dip bon-bon's into mixture. Place on greased baking sheet.
Bake at 300 degrees until crisp.

Hostess: Mary Morgret
Displayer: Polly Lugten

FELOZES
(PORTUGUESE DOUGHNUTS)

4 cups flour
4 large eggs
1/8 teaspoon cinnamon
1/8 teaspoon nutmeg
2 tablespoons sugar
1 teaspoon salt
1 cup milk
1 tablespoon butter
2 packages dry yeast
1/4 cup warm water to dissolve yeast

Beat eggs with sugar, salt, nutmeg and cinnamon. Heat milk and
butter to "warm" and add to egg mixture. Dissolve yeast in warm
water and add to mixture. Then add flour and beat. Cover and
let rise 1 hour. Beat down with spoon. Let rise until it's size
has doubled and then beat down again. Now dip hands in water
or milk and pinch off small ball of dough (about 1/8 cup) and
stretch into size of small pancakes. Deep fry until golden brown;
drain well and then dip both sides in a mixture of sugar and
cinnamon (about 1/4 cup cinnamon and 1 1/2 cups sugar.) Makes
4 dozen. (Leftovers can be wrapped in foil to freeze and then
be reheated in oven before serving. Can also be made ahead
for holidays.)

COATING:
1/4 cup cinnamon
1 1/2 cups sugar

Hostess: Mary Raddingan
Displayer: Claudia Rooker

****
Those who bring sunshine into the lives of others cannot keep
it from themselves. Sir James Barrie
****

PLAIN DONUT

1 cup sugar
1/4 teaspoon salt
2 eggs
1 tablespoon shortening
1 cup sour milk (1 cup milk, 1/2 teaspoon vinegar)
1/3 teaspoon ginger
1 1/4 teaspoon nutmeg
1 teaspoon baking soda
1 teaspoon baking powder
3 2/3 cups flour
1/2 teaspoon vanilla

Roll out dough, cut and fry in deep fat 420 degrees until brown,then
turn over.

Hostess: Helen Bronn
Displayer: Jean Brown

DOUGHNUTS

1 cup sugar
1 cup mashed potatoes
1 egg
1/2 cup milk
1 tablespoon melted butter
3 cups flour (little more)
2 1/2 teaspoons baking powder
Powdered sugar
Mix well and drop into hot cooking oil and fry until brown and
crispy. Cool on brown paper bag. Roll in powdered sugar.

Hostess: Shirley Young
Displayer: Ruth Young

****
Nothing in the world can take the place of persistance.
Talent will not; nothing is more common than unsuccessful men with talent
Genius will not; unrewarded genius is almost a proverb.
Education alone will not; the world is full of educated derelicts.
Persistance and Determination are omnipotent.
****

YUMMY DELIGHT

First Layer:
1 stick oleo or butter
1 cup flour
1/2 cup chopped nuts
Cream this. Add pecans and pat out in 9 x 12 pan and bake 350 degrees for 20 minutes.

Second Layer:
1 8 ounce package cream cheese
1 cup Cool Whip - out of 9 ounce size
1 cup Powdered Sugar
Coconut
Mix and spread over first layer. Sprinkle with coconut.

Third Layer:
2 packages Instant French Vanilla pudding mix
3 cups of milk
Mix and spread over second layer.

Fourth Layer:
Use the remainder of Cool Whip and spread over third layer, then sprinkle with coconut and toasted pecans chopped. Refrigerate.

Topping:
Coconut
Toasted pecans, chopped

Displayer: Marcia Liverman

REFRIGERATOR DESSERT

1 angel food cake
2 tablespoons sugar
2 packages chocolate chips
3 egg yolks
3 egg whites
1 pint whipping cream

Melt sugar, chocolate chips in a double boiler. Cool for 5 minutes, and add beaten egg yolks. Beat whipping cream, and egg whites. Add whipped cream mixture to chocolate mixture then add egg whites. Pour over bite size pieces of angel food cake. Make in two layer pans. Chill overnight.

Hostess: Lynn Richards
Displayer: Linda Gordon

****

It is a thousand times better to have common sense without education than to have education without common sense.

****

PUDDING TORTE

Crust:
1 cup flour
1/2 cup margarine
1/2 cup chopped nuts
Mix together as pie dough and press in oblong pan. Bake at 350 degrees
for 15 minutes. Cool.

First layer:
1 cup powdered sugar
1 cup Cool Whip (or more for thicker layer) from large size.
1 8 ounce package of cream cheese
Mix together and spread on crust.

Second Layer:
2(3 5/8)ounce packages cooked pudding (chocolate)
Use only 3 cups of milk. Cool.

Third Layer:
Spread the rest of your large size Cool Whip.
Sprinkle with chopped nuts.

Hostess: Augie Knor
Displayer: Marilyn Lambie

PUMPKIN ROLL

1) 3 eggs beaten for 5 minutes at high speed.
2) 1 cup sugar
   2/3 cup pumpkin
   Add to above.
3) 3/4 cup flour
   1 teaspoon baking powder
   2 teaspoon cinnamon
   1 teaspoon ginger
   1/2 teaspoon nutmeg
   1/2 teaspoon salt
   Bake on greased and floured cookie sheet at 375 degrees for 15 min.
4) Turn onto towel, floured and powdered sugar.
   Roll while hot. COOL.
5) 1 cup powdered sugar
   2 3 ounce packages cream cheese
   4 tablespoons butter
   1/2 teaspoon vanilla
   Blend.
6) Fold onto roll and chill.

Hostess: Pam Pollock
Displayer: Cheri Scranton

```
****************
```
The sky is the daily bread of the eyes. Emerson.
```
****************
```

4-LAYER DESSERT

1 cup flour
1/2 cup melted margarine
1/2 cup nuts, chopped fine

Mix and pat in 9 x 13" pan. Bake 15 minutes at 350 degrees. Cool.

8 ounce package cream cheese
1 cup powdered sugar
1 cup Cool Whip (from large size)

Mix and spread on crust. Chill 2 hours.

2 packages Instant Butterscotch pudding*
3 cups milk (only)
1 teaspoon vanilla
1 teaspoon Burnt Sugar flavoring (essential)

Mix pudding with mixer according to the package directions, and pour
over filling, chill. Cover with remaining Cool Whip and sprinkle with
chopped nuts. Chill several hours or overnight before serving.
Serves 12 to 18.
* Instant Chocolate Pudding may be used, omitting Burnt Sugar Flavoring.
Coconut Cream Pudding is delicious with toasted coconut sprinkled on top.

Displayer: Margaret Hamler

COCONUT DELIGHT

1 cup flour
1/2 cup butter
1/2 cup chopped pecans
8 ounces cream cheese, softened
1 cup powdered sugar
9 ounce carton whipped topping
2-3 3/4 ounce packages instant coconut pudding
2 cups milk
1/3 cup coconut toasted

Combine flour, butter and pecans. Pat into a buttered 9 x 12" pan.
Bake at 350 degrees for 15 minutes. Cool. Beat cream cheese and
sugar until smooth. Combine instant pudding and milk and beat two
minutes. Add cream cheese mixture and one cup of the whipped topping to pudding and pour over crust: Spread with remaining topping
and sprinkle with toasted coconut. Chill until firm. Cut into
squares to serve. (Freezes well.) Serves 16-24.

Hostess: Sheila Huffman
Displayer: Nance Bennett

PUMPKIN DESSERT

1) 44 Graham Crackers crushed
   1/3 cup sugar
   1 stick oleo melted
   Mix and press into 9 x 13 pan
2) 2 eggs beaten
   3/4 cup sugar
   1 8 ounce package cream cheese
   Beat and pour over crust. Bake 20 minutes at 350 degrees.
3) 2 cups pumpkin
   1/2 cup sugar
   1/2 cup milk
   1/2 teaspoon salt
   1 tablespoon cinnamon
   3 egg yolks
   Mix, cook until thick. Remove from heat.
4) 1 envelope Knox gelatin--disolved in
   1/4 cup cold water
   Add to pumpkin mixture. COOL.
5) 3 egg whites beaten. Add
   1/4 cup sugar
   Dash cream of tarter
   Fold into cooled pumpkin mixture.
6) Pour egg mixture and pumpkin mixture over cream cheese mixture.
7) Spread cool whip over top.
   Top with pecans.

Hostess: Glorene Horder
Displayer: Cheri Scranton

BUTTERSCOTCH DESSERT

Crust:
1 cup flour
1/2 cup butter
1/2 cup chopped nuts
Mix and press in a 9 x 13" pan. Bake 15 minutes at 350 degrees. Cool.

Cream:
18 ounce package cream cheese
1 cup powdered sugar
Fold in 1 cup Cool Whip - spread over cooled crust.

Cook Together:
2 small packages pudding mix
   1 butterscotch
   1 coconut creame
3 cups milk
When cooled, pour pudding mixture over cheese layer and frost with
Cool Whip.

Hostess: Shelly Larson
Displayer: Roberta Steel

134

CHOCOLATE CINNAMON ROLLS

3/4 cup warm water
1 package yeast
1/4 cup shortening
1 teaspoon salt
1/4 cup sugar
1 egg
1/3 cup cocoa
2 1/2 cups flour

TOPPING:
1 tablespoon soft butter
1 1/2 teaspoons cinnamon
3 tablespoons sugar
nuts (optional)

In mixer bowl dissolve yeast in warm water. Add shortening, salt,
sugar, egg, cocoa, 1 cup flour. Beat 2 minutes at medium speed.
Stir in remaining flour. Blend well. Cover and let rise until
double in bulk (about one hour) Roll on floured board and spread
with last 3 ingredients. Bake 350 degrees for 20 minutes.

Hostess: Marge Kautz
Displayer: Dodie Carpenter

4-LAYER DELIGHT DESSERT

1 cup flour
1/2 cup butter
1/2 cup chopped nuts
1 8 ounce package cream cheese
1 cup powdered sugar
9 ounces cool whip
2 3 ounce packages chocolate pudding mix (or favorite)
3 cups cold milk

First Layer: Mix flour, butter, and nuts as for pie crust. Pat
in 9 x 13 pan. Bake 15 minutes at 350 degrees. Cool.
Second Layer: Combine softened cream cheese, powdered sugar, and
one cup Cool Whip. Spread on crust.
Third Layer: Combine pudding, and milk as for pie, when slightly
thickened, add on top.
Fourth Layer: Top with remaining Cool Whip. Refrigerate.

Hostess: Audrey Kavajecz
Displayer: Nancy Dietze

****

Kindness is the golden chain by which society is bound together.

****

135

BAKED PINEAPPLE

1 cup white sugar
3 eggs
2 tablespoons cornstarch
1/2 cup water
2 tablespoons melted butter
large can pineapple (crushed or chunk)

Combine first five ingredients and blend in blender. Pour into
large, buttered casserole dish. Add pineapple and fold into
mixture. Bake at 350 degress for 90 minutes. Stir at 15 minute
intervals.

Hostess: Sharon Pierce
Displayer: Jackie England

PINEAPPLE SOUFFLE

6 slices white bread, cubed
1 1/2 sticks margarine
2 eggs
3/4 cup sugar (or less)
2 #2 cans pineapple tidbits
2 tablespoons flour

Melt butter, pour over cubed bread and toss. Beat eggs, add sugar,
flour, and pineapple, including the juice. In a greased casserole,
layer bread and pineapple mixture, ending with bread. Bake at 350
degrees about 45 minutes. Makes eight generous portions.

Hostess: Barbara Rice
Displayer: Edel Anders

BUTTER BRICKEL DESSERT

1 one pound can peach slices
1 butter brickel cake mix
1/4 pound butter
Preheat oven to 350 degrees. In 9x13" cake pan, put peach slices and
juice in the bottom of the pan. Sprinkle dry cake mix over the top of
peach slices. Melt butter and drizzle it over the top of cake mix.
Bake 35-40 minutes at 350 degrees. Cool and serve with ice cream
or other topping.

Hostess: Annis Fredrickson
Displayer: Roberta Steel

****

Greatness does not depend on the size of your command, but on
the way you exercise it. Marshal Foch.

****

BUTTERFINGER DESSERT

2 cups crushed graham cracker crumbs
1 cup soda cracker crumbs
1 stick melted butter
2 packages instant vanilla pudding
2 cups milk
1 quart vanilla ice cream
Whipped topping (10 ounces)
4 frozen Butterfingers

Combine crumbs and butter. Press 2/3 of the mixture in to bottom
of the pan (9 x 13") Prepare pudding according to the package
directions using only 2 cups of milk. Blend in the ice cream
until smooth. Freeze until partly firm. Remove and cover with
topping. Crush candy and add to the crumb mixture(other 1/3)
Sprinkle on top of the dessert. Refrigerate (do not freeze)
several hours.

Hostess: Vicki Livingston
Displayer: Cher Adams

ICE CREAM DESSERT

1/2 cup butter
2 squares chocolate
Melt together, cool, then add:
2 cups powdered sugar
2 egg yolks, beaten

3 egg whites
1 teaspoon vanilla
Beat the egg whites, then add vanilla, and the first mixture and add:
1 packet graham crackers, crushed.
Spread in 9 x 15" pan, reserve 1/2 cup for topping.
Use 1/2 gallon vanilla ice cream over crumb mixture, then topping.

Hostess: Marvis Johnson
Displayer: Karen Pratt

STRAWBERRY SHERBET
by Linda Carter

9 12 ounce cans Strawberry Drink
3 cans Eagle Brand Milk
3 10 ounce cartons frozen sliced strawberries

Mix together and freeze in 6 quart freezer.

****
Life by the yard is hard - but by the inch it's a cinch.
From "Be Somebody" by Mary Crowley.

SHERBERT DESSERT

1/2 gallon sherbert ice cream (flavor optional)
2 1/2 cups rice chex (crushed)
1 cup brown sugar
1 cup coconut
2/3 cup melted butter
15 Oreos (cookies)

Mix together Rice Chex, brown sugar, coconut, and melted butter.
Place 1 to 1 1/2" of this mixture into bottom of a styrofoam cup.
Soften (just enough to work with easily) ice cream sherbert and
press into cup - close to full. Crush oreos and sprinkle on top
of sherbert 1/2 to 1 inch to top of cup. Garnish with permanent
blossom. This easy and clever desert resmebles your favorite
potted plant.

Hostess: Marce Kollars
Displayer: Marilyn Kathol

LORNA-DOONE DESSERT

1 package Lorna Doone Cookies
1 stick butter
2 small packages instant vanilla or chocolate pudding
2 cups milk
1 quart butter pecan or chocolate ice cream
2 or 3 Heath Bars (crushed)
2 cups Cool Whip

Melt butter in small saucepan and mix with crushed cookies. Pat into
13 x 9" pan like crust. Mix the pudding with the milk and beat until
thick. Add the ice cream to this mixture and pour over crust. Refrigerate until firm. Put Cool Whip on top. Crush the Heath Bars and
sprinkle over the Cool Whip. Keep refrigerated.

Hostess: Pat Ward

****

We search the world for truth,
We cull the good - the true - the beautiful
From graven stone and written scroll,
And all old flower-fields of the soul,
And, weary seekers of the best,
We come back laden from our quest,
To find that all the sages said
Is in the Book our Mothers read..
                    John Greenleaf Whittier

CHOCOLATE NUT CRUMB

1 package Graham Crackers
1 cup ground nuts
1/2 cup oleo (melted)
Mix altoghther. Line pan with half and bake at 400 degrees for 5 min.
1/2 gallon ice cream
1/2 cup oleo
3 squares baking chocolate
2 cups powdered sugar
1 teaspoon vanilla
6 egg yolks
Cream butter and sugar add egg yolks, then melted chocolate and vanilla.
Fold in beaten egg whites. Spread half of mixture on baked crumbs, and
refrigerate 1 hour then spread 1/2 gallon ice cream over mixture, and
repeat.

Hostess: Betty Dufer
Displayer: Carol Davis

MUFFIN CHEESECAKES

2 8 ounce Philadelphia cream cheese (softened)
3/4 cup sugar
2 eggs
1 tablespoon lemon juice
Cherry pie filling
Mix all together. Fill 18 muffin cups. Bake 15 minutes at 375 degrees.
Spoon pie filling into them after they are filled and baked. You can
also put vanilla wafers in the bottom of muffin cups before you bake.

Hostess: Irene Noblin

PEANUT BUTTER CUPS

1 1/2 cups 100% granola cereal
1 cup dry instant milk
1 cup chunky peanut butter
1 cup honey

Place paper liners in 8 to 12 muffin pan cups. Combine all ingredients
in a medium size bowl. Divide mixture evenly among the muffin cups
depending upon the size desired. These are easy, nutritious, and
delicious for those who carry sack lunches.

Hostsss: Reina McCarthy
Displayer: Frances Burger

****
TIME.......is a quality......not a quantity.
From "Be Somebody" by Mary Crowley.
****

BLACK BOSTON CUP CAKES

1 8 ounce package cream cheese (room temperature)
1/3 cup sugar
1/8 teaspoon salt
Combine the above and add:
1 unbeaten egg
1 6 ounce package chocolate chips (optional)
Set aside.

1 1/2 cups flour (sifted)
1/4 cup cocoa
1 cup sugar
1 teaspoon soda
1/2 teaspoon salt
Sift above together.

1 cup water
1/3 cup cooking oil
1 tablespoon vinegar
1 tablespoon vanilla
Mix together, and add to the dry ingredients.
Beat until smooth. Fill paper cups 1/3 full of batter. Top each
with a heaping teaspoon of the cream cheese mixture. Sprinkle top
with sugar and nuts. Bake at 350 degrees for 30-35 minutes.

Hostess: Iris Salmen
Displayer: Connie Becker

CHOCOLATE CHIP CUPCAKES

1 1/2 cups flour
1 cup white sugar
1 teaspoon soda
1/2 teaspoon salt
1/4 cup cocoa
1 cup water
1/2 cup vegetable oil
1 teaspoon vinegar
1 teaspoon vanilla

FILLING:
1 8 ounce soft cream cheese
Pinch of salt
1 cup real chocolate chips
1 egg 1/2 cup white sugar

MAKE FILLING FIRST:
Beat filling mix. Stir in chips. Set batter aside.
BATTER:
Combine dry ingredients. Stir or beat liquid ingredients until smooth.
Fill Paper cups in tins 1/2 full. Add heaping teaspoon of filling
into center of each cup. Bake at 350 degrees for 25-30 minutes.
Makes 20-24 cupcakes.   NOTE: Donna thinks these are best with no frosting
Hostess: Donna Johnson
Displayer: Cathy Brown

140

PECAN TASSEIES

1 3 ounce package cream cheese
1/2 cup butter or margarine
1 cup sifted flour
1 egg
3/4 cup brown sugar
1 tablespoon butter or margarine
dash salt
2/3 cup broken pecans

CHEESE PASTRY:
Let cream cheese and 1/2 cup butter soften to room temperature, chill
about 1 hour after combining them. Put small amounts in ungreased
muffin pans. Press dough evenly against bottom and sides.

PECAN FILLING:
Beat egg, sugar, butter, vanilla, and salt just until smooth.
Divide half the pecans among pastry lined pans; add egg mixture
and top with remaining pecans. Bake in slow oven, 325 degrees,
25-30 minutes. Cool completely before removing from pans.
Makes two dozen.

Hostess: Sandy Bliss
Displayer: Dodie Carpenter

ORANGE SHERBERT SALAD

1 package orange jello
1 pint orange sherbert
1 small can Mandarin oranges, drained
1 small can pineapple, drained but save juice
1 cup boiling water

Add water to package jello. While still hot, add sherbert.
Mix well. Then add oranges and pineapple. Mix and let set
until firm.

TOP LAYER:
2 rounded tablespoons flour   1 small package cream cheese &
1 egg beaten   1 cup whipped cream for topping
1/2 cup sugar
1 cup pineapple juice
2 tablespoons butter

Cook these ingredients until thick. Scortches easily. Cool.
Then add 1 cup whipped cream (or prepared dessert topping.)
Spread on salad. Garnish with 1 small package frozen grated
Philadelphia cream cheese.

Hostess: Malinda Clinton
Displayer: Wanda A. Fowles

OATMEAL CAKE

1 1/2 cups boiling water
1 square butter or margarine
1 cup oatmeal
Stir until butter has melted and let stand 30 minutes.
1 cup brown sugar
1 cup white sugar
1 teaspoon salt
1 teaspoon vanilla
1 1/2 cups flour
1 teaspoon soda
Mix all dry ingredients and add to oatmeal mixture the following:
2 eggs
Combine oatmeal mixture and dry ingredients. Bake at 350 degrees
for 35 minutes.

FROSTING FOR OATMEAL CAKE:
1 square of butter or oleomargarine (1/2 cup)
1 cup brown sugar
1 cup coconut
1/2 cup canned milk
1 teaspoon vanilla
1 cup nut meats
Beat until dissolved and broil a few minutes under broiler on
warm cake. Oatmeal cake is only good with this frosting on it.

Hostess: Jeannine Westmoreland
Displayer: Joan Niernberger

PLUM CAKE

2 cups self-rising flour
1 cup cooking oil
2 small jars of strained Plum baby food
3 eggs
2 cups of sugar
1 teaspoon cinnamon
1 teaspoon cloves
1 cup chopped nuts - sprinkled in bottom of bundt pan

Combine all ingredients and pour into well greased bundt pan.
Bake in 350 degree oven for 55 minutes.

Hostess:Debra Woods
Displayer: Imelda Villancal

142

Appetizers

NUTS AND BOLTS

3 sticks of butter or oleo
1 large tablespoon of Onion Salt
1 large tablespoon of Celery Salt
1 large tablespoon of Garlic Powder
1/4 cup or more of Worcestershire sauce

Put all ingredients together and melt in saucepan, mix.

40 ounce can of peanuts
stick pretzles, broken into small pieces
small box Cheerios
small box Rice Checks

Combine above ingredients in a large roasting pan, stir in the
melted mixture well and bake in oven at 225 degrees, covered, for
45 minutes. Stir about every 15 minutes. Bake 30 minutes longer
without lid. Cool. Put into container to store.

Displayer: Linda Abel

CHEESE BALL

2 8 ounce packages Philadelphia cream cheese
1 jar Old English cheese
2 tablespoons mayonnaise
2 tablespoons lemon juice
2 tablespoons parmesan cheese
1 tablespoon grated onion

Combine all ingredients and roll ball in crushed pecans.

Hostess: Billie Ramsey

CHEESE ROLLS OR BALL

1 pound Velveeta cheese
1/2 pound cheddar cheese
Small cream cheese
1/4 cup chopped pecans
1/2 teaspoon garlic powder
paprika

Mix all above ingredients except paprika together after cheeses
have softened. Roll into 3 rolls, about the size of a quarter
in diameter. After these rolls have been formed, roll each
one in paprika. Wrap each foll in waxed paper and chill until
ready to serve. Slice, serve with assorted crackers. This
is better made 24 hours before serving.

Hostess: Gail Cowan
Displayer: Marie Keel

CHEESE BALL

2 8 ounce packages cream cheese
1 8 ounce can crushed pineapple, drained
1/2 cup bell pepper, finely chopped
1/2 cup onion, finely chopped
2 cups chopped pecans

Mix all ingredients. Shape into a large ball. Roll in pecans,
that have been chopped very fine. Serve with chips or crackers.

Hostess: Kathy High
Displayer: Pat Anderson, Manager

SAUERKRAUT BALL

1 large can sauerkraut, drained and chopped
2 cups grated cheddar cheese
2 tablespoons chopped pimento
2 tablespoons chopped onion
2 tablespoons chopped green pepper
1 hard boiled egg, chopped
1/2 cup dry, very fine, bread crumbs
1/4 cup mayonnaise
1/2 teaspoon salt
1 tablespoon sugar

Combine all ingredients and form into a ball. For frosting: Mix

8 ounces Philadelphia Cream Cheese
2 tablespoons milk
olives and parsley for garnish
Ice ball with cheese mixture. garnish, let stand over night in
refrigerator.

Hostess: Chris McKinley
Displayer: Sandra L. Grabler

POPCORN BALLS

3 cups minature marshmellows
2 teaspoons butter
1/4 teaspoon salt
food coloring
7-8 cups popped popcorn

Melt marshmellows, butter and salt in top of double boiler.
Add food coloring. Pour in popped corn. Stir. Shape into
approximately 12 balls with well buttered hands.

Hostess: Carol Martin
Displayer: Dodie Carpenter

145

WARM CHIP BEEF DIP

2 8 ounce packages Philadelphia Cream Cheese
4 tablespoons milk
1 cup sour cream
4 tablespoons minced onions
4 tablespoons chopped green pepper
1/4 teaspoon pepper
1-2 3 ounce packages chipped beef, chopped

Put in pan, bake 350 degrees for 15 minutes. Keep warm in
chaffing dish. Serve with chips.

Hostess: Dona Balciar
Displayer: Judy Braun

CRAB DIP

1 small can crab
1 small can water chestnuts
1 teaspoon soya sauce
1 skimpy cup mayonnaise

Mix and chill overnight.

Hostess: Christine Content
Displayer: Peanuts Vigario

DILL DIP

1 cup mayonnaise
1 cup sour cream
1 teaspoon beau monde seasoning
1 teaspoon parsley
1 teaspoon onion flakes
1 teaspoon dill weed
pinch salt

Mix together, and store overnight in refrigerator. Use as a
dip for raw fresh vegetables.

Hostess: Chris McNair
Displayer: Nancy Evans

****

Give for the joy of giving...If you only give to get... You are
not giving....you are trading.   From "Be Somebody" by Mary Crowley

****

146

TAPPONAIDE

2 cups mayonaise
1 6 ounce can tuna
2 anchovy fillets, optional
3 tablespoons black olives
1 small onion
2 garlic cloves
1/2 cup chopped celery
1 can cream of potato soup
1/2 teaspoon worchestershire sauce
dash of tabasco, optional

Combine all ingredients at once in blender. Blend until smooth.
Serve with cucumbers, peppers, celery, carrots, etc. Also good
as a chip dip.

Hostess: Connie Anne Hanna
Displayer: Sandra McClure

****

MOTHER TO SON

Do you know that your soul is of my soul such part
That you seem to be fiber and core of my heart?
None other can pain me as you, dear, can do;
None other can please me, or praise me, as you.

Remember, the world is quick with its blame,
If shadows or stain ever darken your name.
"Like mother, like son," is a saying so true -
The world will judge largely of mother by you.

Be yours then, the task - if task it shall be -
To force the proud world to do homage to me,
Be sure it will say, when its verdict you've won:
"She reaped as she sowed; lo, this is her son."

Author and source unknown.

****

LIME PICKLES

Peel large cucumbers, cut in half and hollow out soft seeded part, and cut into strips. Place strips in roaster and cover with <u>one gallon water.</u> Add <u>one cup lime</u>, let stand over night. Next day, drain the lime water off and soak in tap water for three hours. While soaking, mix other ingredients together in another pan and bring to a boil, stir constantly.

1 quart vinegar
5 1/2 cups sugar
1 1/2 tablespoons salt
1 teaspoon whole celery seed
1 teaspoon mixed pickling spices

Add green food coloring to boiling mixture. Drain off tap water from cucumbers, pour boiled solution over them, place on stove, let simmer for 30 minutes. Fill fruit jars while cucumbers are warm so they will seal well.

Hostess: Marvis Johnson
Displayer: Karen Pratt

SHRIMP DIP MOLD

1 can cream of tomato soup
8 ounce package cream cheese
1/2 cup minced onions
1/2 cup minced celery
1/2 cup minced green pepper
2 tablespoons knox unflavored geletin
1/2 cup water
2 cups chopped boiled shrimp
1 cup mayonnaise

Heat soup over low heat. Add cream cheese, melt and let cool. Dissolve gelatin in water, stir in remaining ingredients to soup and cream cheese. Pour into mold and refrigerate over night.

Hostess: Linda Jody
Displayer: Nancy Thompson

CHILI CON QUESO DIP

2-3 Fresh tomatoes, chopped
1 medium onion chopped
1 small can green (El Paso) chiles peppers
1 small can red chiles peppers
1 pound Velvetta cheese, similar to American Cheese

Saute chopped onions and tomatoes. Add chopped chiles. Melt velvetta, add. Should set 2-4 hours before serving. Can be refrigerated. Serve with Doritos Tortilla Chips, or Doritos Taco Chips. Can also be served warm in fondue dish.

Hostess: Doris Stark
Displayer: Sandra Hayes

RUBY RED JAM

5 cups cut up rhubarb
3 cups sugar
1 package raspberry gelatin (3 ounces)
1 package raspberry Kool-Aid

Cook rhubarb and sugar over low heat until slightly thickened.
Remove from heat. Add gelatin and Kool-Aid. Pour in hot jars
and seal with paraffin.

Displayer: Dodie Carpenter

RHUBARB STRAWBERRY JAM

6 cups sugar
6 cups rhubarb
1 10 ounce package frozen strawberries

Chop rhubarb. Start cooking without water on low heat. Add
sugar after rhubarb is juicy. Cook and skim until clear. Add
strawberries, bring to boil. Do not cook after adding strawberries
as they will disolve. Put in pint jars and seal.

Hostess: Mary McKinney
Displayer: Dodie Carpenter

SQUASH PICKLES

8 cups sliced squash
4 medium onions, chopped
2 sweet peppers, red or green, chopped
1/2 cup salt
Cover above with water and ice for 3 hours, drain
3 cups sugar
3 cups vinegar
1 teaspoon celery seed
1 teaspoon mustard seed
Bring to a boil and add all ingredients, boil for 3 minutes,
put in jars.

Hostess: Barbara McDonald

****

Time was - is past; thou canst not it recall;
Time is - thou hast; employ the portion small.
Time future is not and may never be;
Time present is the only time for thee.

****

Entrees

SWEET AND SOUR MEATLOAF

1 can   15 ounces tomato sauce
1/2 cup brown sugar
1/4 cup vinegar
1 teaspoon mustard
2 pounds lean beef
1/2 pound ground pork
2 eggs, slightly beaten
1/2 cup minced onions
1/2 cup breadcrumbs, dry
1 tablespoon salt
1/4 teaspoon pepper

Preheat oven to 350 degrees. Combine tomato sauce, sugar, vinegar,
and mustard in a bowl. Mix well, set aside. Combine remaining
ingredients with 1 cup sauce mixture in a bowl. Mix well. Place
in lightly greased 1 1/2 quart casserole. Pour remaining sauce
evenly over loaf. Bake 1 hour or until done.

Hostess: Norma Jackson and Cheryl Burke
Displayer: Claudia Rooker

BAKED CHOP SUEY

1 1/2 pounds hamburger, browned
2 medium onions
2 cups chopped celery
1 can mushroom soup
1 can cream of chicken soup
1/2 cup uncooked rice, do not use Minute rice.
2 teaspoons soy sauce
2 teaspoons worcestershire sauce
2 cups water

Mix together and bake in greased casserole at 350 degrees for
1 1/2 hours. Top with 1/2 can of Chow Mein noodles and bake
15 minutes more.

Hostess: Bonnie Eisentrout
Displayer: Judy Braun

****

If your purpose is worthwhile enough, and your belief in it is
strong enough, the strength of the purpose will take over and
keep you keeping on even when you are physically exhaused.
                              From "Be Somebody"
****

BEEF STROGANOFF

1 1/2 pounds round steak
1 pound sliced fresh mushrooms
1 cup butter
2 pounds onions, finely chopped
1 can tomato soup
1 6 ounce can tomato paste
1 teaspoon salt
1/8 teaspoon soy suace
1 cup sour cream
minced parsley

Cut meat in very thin strips, trim off excess fat. Brown meat
and mushrooms in butter. Add onions. Combine soup, tomato
paste, and seasoning. Add to meat mixture. Cover, simmer for
1 hour. Just before serving, stir in sour cream. Thicken
gravy if desired. Serve in rings of fluffy hot rice. Garnish
with parsley.

Hostess: Jan McLaughlin
Displayer: Jackie Fetterhoff

QUICKIE BEEF STEW

1 can (1 pound) sliced carrots
1 can (8 ounces) whole potatoes
1 can (8 ounces) cut green beans
1/4 cup all purpose flour
1 envelope (about 1 1/2 ounces) dry onion soup mix
3 cups cut-up cooked beef

Drain vegetables, reserving liquid. Combine flour and soup mix
in large skillet. Add water to reserved liquid to measure 3 cups;
stir into mixture in skillet. Heat to boiling, stirring
constantly. Boil and stir 1 minute. Stir in vegetables and
beef. Cover; cook over low heat about 10 minutes or until it
is heated through. 4 servings, about 1 1/2 cups each.

Hostess: Eunice Armstrong
Displayer: Dodie Carpenter

****

ABOUT CLOSED HANDS

A closed hand can't receive.
Even God himself cannot give you or me any more that we are
mentally, emotionally and spiritually conditioned to receive.

If our hands are already full of ourselves, then God can't
fill them.   From "Be Somebody" by Mary Crowley

****

ENCHILADAS

1 pound ground beef
2 teaspoon salt
1 tablespoon vinegar
1 teaspoon chili powder
1 tablespoon tequilla
1 can kidney beans
3 tablespoon oil
dash of pepper
1 cup of water
flour
cheddar cheese
lettuce
tortillas

Brown ground beef. Add salt, vinegar, chili powder, tequilla, salad oil, pepper and, if desired, hot sauce. Mix well. Add kidney beans and water. Keep over medium heat. Then slowly add flour until mixture thickens. Shred cheese and mix with cut lettuce. Put tortillas in salad oil in frying pan, but do not let fry. Just leave until soft. Put mixture in tortilla, add cheese and lettuce mixture over top. Roll. Spread remaining ingredients over top of rolled tortillas. Heat in oven until cheese on top is melted.

Hostess: Kathy Kaufman
Displayer: Dodie Carpenter

CHILE VERDE WITH MEAT

Round steak, cut in small cube size
garlic powder
onion powder
cominos
salt

Cook the above in an uncovered pan with water approximately 20 min. Add:
1/2 can hot chiles (Ortega)
2 chopped fresh tomatoes
small can tomato sauce
1 1/2 cup water and let come to a boil
Serve with rice on the side and crisp fresh lettuce salad.

CHILE VERDE SAUCE:
Can of chiles (Ortega)
2 fresh tomatoes
garlic powder
onion powder
can tomato sauce

Chop up the chiles with the tomatoes, add the garlic and onion powder and a dash of salt. Mix in bowl with the tomato sauce and a little bit of water. No cooking, ready to serve over rice, noodles, refried beans, etc.

Hostess: Blanca Arias
Displayer: Betty Goertzen, Manager

CHILI

4 pounds chili meat, if you can get meat ground really coarsely
            or cut up into small cubes it makes prettier chili.
8 tablespoons chili powder
4 tablespoons SPANISH paprika, it's richer and darker than Italian
2 teaspoons ground comino
2 teaspoons ground oregano
1 teaspoon sugar
1/2 cup flour
salt to taste
2-3 chopped onions and 6 or 7 buttons of garlic
Saute meat, if meat does not have enough fat, add enough oil to
lighlty cover bottom of pan. Add onions and garlic. Cook until
onion is clear, but not brown. Mix dry ingredients together and
add just enough water to make a paste. Add to meat mixture and
simmer ten minutes. Add water and cook about three hours. Thicken
before serving. This is super chili, and makes great enchiladas,
the receipe can be increased many times without loss of flavor.

Hostess: Mary Jewett

SPANISH ENCHILADAS

1 15 ounce can Hunts tomato sauce
1 dozen corn tortillas
1 can Hormel chili without beans
1 1/2 pounds browned hamburger meat
1 clove garlic
1 small chopped onion
2 cups shredded cheddar cheese

Have all ingredients chopped and in individual containers. Combine
tomato sauce, chili, and garlic, and any other seasonings you might
like. Brown corn tortillas in hot oil, 10 seconds on each side. Dip
tortillas in tomato and chili sauce, add handful of meat, onion, and
cheese. Roll tortilla shells closed and place closed ends on the
bottom. Place in a 9 x 13" baking dish. Place left over hamburger,
onion, sauce, and cheese on top. Bake at 400 degrees for 15 minutes.
Serves 6.

Hostess: Debbie Potts
Displayer: Marilyn Kathol

****

School is a building that has four walls - with tomorrow inside.
                                                    Lon Waters.
                    ****

TORTILLA CHIP SALAD

1 16 ounce can of red kidney beans, drained
1 head of cut lettuce
1 cup diced onions
1 pound cheddar cheese
1 cup thousand island dressing
4 small tomatoes, cut into wedges
1 avacado sliced
1 pound hamburger
1 package taco seasioning mix
1 package tortilla chips, 16 ounce

Break up hamburger into small pieces and brown in skillet. Drain
off excess fat and add taco seasioning mix. Let stand. Shread
the lettuce, wash and drain. Grate the cheese, place all ingredients in a lagre bowl and toss with the thousand island dressing.
Note: Save some tomatoes and avacado slice and chips for a
garnish. Serves 8-12.

Hostess: Trudy DeJung
Displayer: Chloe Resh

TACO SALAD

1 pound ground beef, browned and drained
1 pound can kidney beans, drained
1 large onion, chopped
Mix above ingredients and refrigerate. Then mix:
3-4 chopped tomatoes
1 large head of lettuce
8 ounce grated cheddar cheese
Toss these 2 parts together. Add the next two ingredients at the
last minute.
1 small bag crushed tortilla chips
1 8 ounce bottle russian dressing

SUPER ON BREAD

1 1/2 pounds hamburger
1 cup cheese
1 small can Pet milk
1 egg
small onion
1 cup cracker meal
1 loaf french bread
Mix all together and let simmer. Pack into french bread, after you
cut the top center out. Wrap in foil. Bake 40 minutes at 350 degrees.

Hostess: Marie Keel

LASAGNE

2 boxes lasagne noodles
1 pound ground beef
1/4 cup onion
6 ounces can tomato paste
8 ounce tomato sauce
1 clove garlic, crushed
2 teaspoons Italian seasoning
1 teaspoon salt
1/4 teaspoon pepper
1 1/2 cups water
1 carton creamed cottage cheese
2 eggs
2 large bags mozarella cheese

Cook lasagne noodles as directed on package. Brown beef with onion in skillet. Add tomato paste, sauce, salt, pepper, Italian seasoning and water. Simmer 1 hour. Combine cottage cheese, eggs and mozarella cheese. In baking pan, alternate layers starting with noodles, then meat mixture and lastly cheese mixture. Sprinkle top with parmesan cheese. Bake at 350 degrees for 30 minutes. Remove from oven and let stand for 15 minutes before serving. Serves 10.

Hostesses: Roberta Mullis with Linda Grodon
Displayer: Karen Miller

LASAGNA

FIRST MIXTURE:
2 pounds ground beef
1 clove garlic, minced
1 1/2-2 tablespoons parsley
1/2 teaspoon basil
1 teaspoon oregano
2 teaspoons salt
1 1 pound can tomatoes
1 12 ounce can tomato paste
2 12 ounce cans tomato sauce
10-12 ounces lasagna noodles

SECOND MIXTURE:
3 cups creamed cottage cheese
2 beaten eggs
2 teaspoons salt
1/2 teaspoon pepper
2 teaspoons parsley flakes
1 3 ounce can parmesan cheese
1 pound mozeralla cheese, grated

Slowly brown meat, drain off excess fat. Add next seven ingredients. Simmer uncovered for 30 minutes. Stir occasionally. Cook noodles in boiling, salted water until tender. Drain noodles then rinse in cold water. Meanwhile, combine cottage cheese and eggs, seasoning and parmesan in a medium sized bowl. Place 1/2 cup noodles in a 13 x 9 x 2 buttered dish. Spread 1/2 of cottage cheese mixture over noodles; then 1/2 of meat sauce; then 1/2 of mozeralla. Repeat layers. Bake at 375 degrees for 30 minutes. Let stand 10 minutes. Serve with salad and french bread. Serves 12.

Hostess: Gayla Moates
Displayer: Jo Shnell

ITALIAN SPAGHETTI AND MEAT BALLS

1 small onion
small amount of olive oil
4 cans tomato sauce
4 cans water
1/8 teaspoon ground cloves
1/4 to 1/2 teaspoon oregano
1/2 teaspoon celery salt   or 2 sticks celery
1/4 teaspoon pure garlic juice or 1/2 teaspoon garlic salt
2 tablespoons parmesan cheese
2 tablespoons Italian seasoning
1 egg
3 pounds ground beef
salt and pepper
1 tablespoon parmesan cheese
cracker crumbs

Prepare sauce in dutch oven or large heavy pan. Chop onion
very fine and cook to transparency in olive oil. Add tomato
sauce, cloves, oregano, celery salt, garlic juice, parmesan
cheese. Wrap Italian seasoning in small piece of cheese
cloth or other clean soft rag and drop into sauce. Cook on
simmer for 30-40 minutes while sauce thickens and you are
preparing meatballs. Make paste of cracker crumbs and egg
and add to ground beef, season with salt, pepper, parmesan
cheese. Shape into balls and drop into hot fat; allow to
brown on all sides. Drain and drop into sauce to simmer
4-6 hours. After sauce has thickened you may put it and
meatballs into crock-pot and cook on low all day or all
night.

Hostess: Jean Landrum
Displayer: Edwana Lee

LASAGNE

1 pound ground beef
1 onion
1 large can tomato sauce
salt and pepper to taste
1 pound cottage cheese
1 pound mozzarella cheese
1 pound lasagne noodles

Brown ground beef and onions together. Add tomato sauce and
simmer. Add cottage cheese and set aside. Boil noodles in
boiling water. Drain and layer in baking dish sauce, lasagne
noodles, mozzarella cheese, continue until all is used up. Bake
about 25 minutes or until heated thoroughly at 375 degrees
uncovered.

Hostess: Darlene Elerick

MEAT BALLS IN ONION SOUP

1 pound ground beef
3/4 cup rolled oats, quick or regular
1 egg
1/2 cup milk
1 teaspoon salt
1/2 teaspoon tarragon, optional
1/3 cup flour
2 tablespoons fat
1 envelope dry onion soup mix
2 1/4 cups water
1/2 cup dry wine, optional
shredded parmasan cheese

Combine beef, rolled oats, eggs, milk, and seasoning. Blend
thoroughly. Shape into 18 medium sized balls, and roll lightly
in flour, save excess flour. Melt fat in frying pan, brown
the meat balls at moderate heat. Dissolve onion soup in 2
cups water and add to meat balls. Cover, cook over low heat
until done, 20-25 minutes. Mix remaining flour and water to
a smooth paste and stir into onion soup. Cook until thick
and smooth. If desired, five minutes before serving, sprinkle
with cheese.

Hostess: Dorothy Eckert
Displayer: Nancy Dietze

HAWAIIAN MEAT BALLS

1 pound ground round
1/2 pound pork sausage
3/4 cup bread crumbs
3/4 cup milk
1/2 cup chopped onion
1 egg slightly beaten
3/4 teaspoon salt and pepper
2 tablespoons salad oil, heated
Make small meatballs from above ingredients, brown a few
at a time in the oil. Put the following in a saucepan:
1/2 cup pineapple juice
1/2 cup wine vinegar
1/4 cup white sugar
3 tablespoons brown sugar
1 teaspoon soy sauce
When juices reach boiling, add cornstarch and water til smooth.
3/4 teaspoon cornstarch and 1 teaspoon cold water, blended.
After all meatballs are brown, add:
2 tablespoons green pepper, chopped
clove of garlic
After all meatballs are brown, add green pepper and garlic and
cook for five minutes. Remove garlic, add this mixture to
the juices and pour over meatballs. Bake at 325 degrees
for 45 minutes in a covered casserole.
Hostess: Joyce Kissler
Displayer: Karen Greenwood

MEATBALLS

4 pounds hamburger
4 teaspoons cumin
1 teaspoon garlic powder
2 tablespoons worcestershire sauce
1 tablespoon onion powder
salt and pepper to taste
1 large can pineapple chunks

Combine first 6 ingredients together. Shape into one inch
balls. Brown some chopped onion and meatballs together in
a large skillet. Drain off fat. Drain pineapple, reserving
syrup; set pineapple aside. Pour syrup over meatballs. Bring
to a boil. Cover, simmer 10 minutes. Serve on toothpicks,
with one chunk of pineapple and one meatball on each toothpick.
May be served cold or hot.

Hostess: Pearl Edmondson
Displayer: Diana M. Herrera

COCKTAIL MEATBALLS

1/2 cup cornflakes crushed
1 small onion grated
1 clove garlic, crushed
2 eggs, beaten
2 pounds ground beef
salt and pepper to taste
1 bottle chili sauce
1 6 ounce jar grape jelly
juice of 1 lemon

Combine first six ingredients together. Shape into 1/2 inch
balls and place on a baking sheet. Bake at 500 degrees until
browned. In a saucepan add chili sauce and grape jelly and
lemon juice. Mix until well blended over low heat. Add
meatballs to mixture. Pour into fondue dish (must be kept
warm for better flavor) and serve.

Displayer: Diana M. Herrera

****

Blessings are not to hoard, but to share.

As Christians we are blessed to share our blessings with others.

From "Be Somebody" by Mary Crowley.

****

158

CHILI MARVEL

2 pounds hamburger
2 medium onions
salt to taste
pepper to taste
2 medium cans kidney means
2 big cans tomatoes
1 large can tomato juice

Brown slowly together the hamburger and onions. Add salt
and pepper to taste, then add remaining ingredients. Simmer
1 1/2 to 2 hours.

Hostess: Marge Anderson
Displayer: Susie Mullinix

HAMBURGER MEDLEY SOUP

1 1/2 pounds ground chuck
6 onions, sliced
4 stalks celery
4 carrots
4 potatoes
3 tablespoons margarine
6 cups water
1 large can tomatoes
salt and pepper to taste

Simmer meat, pour off excess grease. Add margarine, sliced
onions and water and cook 1 1/2 hours, then add tomatoes and
cut up vegetables and seasoning. Cook until done, about one
hour.

Hostess: Trin Jones

PORCUPINES

1/2 cup uncooked rice
1 1/2 pound ground beef
1/2 cup chopped onion
1/2 cup chopped green peppers
1/2 cup chopped celery
1 egg, beaten
2 teaspoons prepared mustard
1 teaspoon salt
2 cans tomato soup
2 soup cans water

Mix everything together except soup and water. Make balls at
least 2" in diameter. Place in baking dish. Pour soup and
water over it. Bake covered at 350 degrees for 1 1/2 hours.
Makes 6 servings.

Hostess: Susan Ewald

STUFFED BURGER BUNDLES

1 cup herbed seasoned stuffing mix
1/3 cup evaporated milk
1 pound ground beef
1 10 1/2 ounce can condensed cream of mushroom soup
2 teaspoons worcestershire sauce
1 tablespoon ketchup

Prepare stuffing according to package directions. Combine
evaporated milk and meat. Divide into 5 patties, on wax
paper pat each patty into a 6 inch circle. Put 1/4 cup of
stuffing in center of each patty. Bring sides of patty up,
seal over stuffing. Place in 1 1/2 quart casserole dish.
Combine remaining ingredients. Heat and pour over meat.
Bake uncovered, 45 minutes at 350 degrees.

Hostess: Sandra Welch
Displayer: Elsie Wierwille

DINNER BEEF PATTIES

1 large bermuda onion
2 tablespoons butter or margarine
1/4 cup water
3 tablespoons brown sugar
paparika
2 pounds ground beef
2 teaspoons salt

Peel onion and cut crosswise into 4 thick slices. Saute in
butter or margarine until lightly browned on bottom. Turn
carefully. Add water and brown sugar, cover. Simmer 10
minutes, or just until tender. Sprinkle with paprika. Keep
hot while fixing and cooking meat. Mix ground beef lightly
with salt, shape into 4 large and 4 medium size patties about
1 inch thick. Pan fry over medium heat 8 minutes, turn, cook
5 minutes longer. Spoon chile glaze (receipe below) over,
continue cooking, basting with glaze in pan, 3 minutes longer
for medium, or until meat is done as you like it. Put one
each large and medium size pattie together with onion slice
between on a plate. Top with any sauce left in pan.

CHILE GLAZE:
Combine 1/2 cup chile sauce with 1/2 cup water, 1 tablespoon
corn syrup, and 1 tablespoon worcestershire sauce in a 2 cup
measure. Makes 1 cup.

Hostess: Mrs. Bonnie Broadhurst
Displayer: Rita Brown

BEEF STEW BURGUNDY

2 pounds beef stew meat
2 tablespoons cooking oil
3 tablespoons flour
1 medium onion
1 clove garlic
1 cup red wine, Burgundy or other dry red wine
1 cup water
1/2 teaspoon thyme
1 bay leaf
parsley and celery leaves
salt and pepper
1 bouillon cube
1 pound mushrooms or 1 large can and liquid
6 carrots
4 large potatoes
15 small white onions, peeled or 1 can onions
1 bell pepper, cut into 1/2 inch squares, about 1/2 cup

Shake meat cubes in bag with flour, salt and pepper until meat
is well coated. Brown in hot oil, or shortening, in skillet.
When the chunks are a rich brown on all sides, remove them
with kitchen tongs to a dutch oven. In the remaining fat in
the skillet cook the onions and garlic over low heat, just
until tender, not brown, stirring constantly. With slotted
spoon transfer them to the dutch oven along with the meat,
and add the water, bouillon, wine, mushrooms, dry herbs,
parsley and celery leaves and simmer over low heat for about
2 hours. The last 45 minutes, add the carrots, potatoes,
onions, and bell pepper. Continue simmering until meat and
vegetables are tender. Season to taste. Serve hot with a
tossed salad and french bread. If there are any left-overs,
serve them the next day on steamed rice. Variations; Add
green beans, peas, or stock of celery.

Hostess: Deidre Meyers
Displayer: Agnes Avolicino

CHEESBURGER PIE

2 1/2 pounds ground beef   1 pie crust
1/2 cup chopped onions
3/4 can of cream of mushroom soup
cheese slices
Mix ingredients together and pat into a 9 x 13" pan. Then add
one layer of cheese slices over hamburger mixture. Then cover
with your favorite pie crust. Bake at 325 degrees for 1 hour.

Hostess: Bernie Kolbo
Displayer: Carol Post

SHORT RIBS WITH LIMA BEANS

2 cups large dry lima beans
5 cups water
3 pounds short ribs
1/2 cup catsup
1/2 cup chopped onions
1/2 cup chopped celery and tops
1 clove garlic, minced, or 1 teaspoon garlic salt
3 teaspoons salt
pepper to taste

Rinse limas, add the 5 cups of water. Boil 2 minutes, remove
from heat and let stand 1 hour. Brown ribs in skillet, remove
excess fat. Bury ribs in limas and add remaining ingredients.
Cover and cook gently until meat and limas are tender. If
needed, add more water, season with salt and pepper to taste
in the last 1/2 hour.

Hostess: Paula Barton
Displayer: Sandra Hayes

SLEMISH CARBONNADES
(Crock pot recipe)

2 pounds round steak, 1 inch thick
1/4 cup flour
1 teaspoon sugar
1/8 teaspoon pepper
6-8 small new potatoes, peeled
1 envelope or 1 1/2 ounce dry onion soup mix
3/4 cup beer

Trim round steak. Cut into serving portions. Combine flour,
sugar, and pepper. Toss with steak to coat thoroughly. Place
potatoes in crock pot and cover with steak pieces. Thoroughly
combine soup mix and beer. Pour over steak, moistening well.
Cover and cook on low setting 8-12 hours. Thicken gravy
before serving if desired. 4-6 servings.

Hostess: Cindy Halsey
Displayer: Marilyn Kathol

****

Attitude is the mind's paint brush, it can color a situation
gloomy or gray or cheerful and gay.

****

162

BAKED ZUCCHINI

Ground hamburger or sausage, browned
onion
poultry seasoning
garlic powder
salt
pepper, as desired for all spices
package seasoned stuffing mix
parmasan cheese

Cut zucchini in half lengthwise and spoon out center; put it in
frying pan with hamburger or sausage, onion and seasonings.
Simmer until about half done. Put package seasoned stuffing
mix in large bowl, add mixture from frying pan, add parmasan
cheese (as much as desired) mix well. If dry, add small amounts
of hot water until moist. Now sprinkle cheese into zucchini
shells and stuff. Sprinkle cheese on top, if desired, and
wrap each half in foil separately. Place on cookie sheet and
bake at 375 degrees until tender. Pierce bottom of zucchini
with large fork to check for tenderness. Large zucchinis take
about 1 hour, smaller ones about 1/2 hour.

Hostess: Mary Schwarm

BEEF ZUCCHINI CASSEROLE

1 1/2 pounds ground round
1/2 cup chopped onion
1/4 teaspoon garlic powder
1/2 teaspoon salt
1/8 teaspoon pepper
1/8 teaspoon oregano
1/2 cup bread crumbs
1/4 cup flour
1/4 cup butter
1/4 teaspoon salt
1/4 teaspoon pepper
2 cups milk
1 cup grated cheddar cheese
6 or 8 medium zucchini squash

Grease two quart casserole, wash and cut ends of squash and boil
in lightly salted water just till tender. Slice 1/2 inch or
larger. Cook onions, ground round and pour off excess drippings,
stir in bread crumbs and spices, consistancy will be dry. Remove
from heat. In sauce pan put butter and let melt, add flour, salt,
pepper, and milk. Then add cheese, and cook till thickened.
Begin to layer, placing squash on bottom, then a layer of meat,
then a layer of cheese sauce and repeat layers. Grate an extra
amount of cheese, sprinkle on top and paparika may be added also.
Bake at 350 degrees for 1/2 hour. Serves 6-8.

Hostess: Marietta Mullenaux
Displayer: Patsy O'Rourke

SHARON'S CHEROKEE CASSEROLE

1 pound ground beef
1 can cream of mushroom soup
1 pound can whole tomatoes
1/4 cup chopped onions
1 1/2 teaspoons salt
dash of pepper
1/8 teaspoon garlic
1/8 teaspoon of oregano
1 cup minute rice
3 slices american cheese

Brown ground beef and onions, drain. Stir in seasonings.
Add tomatoes, mushroom soup and rice. Mix well. Simmer
5 minutes, stirring occasionally. Top with cheese. Replace
top and simmer 2-3 minutes. Serves 4-6, takes 15-20 minutes.

Displayer: Sharon Adcock

****

HOME INTERIORS CODE OF ETHICS

We believe in the dignity and importance of women,
We believe that everything woman touches should be ennobled
    by that touch,
We believe that the home is the greatest influence on the
    character of mankind,
We believe that the home should be a haven - a place of
    refuge, a place of peace, a place of harmony, a place
    of beauty,
No home in America ever need to be dull and unattractive,
We are dedicated to doing our part to make every home have
    ATTRACTION POWER.

****

****

When the Lord created the world, he looked at it and said,
"Thats good."

Then he created man, looked at him and said, "That's good but
I believe I can do better."

So - He created woman.

From "Be Somebody"   Mary Crowley

****

164

HAMBURGER POTATO PIE

1 pound ground beef
1 medium onion
1 cup cooked peas
2 cups tomatoes
1/2 cup catsup
2 tablespoons butter
1/2 teaspoon salt
1/2 teaspoon pepper
5 potatoes, cooked and mashed
1 egg

Brown the chopped onion in butter. Remove onion and brown
ground beef with salt and pepper. Place ground beef and
onions, peas, tomatoes, and catsup in a casserole to combine. Mash potatoes, beat in 1 egg and spoon potatoes on
top of other mixture. Brown in 375 degree oven till peaks
are golden.

Hostess: Barbara McDonald

HAMBURGER NOODLE STROGANOFF

1 pound ground beef
1/2 cup chopped onion, can also use onion flakes
1 can cream of mushroom soup
1/2 cup sour cream
1/2 cup water
1/2 teaspoon salt
1/8 teaspoon pepper
1/2 teaspoon paparika, optional
2 cups cooked noodles

Brown beef and cook onion until tender in skillet. Stir to
seperate meat and pour off fat. Add remaining ingredients.
Pour into 1 1/2 quart greased shallow baking dish. Bake at 400
degrees for 25 minutes. Remove from oven and stir. Garnish
with tomato slices and buttered bread crumbs. Place in oven for
5 minutes of baking. Makes 4 1/2 cups.

Hostess: Doris Carey
Dislpayer: Marilyn Kathol

****

Advice to a wife about her husband: You have to lean on him
on one side...and prop him up on the other.
                                    From "Be Somebody"
****

HAMBURGER CASSEROLE

1 pound ground beef
2 tablespoons butter
4 medium sized potoates
2 onions
1 teaspoon salt
dash pepper
1 cup tomato soup

Brown the beef in skillet with butter. Cut potatoes in 1/2
inch cubes and spread in a baking dish. Cover with half the
meat. Add half the soup and a sliced onion. Season with salt
and pepper. Repeat, using remaining ingredients. Bake 1 1/2
hours in a 350 degree oven. More soup may be added during
baking if needed

Hostess: Barbara McDonald

MORE BEEF CASSEROLE

1 8 ounce package noodles
1 pound lean ground beef
1/4 cup chopped onions
1 tablespoon cooking oil
1 cup of tomato sauce or tomato catsup
1 8 1/2 ounce can cream-style corn
1/2 cup of chopped green pepper
1 tablespoon chili powder
1/2 cup shredded cheese

Cook noodles according to package directions. Cook beef and
onions in cooking oil until meat turns white. Add tomato sauce
or catsup, corn, green pepper and chili powder to meat mixture,
and cook about 10 minutes. Put a layer of noodles in a 2 quart
casserole dish, then a layer of meat mixture. Bake for 20 minutes
at 325 degrees. Add shredded cheese and continue cooking until
cheese melts. Yield 6-8 servings.

Hostess: Barbara McDonald

****

If you are doing more for others, they will be drawn to you.
If you help other people get what they want out of life,
You will get what you want out of life.

From "Be Somebody"
****

166

GOOD, GOOD SANDWICH

Roman Meal Bread, or any whole grain bread
Monterey Jack Cheese
Alfalfa sprouts, less expensive if bought in a health food store
Tomatoes
Bacon
Durkee's dressing

Grill bread in butter with cheese, but do not melt cheese
too soft. Pull bread apart and add other ingredients. If
desired add salt and a little garlic powder.

Hostess: Rossie Harwell

NOODLE CASSEROLE

2 cans onion soup
2 cans beef consomme
1/2 pound oleo
8 ounces very small noodles
2 tablespoons soy sauce
2 cans water chestnuts or mushrooms

Place _uncooked_ noodles in butter and brown, using any skillet
large enough to stir this mixture easily. After brown, put in
casserole. Add onion soup and consomme; then soy sauce. Stir
sliced water chestnut or mushrooms into this mixture. Bake 45
minutes at 350 degrees. This serves 10-12 poeple and can be
divided into 5 or 6 servings so easily.

Hostess: Mary Ann Mansker
Displayer: Marge Fritsche

CRUNCHY CORN DOGS

1 cup pancake mix
1 cup milk
1/2 cup corn meal
2 teaspoons chili powder
1/4 teaspoon salt
1/8 teaspoon pepper
12 skewers
12 frankfurters
vegetable oil
Combine pancake mix, milk, corn meal, chili powder, salt and
pepper; mix until batter is fairly smooth. Insert wooden
skewers into franks. Dip into batter; drain off excess. Fry in
deep hot oil (375 degrees) 1-2 minutes, until golden brown. Drain
on absorbant paper. Serve with mustard.

Hostess: Miriam Sumner
Displayer: Linda Gordon

RICE CASSEROLE

1 pound ground meat
1 1/2 cups rice
1/4 cup chopped onions
1/4 cup bell peppers
1/4 cup celery
1 teaspoon celery salt
1 teaspoon garlic salt
1 1/2 teaspoons black pepper
1/2 jalapeno pepper
1 slice cheese
1/4 cup parsley
1 1/2 teaspoons salt
Cook rice until done, set aside. Saute the onions, bell peppers
and celery. Brown meat, add peppers and seasonings and rice,
adding cheese when it is well mixed. Cook on top of stove.

Hostess: Brenda Gipson
Displayer: Izella Allen

CALICO BEANS

1/4 pound bacon, cut in bite sizes
1 pound hamburger meat
1/2 cup chopped onion
Brown these ingredients together, do not drain.

1/2 cup brown sugar
1/2 cup ketsup
2 tablespoons vinegar
1 tablespoon prepared mustard
1 pound can butter beans
1 pound can red beans, not kidney beans, use pinto beans
1 pound can pork and beans
Do not drain beans. Stir together. Mix both mixtures together.
Bake uncovered 1 1/2 hours at 300 degrees.

Hostess: Wanda Copeland
Displayer: Sandy Webb

MACARONI & CHEESE CASSEROLE

12 ounces elbow macaroni
9 cups water
4 1/2 tablespoons butter, 1 block
4 1/2 tablespoons flour
3/8 teaspoons salt
dash of pepper
1 1/2 cups of milk
1 large can carnation milk
1 16 ounce block Kraft american cheese

Cook macaroni in water until tender. Do not add salt. Drain.
Melt butter in small pan; stir in flour; salt and pepper. Add
milk slowly, cook, stirring constantly until blended. Grate
block of cheese and put 1 cup of cheese aside for topping of
casserole. Add remaining grated cheese to milk, cooking and
stirring until melted. Blend together cheese sauce and macaroni
and place in casserole dish; sprinkle 1 cup grated cheese over
macaroni casserole. Bake at 325 degrees until cheese on top is
browned.

Hostess: Patricia R. Lormand

PIZZA

Bridge Port Bread (store freezer type)
Oregano leafs, 1 teaspoon for each pizza
2 1/2 6 ounce can tomato paste
Garlic powder
1 1/2 cups diced onion
1 1/2 Victor brand salami
Parmesan grated cheese
Mushrooms, fresh or canned
1 1/2 packages Monterrey Jack cheese, grated
1 1/2 packages Mozzarella cheese, grated

Section bread into five balls, in each ball sprinkle oregano
leaves, then roll out dough, spread tomato paste, sprinkle
garlic powder and then onions. After the onions place the
salami, the Jack cheese, the Mozzarella cheese, then the
parmesan cheese, spread mushrooms on top. Sprinkle a few
oregano leaves on top of mushrooms. Make sure your oven is
at 450 degrees, bake 15 minutes. Each pizza serves 6-8.
Recipe makes 5 medium pizzas.

Hostess: Pat Dillard
Displayer: Claudia Rooker

****

One person with a belief is equal to ninety-nine with only
interest.   "Be Somebody" by Mary Crowley

****

CHICKEN AND VEGETABLES

1 onion, diced
1/2 head of cabbage, chopped
1 cup of sliced celery
1 cup of sliced carrots
1 teaspoon of tumeric
2 chicken boullion cubes
salt and pepper to taste
1 cut up chicken pieces

Place all in large soup pot, cover, simmer slowly for 1 hour,
add 1/2 cup water or chicken broth.

Hostess: Maylene Flagg
Displayer: Marion Casalan

OVEN FRIED CHICKEN

3 pound young frying chicken, cut up as for frying
salt
flour
1/2 cup melted butter
homogenized sweet milk

Salt and roll chicken in flour, put melted butter in baking pan.
Place chicken in pan and cover with milk, sprinkle with pepper.
Bake until tender, turning so it will brown on all sides. You'll
find this is a change and delicious. Makes it own gravy. Bake at
400 degrees, 1 to 1 1/2 hours.

Hostess: Carla J. Gragus
Displayer: Diane Armstrong

BARBEQUED CHICKEN

1 large frying chicken, cut up
2 bottles hickory-smoked Open Pit barbeque sauce
garlic and onion salt and regular salt

Put chicken in roaster or deep pan. Pour sauce over chicken.
Rinse bottle with a little water and add also. Sprinkle
garlic and onion salt and regular salt to taste over sauce.
Bake at 325 to 350 degrees at least 1 hour or until done.
Can be covered. Also for country style ribs instead of chicken.

Hostess: Oneth Lovetinsky
Displayer: Rovona Miller

****

Curiosity is the wick in the candle of learning. William A. Ward.

****

HOT BEEF SANDWICHES
Makes six dozen

15 pounds lean beef, cubed
2 pounds onions
2 ounces McCormick beef flavor
2 ounces flavored croutons
2 6 ounce cans mushrooms
12 ounces white wine

Cover this mixture with water. Cook 1 1/2 days in crockpot on
high during the day and on low overnight. (36 hours) Stir with
fork after 6 hours. It will thicken by end of cooking time.May
also be cooked in oven at 450 for 10 1/2 hours. 1/2 of this
receipe makes three dozen sandwiches.

Hostess: Jean Hoffman
Displayer: Karen Greenwood

CHILI

5 pounds meat
1 large onion
2 cans tomato paste
2 1/2 teaspoons comino seed
5 tablespoons chili powder
1 teaspoon black pepper
5 teaspoons salt
2/3 cup flour
3/4 teaspoon garlic powder

Brown meat, onion, and comino seed with salt, pepper and garlic
powder. Then add chili powder and mix thoroughly, add tomato
paste and equal amount of water. Simmer about 2 hours, adding
water as needed. About 20 minutes before chili is done, mix
flour in a glass of water and add to mixture. Stir to thicken.

Hostess: Mrs. Juan Gonzales
Displayer: Joyce Moore

****

Resolve to be tender with the young, compassionate with the aged,
sympathetic with the striving, and tolerant with the weak and the
wrong. Sometime in life you will have been all of these.
"Dandy Lion", quoted by Bob Goddard in St. Louis Globe-Democrat.

****

CHICKEN ENCHILADAS

2 whole chickens
2 4 ounce cans ortega diced green chiles
2 4 1/2 ounce cans chopped olives
1 small onion chopped
2 1/2 to 3 dozen corn tortillas
1 cup oil
1 pound chedder cheese
3 tablespoons flour
3 tablespoons shortening
3 cups water
1 19 ounce Las Palmas enchilada sauce
3 8 ounce cans tomato sauce

Melt shortening, add flour, brown. Add water, enchilada sauce, simmer 10 minutes. Set aside. Boil chicken til done, cool, bone. Add chiles, olives and onion. Mix well with hands. Put aside. Heat oil, dip each tortilla quickly, to soften. Set aside. Put filling in, roll up, add sauce and sprinkle cheese on top. Bake 15 minutes at 350 degrees. Makes servings for 12.

Hostess: Debbie Delgado
Displayer: Susan Klepar

CHIPPED BEEF CASSEROLE

1 cup dry (uncooked) shell macaroni
1 can cream of mushroom soup
1 cup milk
1 cup sharp Cheddar cheese, shreaded
1/4 onion, minced
1 40 ounce package chipped beef, snipped fine

Place macaroni in buttered baking dish. Pour the other ingredients over macaroni. Do not stir. Cover and place in refrigerator 6 to 8 hours or overnight. When ready to bake, take a spoon and go to the bottom of the casserole in several places, without stirring. Bake 1 hour at 350 degrees.

****

"I never go out to meet a new day
Without first asking God as I kneel down to pray
To give me the strength and courage to be
As tolerant of others as He is to me."
Ned Nichols

****

BAKED SPAGHETTI

1 onion
garlic
1 pound ground beef
1 teaspoon salt
pepper, to taste
1 envelope spaghetti seasoning
1 large jar Ragu
1 cup water
1/2 pound uncooked spaghetti
1 cup grated cheese

Brown meat, adding onion and garlic, salt and pepper. Stir in seasoning, sauce, and water. Cover, simmer 25 minutes. Break half spaghetti (raw) into lightly greased casserole, cover with half sauce and half the cheese. Repeat layers. Cover and bake at 350 degrees 30 minutes covered, 15 minutes uncovered.

Hostess: Susan Bahner
Displayer: Linda Gordon

ITALIAN SPAGETTI

1 medium onion, chopped
1 pound hamburger
Brown together in skillet
Pour over this mixture:
1 15 ounce can tomato sauce or tomato juice
1 6 ounce can tomato paste
salt and pepper to taste
ADD:
1 teaspoon chili powder
1/2 teaspoon salt
1/2 teaspoon parsley flakes
1 teaspoon white sugar
1 to 3 bay leaves
garlic salt if desired
Simmer for 1 hour. Serve on cooked spagetti. Serves 6.

Hostess: Gayle Gieselman
Displayer: Marilyn Kathol

****

Every morning lean your arm a while upon the window sill of Heaven and gaze upon your God. Then with that vision in your heart, turn strong to meet the day.
From "Be Somebody" by Mary Crowley.

****

GREENBEAN CASSEROLE

2 pounds ground beef
1 can green beans, drained
1 onion, chopped
2 cans tomato soup, no water
6 potatoes, whip with butter and 2 eggs

Brown meat and onion, add green beans and tomato soup.
Put into casserole dish. Spoon potato mixture on top. Bake
at 350 degrees until bubbly. About 20 minutes.

Hostess: Becky Clubb
Displayer: Sandra Hayes

EVERYDAY MEATLOAF

2/3 cup dried bread crumbs
1 cup tomato juice or milk
1 1/2 to 2 pounds ground beef
2 beaten eggs
1/4 cup of onion
1/2 teaspoon sage
1 teaspoon salt
dash pepper
Soak crumbs in juice or milk, add ground beef and other ingredients.
Mix well, form into individual loafs, and cover with
piquant sauce. Bake at 350 degrees for 45 minutes.

PIQUANT SAUCE:
3 tablespoons brown sugar
1/4 cup of catsup
1/4 teaspoon nutmeg
1 teaspoon dried mustard, optional

Hostess: Gloria Crenshaw
Displayer: K. Selby

****

Judge not another from your high and lofty seat,
Step down into the arena, where he and his problems meet.
From "Be Sombody" by Mary Crowley.

****

****

Man - by himself is priced. For thirty pieces Judas sold himself,
Not Christ.   "Be Somebody" by Mary Crowley.

****

HAM ROLL UPS

2 packages pressed ham
6 ounces philadelphia cream cheese
1 teaspoon mayonnaise
Horse radish to taste
salt and pepper
dash garlic salt

Put ham slices between paper towels to dry. Mix other ingredients
together to spreadable consistency. Spread mixture on ham slices,
roll, and stick with 5 toothpicks. Refrigerate overnight and slice
between toothpices. Serve attractively.

Hostess: Marge Moore
Displayer: Mary Kuzmanich

DUMPLINS

1 1/2 cup flour
1/4 cup crisco
1/2 teaspoon salt
1/4 cup milk
1 egg

Cut flour, crisco, salt in mixing bowl until it resembles cornmeal.
Add milk and egg. Roll out on floured board and cut into strips.
Let dry for 30 minutes before placing over your boiled and deboned
chicken. Cook for 20 minutes without taking the lid off the pan.

Hostess: Cynthia Waters
Displayer: Pat Anderson

DRESSING

1 can campbell onion soup
1 can campbell celery soup
1 can campbell mushroom soup
4 eggs
corn bread
sage to taste
2 or 3 cans chicken broth
Bake at 350 degrees till light brown. An easy but delicous dressing.

Hostess: Charlotte Matthews
Displayer:

****

To ease another's heartache is to forget one's own. Abraham Lincoln.

****

JAMALAYA

2 pounds smoked pork sausage, cut into small peices
8 pork chops, cut into 1 inch pieces
chicken pieces, use the meaty pieces such as thighs and drumsticks
salt & pepper to taste, about 1 tablespoon salt, 1/2 teaspoon cayanne pepper
3 large onions, chopped
1 bunch celery, chopped
2 tablespoons parlsey
3 beef bouillon cubes
3 chicken bouillon cubes
1 teaspoon kitchen bouquet
4 cups long grain rice
3 tablespoons lemon juice

Brown all the meat seperately and remove from the pot, preferable
an iron one. Brown seasonings in the same pot as the meat. Dissolve
bouillon cubes in water and add kitchen bouquet to the mixture. Add
other seasonings to taste. Measure rice and place in a large roasting
pan. Pour 8 cups liquid over this. Use the bouillon water and plain
water to make 8 cups. Layer the meat and the sauteed seasonings over
the rice. Add lemon juice and stir. Place into a 350 degree oven
until all the liquid is absorbed by the rice. Lift the cover of the
pan only to check the absorbtion. This is a large receipe, but it
freezes extremely well. Just freeze in casserole dishes, and reheat
in a preheated 350 degree oven until hot. It is sometimes a good
idea to have the casserole partially thawed before you heat it.

Hostess: Dorothy Cutrer

QUICK PORK AND POTATO BAKE

6 pork chops or steaks
salt and pepper
1 can cream of mushroom soup
medium sharp cheese, grated
chopped onion
Tater-Tots, frozen

Place pork chops in an oblong cake pan. Salt and pepper lightly.
Spoon soup over top of chops, grate cheese all over lightly. Sprinkle
with a little chopped onion. Place frozen Tater-Tots in order all
over the top of this so meat is completely covered. Sprinkle more
cheese over this. Bake 1 hour at 350 degrees. Turn heat down to
200 degrees for an additional 15 minutes. Serve with cottage cheese,
or tossed salad for a complete meal.

Hostess: Nell Herrington

****

HAM LOAF

2 1/2 pounds smoked ham, ground
1/2 pound fresh ham, ground
2 eggs
1 cup cracker crumbs, rolled
Mix well, make loaf in 9 x 13 pan, bake at 350 degrees for 1 1/4
hours. Drain drippings and add glaze, basting every five minutes
for 30 minutes.

GLAZE:
1/2 cup brown sugar
1/2 cup vinegar, scant
1/2 cup water
3/4 teaspoon dry mustard
1/3 cup pineapple juice

Hostess: Helen Taylor

GRANDMA ROY'S MEAT PIE

2 pounds ground pork
1 pound ground beef
Cook above with water
1/2 teaspoon cloves
1/2 teaspoon cinnamon
1/2 teaspoon poultry seasoning
2 cup up onions, fried in butter
3 large potatoes, mashed
Pastry shell
Combine all ingredients, pour into pastry shell, top with shell and
bake until golden brown at 350 degrees.

Hostess: Karen Orr
Displayer: Eleanor Sheehe, Manager

BARBECUED PORK

6 pork steaks, cubed
2 onions, diced
3 cloves garlic, sliced
3 stalks celery, diced
2 small green peppers, diced
3 cups catsup
6 tablespoons tarragon vinegar
3 tablespoons worcestershire sauce
3 teaspoons salt
3/4 teaspoon pepper
Rub a small amount of fat from meat over bottom of fry pan, add meat
and brown well on stove. Combine all other ingredients and pour
mixture over the meat. Cover, reduce heat to simmer and cook for
45 minutes or until meat is tender. Turn occassionally during
cooking. Serve over rice. Serves about 7.

Hostess: Marilyn Smith
Displayer: Janet Sroka

CHOPSTICK TUNA

1 can condensed cream of mushroom soup
1/4 cup water
2 cups chow mein noodles
1 6 1/2 or 7 ounce can tuna, drained and flaked
1 cup sliced celery
1/4 cup chopped onion
dash pepper

In mixing bowl, combine the soup and water. Add 1 cup of the
chow mein noodles, the tuna, celery, onion, and pepper. Toss
lightly. Turn into 10 x 6 x 2 inch baking dish. Sprinkle
remaining noodles atop. Bake in 375 degree oven for 30 minutes
or till casserole is heated through. Makes 4 servings.

Hostess: Mrs. Audrey Jean Warner
Displayer: Genendal Raines

TUNA CHEESE SANDWICHES

2 cans (6 1/2 ounce) tuna, drained
3 hard boiled eggs, chopped
1/4 cup finely chopped onions
1 cup small cubed cheese, cheddar or other favorite
1/4 teaspoon celery salt
salt and pepper to taste
Mayonnaise
12 slices bread or 6 hamburger buns, halved

Mix tuna, eggs, onion, cheese, celery salt, salt, and pepper. Mix
with mayonnaise until of right consistancy. Spread on top of bread
or buns. Place in oven and broil 4-5 inches from heat 3-5 minutes
or until cheese bubbles. Serve immediately.

Hostess: Lynn Letarski
Displayer: Nancy Dietze

****

"Bless the Lord, O my soul; and all that is within me, bless his
holy name. Bless the Lord, O my soul, and forget not all his
benefits."   Psalm 103:1,2.

****

SCALLOPED OYSTERS

2 cans oysters (canned)
2 cups cracker crumbs
1/2 cup melted butter
1/2 teaspoon salt
dash pepper
3/4 cup cream
1/4 cup juice from oysters
1/4 teaspoon worcestershire sauce

Drain oysters, save juice. Combine cracker crumbs with butter, salt, pepper, and worcestershire sauce. Layer oysters in bottom of pan. Add layer of crumb mixture. Make three layers like this ending with top layer cracker crumbs. Mix cream and oyster juice and pour over top of layers. Bake at 350 degrees for 40 minutes.

Hostess: Andrea Crumly
Displayer: Marilyn Kathol

SHRIMP-TOMATO ASPIC MOLDED SALAD

1 box lemon gelatin
2 cups tomato juice
2 tablespoons worcestershire sauce
2 tablespoons vinegar
1 avocado, chopped
5 green onions, chopped
3/4 cup celery, chopped
1 can shrimp

Dissolve gelatin in 1 cup boiling tomato juice. Add 1 cup cold tomato juice, stir well. Add remaining ingredients and pour into a mold. Chill until set. Unmold. Serves 6 to 8.

Hostess: Carol Penner
Displayer: Lurae Cox

TAPPONAIDE

2 cups mayonnaise
1 6 ounce can tuna
2 anchovy fillets, optional
3 tablespoons black olives
1 small onion
2 garlic cloves
1/2 cup chopped celery
1 can cream of potato soup
1/2 teaspoon worcestershire sauce
dash of tobasco, optional
Combine all ingredients at once in blender. Blend until smooth. Serve with cucumbers, peppers, celery, carrots, etc. Also good as a chip dip.

Hostess: Connie Anne Hanna
Displayer: Sandra McClure

SHRIMP CREOLE

1 1/2 cups chopped onoin
1 cup finely chopped celery
2 medium green peppers, finely chopped
2 cloves garlic, minced
1/4 cup butter or margarine
1 can(15 ounce) tomato sauce
1 cup water
2 teaspoons snipped parsley
1 teaspoon salt
1/8 teaspoon cayenne red pepper
2 bay leaves, crushed
14-16 ounces fresh or frozen cleaned raw shrimp
3 cups hot cooked rice

Cook and stir onion, celery, green pepper and garlic in butter
until onion is tender. Remove from heat; stir in tomato sauce,
water and seasonings. Simmer uncovered 10 minutes add water if
needed. Stir in shrimp. Heat to boiling. Cover and cook on
medium heat 10-20 minutes or until shrimp are pink and tender.
Serve over rice. Makes 6 servings. Rinse frozen shrimp under
running cold water to remove ice glaze.

Hostess Helen Whitaker
Displayer: Dianna Doyle

SHRIMP MOLD

1 can tomato soup
1 large 8 ounce package Philadelphia Cream Cheese
1 1/2 tablespoons Knox Unflavored gelatin (1 pack)
2 cans medium shrimp (or 1 pound shrimp)
1/2 cup mayonnaise
3/4 cup chopped celery
1/4 cup onions

Soak gelatin in 1/4 cup cold water. Heat tomato soup to boiling
point and dissolve cream cheese in soup. Add gelatin and then let
cool, grind celery and onions together. Add mayonnaise, celery,
and onions to soup then season to taste. Grind shrimp and when
mixture begins to thicken, add shrimp. Mold and cool in
refrigerator, serve as a dip or with crackers or as a sandwich
spread.

Hostess: Patricia Lormand

****

Every evening I turn "worries" over to God. He's going to be
up all night anyway.   From"Be Somebody" by Mary Crowley.

****

180

GREEK BAKED FISH WITH VEGETABLES

3 pounds whole fish (Turbot is inexpensive)
1/4 cup crisco oil
1 1/2 cup chopped onion
2 cloves garlic, minced
1 1/2 cup canned tomatoes
1/2 cup snipped parsley
1/2 teaspoon salt
1/4 teaspoon pepper
2 tablespoon lemon juice
1 pound fresh spinach
1/2 cup dry white wine (optional)
1/4 cup snipped fresh dill or 1 tablespoon dry dill weed

Heat oven to 350 degrees. In skillet saute onions in oil until soft.
Add garlic, tomatoes, parsley, dill, salt, and pepper; cook 10
minutes (simmer) Sprinkle fish lightly with salt to taste and lemon
juice. Arrange tomato mixture in 9 x 12 baking dish. Lay fish on top.
Arrange spinach on top of fish. Pour wine over all. Cover with foil
and bake for 50 minutes. Uncover and bake another 15 minutes. Serves
4-6. Serve with cornbread.

Hostess: Betty Cantrell

CRAB-RICE MIXTURE ON TOMATOES

1 package (6-8 ounces) frozen crab meat or 7 1/2 ounces (1 can)
     crab or chicken
1 1/4 cooked, chilled rice
1/3 cup chopped celery
2 green onions, chopped
1 tablespoon lemon juice
1/2 teaspoon soy sauce
1/4 teaspoon salt
1/8 teaspoon pepper
1/2 cup mayonnaise
6 medium tomatoes
crisp lettuce

Drain crab. Break into pieces. Combine crab with rice, celery and
onions. Mix lemon juice and seasonings with mayonnaise. Add to
crab mixture and toss to coat lightly. Chill well. Fill tomato
rossettes with crab mixture. Serve on bed of crisp lettuce.
Serves 6.

Hostess: Ann Kottmier
Displayer: Nancy Evans

****

CHICKEN PAPRIKA

1 chicken cut up
salt and pepper
2 tablespoons crisco
2 tablespoons oleo
1 onion chopped up
1 teaspoon paprika
1 cup water
1 tablespoon flour
2 tablespoons cold water
1/2 cup sour cream

Melt oleo and crisco. Brown chicken and remove from pan. Add
more crisco and oleo if needed. Brown chopped onion then
add water and paprika. Put the chicken in and cook until done,
about an hour. Make paste and pour over chicken. Cook about 10
minutes.

DUMPLINGS:
2 eggs
1/2 cup milk
1 teaspoon salt
1 cup flour
salt and pepper
Mix to a firm batter. Drop by teaspoon into boiling water. Cook
10 minutes or until they are tender. Add to chicken and paprika.

Hostess: Karen Rieuitti
Displayer: Karen Greenwood

SALMON CASSEROLE

1/4 cup onion
1/4 cup celery
1 tablespoon butter
2 #303 cans salmon
1 can mushroom soup
1/2 cup shredded cheese
2 cups cooked rice
Combine salmon, soup, cheese and rice.
Saute onion and celery in butter. Add celery and onions to salmon
mixture. Pour in casserole. Top with corn flake crumbs or bread
crumbs. Bake 30 minutes at 350 degrees.

Hostess: Julie Jones
Displayer: Linda Gordon

****

Kindness is a lanquaqe which the deaf can hear and the blind can read.
                                                        Mark Twain.
****

CHICKEN FRICASSEE WITH DUMPLINGS

4 1/2 to 5 pound stewing chicken, cut up
1 cup all purpose flour
2 teaspoons salt
1/4 teaspoon pepper
2 teaspoons paprika, if desired
shortening or salad oil
1 cup water
3 tablespoons flour
Milk
Dumplings (below)

Wash chicken pieces and pat dry. Mix 1 cup flour, salt, pepper, and paprika. Coat chicken with flour mixture. Heat thin layer of shortening in large skillet; brown chicken on all sides. Drain off fat and reserve. To skillet, add water and if desired, chopped onion, lemon juice or herbs, such as rosemary or thyme leaves. Cover tightly; cook chicken slowly 2 1/2 to 3 1/2 hours or until fork-tender, adding water if necessary. Remove chicken to warm platter; keep warm. Pour off liquid in skillet; reserve. To make gravy, heat 3 tablespoons reserved fat in skillet. Blend in 3 tablespoons flour. Cook over low heat, stirring until mixture is smooth and bubbly. Remove from heat. Add enough milk to reserved liquid to measure 3 cups; pour into skillet. Heat to boiling, stirring constantly. Boil and stir 1 minute. Return chicken to gravy. Prepare dough for Dumplings, drop by spoonfuls onto hot chicken. Cook uncovered 10 minutes; cover and cook 20 minutes longer.
Note: To fricassee a broiler-fryer chicken, select 3-4 pound broiler-fryer chicken and cook slowly 45 minutes or until fork tender.

DUMPLINGS:
1 1/2 cups all purpose flour
2 teaspoons baking powder
3/4 teaspoon salt
3 tablespoons shortening
3/4 cup milk

Measure flour, baking powder and salt into bowl.
If desired, add 3 tablespoons snipped chives. Cut in shortening thoroughly until mixture looks like meal. Stir in milk.

Hostess: Sharon Pierson
Displayer: Dodie Carpenter

****

A careless word may kindle strife,
A cruel word may wreck a life,
A bitter word may hate instill,
A brutal word may smite and kill,
A gracious word may smooth the way,
A joyous word may light the day,
A timely word may lessen stress,
A loving word may heal and bless.

****

CHICKEN AND BROCCOLI CASSEROLE

2 10 ounce frozen broccoli pieces
2 cups cooked diced chicken breasts (about 3)
2 cans creme of chicken soup
1 cup of mayonnaise
1 teaspoon lemon juice
1/2 teaspoon curry powder
1/2 cup bread crumbs
1/2 cup shredded cheddar cheese

Cook broccoli, drain most liquid, place in casserole dish. Cut
up cooked chicken, layer oven broccoli in casserole. Combine
soup, mayonnaise, lemon juice, curry powder. Mix well and pour
over chicken and broccoli. Cover top with bread crumbs, sprinkle
on cheddar cheese. Bake at 350 degrees for 30 minutes or until all
is hot through. This can be prepared and refrigerated earlier in
the day but must be baked a little longer if chilled.

Hostess: Kathy Herman
Displayer: Doris Roper

CHICKEN SUPREME SANDWICH

4 cooked chicken breasts (or approximately the same amount of any
     meat part of the chicken you may have left over)
1 can Franco American chicken gravy
1 can cream of mushroom soup
1 jar pimento, optional
1 can water chestnuts, sliced
2 tablespoons chopped onions

Mix all together, cut the crust off one loaf of sandwich bread
and make sandwiches using two slices of bread with filling inside.
Wrap in foil and freeze.

1 twin pack potato chips
6 eggs
4 tablespoons milk
Mix beaten eggs and milk together, crush potato chips. When
ready to make sandwiches, dip frozen sandwiches into the egg
batter and then into the crushed potato chips. Place on well buttered cookie sheet and bake for one hour at 300 degrees.

Hostess: Mary Whisenhunt
Displayer: Betty Goertzen, Manager

****

The smallest deed is better than the grandest intention.
                                            Larry Eisenberg
                    ****

CHICKEN WILD RICE CASSEROLE

2 cups cooked and diced chicken
1 box long grain wild rice
1 can mushroom soup
1 can mushrooms
1/2 pound cheddar cheese
2 tablespoons butter or margarine
2 tablespoons flour

Melt margarine in pan and add all flour. Mix well and add mushroom
soup. Add mushrooms. Set aside but keep warm. Buy the cut of
chicken you prefer. Boil, remove from bone, cut up and set aside.
Take 2 1/2 cups of the broth from the chicken and cook the rice by
using directions on package, using broth instead of water. Use
a casserole dish and layer the mushroom mixture, chicken, and
the wild rice. Alternate till all is used. Put slices of cheese
on top. Put in oven long enough to melt cheese. Serves 4.

Hostess: Nancy Howard
Displayer: Jean Brown

TURKEY OR CHICKEN RICE CASSEROLE

4 tablespoons butter
2 cups bullion or mushroom juice
1 cup whipping cream or evaporated milk
5 tablespoons flour
1 1/2-2 cups cooked rice
8 ounce can drained mushrooms
1 10 ounce box frozen peas
2-3 cups cooked chicken or turkey
Paprika   and bread crumbs
Mix rice, mushrooms, peas, and chicken or turkey together in
baking dish. Mix butter, bullion, milk, and flour together and
pour over chicken mixture. Sprinkle with bread crumbs and paprika.
Bake at 325 degrees for 30 minutes. Serves six.

Hostess: Donna Parsley
Displayer: Darlene Simpson

****

Today is the only day I have for family tenderness -
for graciousness - for kindness - for love.
Say "I love you" to someone today.

****

CHICKEN AND SAFFRON RICE

1   2 1/2-3 pound broiler/fryer chicken, ready to cook, cut up and salted
1 clove garlic, minced
1/4 cup salad oil
1 cup uncooked long grain rice
1   12 ounce can vegetable juice cocktail (1 1/2 cups)
3/4 cup water
1   3 ounce can (2/3 cup) broiled sliced mushrooms, undrained
1 cup chopped celery
1 cup chopped onion
1 teaspoon salt
1/4 teaspoon pepper
1 teaspoon dried marjoram (crushed)
pinch powdered saffron
1/3 cup halved ripe olives
1/2 10 ounce package frozen peas, thawed (about 1 cup)
1 tomato cut in wedges

Season chicken pieces with salt. Heat garlic in oil. Brown
chicken slowly in hot oil; remove chicken. Add rice, brown slowly
stirring occasionally. Stir in vegetable juice, water, undrained
mushrooms, chopped celery, onion, salt, pepper, marjoram, saffron,
and olive halves. Bring to boiling. Turn mixture into a
13 x 9 x 2" baking dish. Top with the chicken pieces. Cover dish
tightly with foil. Bake at 375 degrees about 1 hour. Uncover and
sprinkle thawed peas around chicken. Top with tomato wedges,
season with salt and pepper. Cover dish again and bake 15 minutes
longer. Makes 6 servings.

Hostess: Jan Brodl
Displayer: Bernie Lorraine

CHICKEN AND RICE CASSEROLE

1 1/2 cubes margarine (3/4 cup)
4 beef bouillon cubes
1 package dry onion soup mix
2 cups regular long grain white rice
4 cups water
1 whole chicken, cut up

Melt margarine and bouillon cubes then add soup mix, rice, water.
Mix well and pour into buttered casserole dish. Salt and pepper
drained chicken and place on top of rice mixture. Bake in covered
casserole at 350 degrees for 1 1/2 hours. Serves 8.

Hostess: Gail Scott
Displayer: Nancy Evans

****

What sunshine is to flowers, smiles are to humanity. Joseph Addison.

****

186

CHICKEN SUPREME

1 cup of dry rice
6 pieces of chicken
1 cup of cooking sherry
1 can of mushroom soup
1 can of celery soup
1 package of dry onion soup

Put rice in bottom of pan and lay chicken parts on top. Mix sherry,
mushroom soup and celery soup. Pour over rice and chicken. Sprinkle
dry onion soup on top and bake at 350 degrees for two hours.

Hostess: Carol Mrvan
Displayer: Helen Barnett

CHICKEN CASSEROLE

1 boiled and deboned chicken
1 can of chicken soup
1 can of celery soup
1 can of chicken broth
1 small diced onion
salt and pepper to taste
1 can of Chou-Mein Noodles
2 cups potato chips

Mix chicken, soup, broth, onion, and salt and pepper. Add the
noodles, in a buttered casserole dish. Top with crushed potato
chips. Bake 370 degrees for 1 hour.

Hostess: Marge Christian
Displayer: Pat Anderson

CHICKEN NOODLE CASSEROLE

1   4 pound chicken
1 large package noodles
1 can cream of mushroom soup
1 cup crushed corn flakes for top

Cook chicken until tender. Cook noodles in salt water, until
tender. Drain, add chicken and soup to noodles, make a gravy
with broth, add to chicken, soup, and noodles. Mix well, turn
into pan and top with corn flakes. Bake at 350 degrees for
30 minutes.

Hostess: Stella Sterling
Displayer: Dodie Carpenter

EASY CHICKEN DIVAN

3 cans asparagus, long stalk, drained
4 chicken breasts, cooked and boned
2 cans condensed cream of chicken soup
3/4 cup mayonnaise
1 teaspoon lemon juice
1/2 cup shredded sharp cheese
1 cup soft bread crumbs
1 tablespoon melted butter

Arrange asparagus in greased 12 x 7 1/2 x 2 baking dish. Layer chicken atop of asparagus. Combine soup, mayonnaise and lemon juice. Pour over chicken and asparagus. Sprinkle with cheese. Combine bread crumbs and butter, sprinkle over all. Bake 350 degrees for 35 minutes. 8-10 servings.

Hostess: Rita Angelo
Displayer: Agnes Avolicino

CHICK AND CHIPS

1 can (1 1/4 cup) condensed cream of chicken soup
1 cup cubed cooked chicken (5 ounce can boned chicken)
1/2 cup milk
1 1/4 cups crushed potato chips
1 cup cooked green peas, drained

Preheat oven to 375 degrees. Empty soup into a 1 quart casserole dish and add milk, mix thoroughly. Stir in chicken (or you may use tuna) and 1 cup of potato chips and peas. Sprinkle top with remaining 1/4 cup of chips. Bake for 25 minutes at 375 degrees.

Hostess: Irma Holzworth
Displayer: June Lackey

CHICKEN CASSEROLE

2 large fryers, boiled and boned, season to taste
Butter casserole dish, put in chicken in small serving pieces. Add:
1 can of cream of mushroom soup
1 can cream of chicken soup
2 cups chicken broth
Pepperidge Farm stuffing mix over all then:
dot with butter.
Cook at 350 degrees for 30 minutes. Serves 8-10 people.

Hostess: Irene Noblin

****

You have freedom of choice, but not freedom from choice. Wendell Jones.

****

CHICKEN GUMBO

3 1/2 pound broiler-fryer chicken, cut up
2 cups water
1 clove garlic, finely chopped
2 teaspoons salt
1 large bay leaf, crumbled
2 large stalks celery, with leaves, cut diagonally making about 1/2 cup
1/2 cup chopped onion
1   28 ounce can whole tomatoes
1   10 ounce package frozen okra
1   7 ounce can whole kernel corn
1/3 cup uncooked regular rice
1/2 teaspoon red pepper sauce

Heat chicken pieces, water, salt, garlic, and bay leaf to boiling
in Dutch oven, reduce heat. Cover and simmer until chicken is done,
about 45 minutes. Remove chicken from broth, strain broth.
Refrigerate chicken and broth. When cool, remove chicken from
bones, skin may be removed, if desired. Cut chicken into bite-
size pieces. Skim excess fat from broth and place broth and chicken
in Dutch oven. Stir in celery, onion, and tomatoes, with liquid,
break up tomatoes with fork. Heat to boiling, reduce heat. Cover
and simmer until okra and rice are tender, 20-30 minutes. Garnish
with snipped parsley.

Hostess: Donna Borland
Displayer: Karen Miller

SPIFFY SPANISH CHICKEN

2 chickens, quartered
1/2 tablespoon kitchen bouquet
2 tablespoons tomato sauce
garlic powder
salt
oregano
6 potatoes, cut into quarters
1/2 cup olive oil
1 small can tomato sauce
2 cloves garlic, chopped
1 large onion chipped
1 large green pepper in rings
1 small bottle olives, pitted
1 tablespoon capers
1 cup water

Preheat oven to 325 degrees. In large baking pan, arrange chicken
pieces. Mix together kitchen bouquet and 2 tablespoons tomato sauce,
brush chicken covering well with mixture. Sprinkle with garlic powder,
oregano and salt. In sauce pan, heat olive oil and quickly brown
potoates, drain and place around chicken. Add garlic, onion, and
peppers to olive oil and saute until golden brown. Add tomato sauce,
olives and capers and cook slowly for 10 minutes, add water and salt
to taste. Bring to boil and then pour over chicken. Cover tightly and
cook 1 hour at 325. Serve over rice with peas. Yields 8 servings.
Hostess: Dorothy Gonzalez   Displayer: Doris Weaver

CURRY CHICKEN

1 whole chicken
3/4 ounce curry
1 medium size onion
4 large fegs of garlic
1/2 teaspoon poultry seasoning
1 tablespoon tomato paste or ketchup
2 tablespoons vegetable oil or crisco

Cut chicken up into eight or ten pieces, removing fat as much as possible. Add salt, lemon juice or vinegar, and rub in well about an hour before cooking. Wash thoroughly and squeeze all the water out when ready to cook. Mix curry powder into smooth paste with water, adding part of onion finely chopped or grated with chopped or grated garlic, and poultry seasoning. Put oil to heat. When hot, add curry stirring well until slightly brown, then add chicken stirring very well. Cook until moisture is out. When chicken starts to fry, add water covering the chicken. Add tomato paste or ketchup and salt to taste. Boil chicken to whatever thickness of sauce you require, and chicken is properly cooked. It goes well with rice.

Hostess: Mrs. Dhanmatty Menzies
Displayer: Rita Brown

CHICKEN AND DRESSING CASSEROLE

1 3 pound chicken, cooked, deboned, and skinned
Spread the following over chicken in long cake pan or casserole dish:
1 can cream of chicken soup
1 can cream of celery soup
1 small can pet milk
Mix and add:
1 tablespoon sage
1 package Pepperidge Farms corn bread mix.
1 cup chicken broth
Add corn bread last so that it will be on the top. Bake at 450 degrees for 20 minutes.

Hostess: Darla Givens

****

When one tugs at a single thing in nature, he finds it attached to the rest of the world.   John Muir

****

PEPSI CHICKEN

1 stick oleo
1 can pepsi
1 20 ounce bottle ketchup
1 cut up chicken
salt and pepper to taste

Melt oleo in electric skillet. Place chicken in skillet and pour
pepsi and ketchup over chicken. Cook at 205 degrees for 2 hours.
Serves 4.

Hostess: Cheryl Cape
Displayer: Nancy Bennett

SWEET AND SOUR CHICKEN

2 1/2 pounds chicken, cut into eights
1/4 cup all purpose flour
1 teaspoon salt
1/4 cup oil
1 can (1 pound)tomatoes, broken up
    or 2 small cans of tomato sauce
1 tablespoon brown sugar
1 tablespoon worcestershire sauce
1 1/2 teaspoons lemon juice

Dredge chicken with flour and salt. Heat oil in skillet. Simmer
covered 45 minutes.

Hostess: Barbara McDonald

EXTRA SPECIAL CHICKEN

3 ounces sliced dried beef
3 large chicken breasts (skinned and deboned and cut in half)
6 sliced of bacon
1 can of condensed cream of mushroom soup
1 cup sour cream

Run cold water over dried beef and drain. Place in bottom of a
12 x 8 x 2" dish. Place chicken over beef. Salt and pepper.
Top each half of chicken breast with a slice of bacon. Bake
uncovered in a 350 degree oven for 30 minutes. Stir soup and
sour cream together. Spoon over chicken. Bake uncovered 25
minutes. Serve.

Hostess: Gail Gibbs
Displayer: Charlyn K. Travers

****

Success does for living what sunshine does for stained glass.
                                              Bob Talbert
                    ****

191

Colonial·JETTON'S Formerly Jetton's of Texas **,INC.**

P. O. BOX 2018
1700 ROGERS ROAD
FORT WORTH, TEXAS 76101
(817)335-9372

William A. Horan, *President*
Grant Linder, *Vice President*
John C. Horan, *Vice President*

PORK RIBS BARBECUED

Sprinkle well with Jetton's Dry Seasoning for Ribs.
Place ribs on open pit, fired with charcoal, turn as
needed until brown on each side.

Slice and serve hot.

Given by Mrs. Moore of Jetton's---
The girls asked for this recipe after the scrumptious
Barbeque Ribs at the Carter Ranch at Dallas Displayers Day.

PAN FRIED BARBECUED CHICKEN

1 frying chicken cut up
1 can tomato soup, undiluted
1/2 cup brown sugar
1/2 cup chopped celery
3 teaspoons garlic salt
3 tablespoons prepared mustard
3 tablespoons worcestershire sauce
few drops tabasco sauce

Brown unfloured chicken in frying pan. An electric frying pan is
nice to use with this recipe. Add barbecued sauce which has
previously been mixed in a bowl. Cook slowly until chicken and
celery are well done. Delicious.

Hostess: Maxine Maycock
Displayer: Joan Niernberger

BARBECUED CHICKEN

2 pounds chicken parts
2 tablespoons shortening
1 can tomato soup
1/3 onion, celery
2 tablespoons brown sugar
2 tablespoons worcestershire sauce
2 tablespoon lemon juice
2 teaspoon prepared mustard
2 to 4 drops tobasco sauce

In skillet, brown chicken parts in shortening. Mix together
and stir in remaining ingredients. Cover, simmer 45 minutes
until chicken is tender, stirring now and then.

CHICKEN ELEGANTE

1 chicken breast per person, halved and de-boned
Leo's spicy or sliced beef
garlic, salt, and pepper to taste
bacon
cream of mushroom soup
1/2 pint sour cream

Line baking dish with spicy or sliced beef. Sprinkle chicken with
garlic, salt, and pepper. Wrap with one slice of bacon. Place in
baking dish. Pour one can of cream of mushroom soup mixed with one
half pint sour cream over chicken. Bake one and one-half hours at
350 degrees. Serve on bed of parsley and rice.

Hostess: Dorothy Risner
Displayer: Nancy Thompson

ELEGANT CHICKEN

4-5 chicken breasts split
4 ounce package dried beef
8 ounce carton sour cream
1 can cream of mushroom soup
paprika

Grease large baking dish and line bottom with dried beef. Place
chicken on top of beef. Mix sour cream and mushroom soup together.
Pour mixture over chicken and sprinkle with paprika. Do not add
salt as the beef is salty. Bake uncovered at 275 for three hours.
(This dish will "hold" nicely up to 45 minutes.)

Hostess: Ernestine Embrey
Displayer: Donna Andes

****

Nothing in life is to be feared. It is only to be understood.
Marie Curie.
****

MEXICAN RECEIPE - FLAUTAS

1 pound roast beef
1 dozen corn tortillas
2 avacados
2 jalapeno peppers
1/4 cup mayonaise
1/4 small onion
3 cloves garlic
1/4 teaspoon oregano
1/4 teaspoon salt
1/4 teaspoon lemon juice
oil

Begin by cooking beef with 2 cloves of garlic, 1/4 teaspoon oregano, break beef into small stringy pieces. Put shreaded beef inside tortilla, roll and hold together with a toothpick. Pass rolled tortilla through hot oil, leaving it there until hard, one at a time. Prepare guacomole topping. Roast jalapeno peppers, peeled and chopped. Mix together mashed avacados, jalapeno peppers, onions, garlic, salt, lemon juice and mayonaise. Spread topping on prepared tortilla. Dish can be served with a side of Spanish rice and salsa.

Hostess: Dora Padilla
Displayer: Diana M. Herrera

MEXICAN CHICKEN CASSEROLE

1 whole chicken
1 large package crushed taco flavored doritos
4 chopped jalapeno peppers
1 can cream of chicken soup
1 can cheddar cheese soup

Boil chicken until done. Bone when cool. Crush doritoes.
Dilute chicken soup with 1/2 can of broth from boiled chicken.
Layer crushed doritoes, chicken, peppers, and chicken soup. On top of this, spread the can of cheddar cheese soup. Sprinkle with a few of the crushed doritoes. Bake in a 325 degree oven until it is bubbly. Serve with a salad and doritoes.

Hostess: Betty Whitehouse
Displayer: Tonya Pember

****

If righteousness is in the heart, there will be beauty in the character;
If beauty is in the character, there will be harmony in the home;
If harmony is in the home, there will be order in the nation;
If order is in the nation, there will be PEACE IN THE WORLD.
                                    From "Be Somebody" by Mary Crowley
****

194

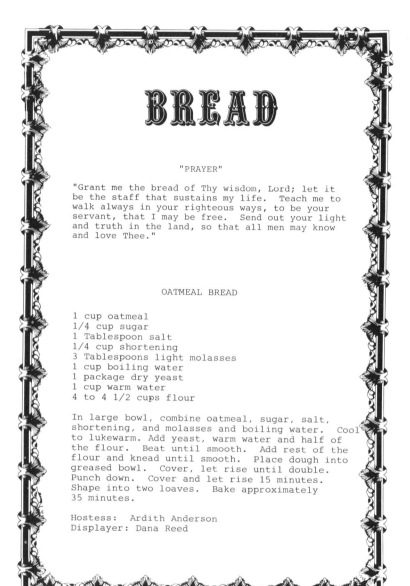

BREAD

"PRAYER"

"Grant me the bread of Thy wisdom, Lord; let it be the staff that sustains my life. Teach me to walk always in your righteous ways, to be your servant, that I may be free. Send out your light and truth in the land, so that all men may know and love Thee."

OATMEAL BREAD

1 cup oatmeal
1/4 cup sugar
1 Tablespoon salt
1/4 cup shortening
3 Tablespoons light molasses
1 cup boiling water
1 package dry yeast
1 cup warm water
4 to 4 1/2 cups flour

In large bowl, combine oatmeal, sugar, salt, shortening, and molasses and boiling water. Cool to lukewarm. Add yeast, warm water and half of the flour. Beat until smooth. Add rest of the flour and knead until smooth. Place dough into greased bowl. Cover, let rise until double. Punch down. Cover and let rise 15 minutes. Shape into two loaves. Bake approximately 35 minutes.

Hostess: Ardith Anderson
Displayer: Dana Reed

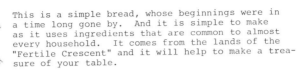

This is a simple bread, whose beginnings were in
a time long gone by. And it is simple to make
as it uses ingredients that are common to almost
every household. It comes from the lands of the
"Fertile Crescent" and it will help to make a treasure of your table.

SUN BREAD

2 cups yellow cornmeal
4 to 5 cups whole grain wheat
1 cup millet
1 cup chopped sunflower seeds
1/2 cup golden raisins
1/2 cup chopped almonds
2 cups water
1/4 cup sesame oil
salt

Very simply put, this requires more muscle than
imagination, but like many of the Lord's creations,
it is a labor of love, and the rewards are the en-
joyment of his bounty!
Simply stir all the ingredients together until they
are very well mixed. Form into two loaves, making
certain that the dough is thick enough so the loaves
won't fall apart when baking. Bake at about 350-F
for about 1 1/2 hours. Those who prefer health
food will find this filled with nutrition and it can
be eaten with Grace from the Lord's table.

MILLET: A generic term somewhat loosely applied
to a group of small grain cereals. In the early
days of the world's history, Millet held a very
high place as a food grain.

> THEN I WILL GIVE YOU RAIN IN DUE
> SEASON, AND THE LAND SHALL YIELD
> HER INCREASE, AND THE TREES OF THE
> FIELD SHALL YIELD THEIR FRUIT.
> AND YOUR THRESHING SHALL REACH
> UNTO THE VINTAGE, AND THE VINTAGE
> SHALL REACH UNTO THE SOWING TIME:
> AND YE SHALL EAT YOUR BREAD TO
> THE FULL, AND DWELL IN YOUR LAND
> SAFELY.
>   LEVITICUS 26:4,5

MONKEY BREAD

1 quart scalded milk
1 cup sugar
1 cup oleo
2 packages dry yeast dissolved in 1/2 cup water
8 cups flour
1 cup flour
3 teaspoons salt
2 teaspoons baking powder
1 teaspoon soda

Pour milk over sugar and oleo. Cool, add dissolved yeast, add 8
cups flour, one at a time, let rise double, add 1 cup flour and
other ingredients. Let rise double. Punch down and store in
refrigerator in a covered container. Will keep up to two weeks.
When ready to make bread, roll out thin. Cut into strips.
Melt oleo in pan and then fill pan one half full with strips dipped
in the melted oleo. Let rise and bake. 425 degrees, 10-15 minutes.

Hostess: Fay Shumway
Displayer: Nancy Thompson

POPPY SEED BREAD

3 cups flour
1 1/2 cups milk
1 1/2 teaspoon vanilla
2 1/2 cups sugar
3 eggs
1 1/2 teaspoon baking powder
1 1/2 tablespoon poppy seeds
1 1/2 teaspoon salt
1 cup plus 2 tablespoons salad oil
1 1/2 teaspoon almond extract
GLAZE:
3/4 cup powdered sugar
1/4 cup orange juice
2 teaspoons butter, melted
1/2 teaspoon almond extract

Combine all ingredients and beat 2 minutes. Pour into 2 greased loaf
pans, bake 1 hour at 350 degrees. Pour glaze over loaves while still
warm.

Hostess: Sharon Lovig

****

What we learn with pleasure, we never forget. Alfred Mercier.

****

197

QUICK ROLLS

1 teaspoon baking powder
1/2 teaspoon salt
1/4 cup shortening
1/4 cup lukewarm water
flour, 4 cups minimum
2 tablespoons sugar
1/4 teaspoon soda
1 package or cake yeast
sour milk or buttermilk

Sift 3 cups flour with baking powder, sugar, salt, and soda. Cut
in the shortening. Dissolve yeast in the water and add enough sour
milk to make 1 cup of liquid. Add to the dry ingredients. Stir in
additional flour to make a stiff dough. Turn out on board and knead
for 1 minute. Roll out 1/2 inch thick and cut with biscuit cutter.
Place in pan and let rise 1 hour. Bake about 15 minutes at 425 degrees.

Hostess: Barbara McDonald

HOT ROLLS

1/4 cup sugar
1/4 cup oil or melted shortening
1 teaspoon salt
1 egg
1/2 cup boiling water
1 package yeast, dissolved in 1/2 cup lukewarm water
3 cups flour

Put sugar, oil, salt, egg in bowl and mix together. Add boiling water
to above, then add yeast, and 3 cups flour. Let rise 45 minutes.
Bake at 350 degrees until brown.

Hostess: Sue Engman
Displayer: Glenda Engman

****

Success is like housework - it is so daily. You have to do it
all over again every morning.   "Be Somebody" by Mary Crowley

****

****

You can't rest on your laurels - If you do, they will wilt.
"De Somebody" by Mary Crowley.

****

YEAST ROLLS

1 cup crisco
1 cup sugar
1 teaspoon salt
1 cup boiling water
Mix above in a large mixing bowl and cool. Then mix:
1 cup lukewarm water
2 packages dry yeast
2 beaten eggs
Mix all together, let stand until cool. Mix with first mixture.
Add 6 or 7 cups flour to liquid mixture. Place on floured board.
Knead about 12 times. Make into clover leaf rolls, let rise only
once. Bake in moderate oven at 375 degrees until brown. Yield 36.
You can refrigerate for 2-3 days in a large bowl with loose fitting
lid.

Hostess: Janie Reeves
Displayer: Pat Anderson, Manager

NO KNEAD YEAST ROLLS

2 large or 3 small eggs
2 teaspoons salt
3/4 cup sugar
3/4 cup shortening, half butter
3 cups warm water
2 packages dry yeast
8-10 cups flour

Mix together eggs, salt, sugar, and shortening. Dissolve yeast in
water and add to above mixture. Add flour 2 cups at a time and stir
well. Don't get dough too stiff, add just enough for easy handling.
Place in greased bowl and let rise for several hours, punching down
when it gets to top of bowl. Roll out about 1/2 inch for cinnamon
rolls, spread with mixture of 1 cup sugar, 1/2 cup melted butter,
and 3 teaspoons cinnamon; then roll up and cut into 1 inch slices.
Put into pan cut sides down and let rise till double and bake 20
minutes. This receipe can be used for 4 loaves of bread; shape
dough into four loaf pans, let rise till double and bake at 375
degrees for about 35 minutes. This receipe makes good dinner rolls
and sweet rolls with your favorite glaze.

Hostess: Donna Ruckman
Displayer: Darlene Simpson

****

The parent's life is the child's copybook. Jewels of Home (Gibson)

****

199

UNA'S BREAD

4 eggs, well beaten
1 cup milk
1/2 cup wesson oil
1/2 cup honey
1 pakcage dry yeast
1 teaspoon salt
2 cups flour
2 1/2 cups flour

Combine liquid ingredients, then add yeast, salt, and 2 cups flour.
Beat with elect.ic mixer. Add 2 1/2 cups flour, work with hands,
shape grease and leave in covered bowl 2 hours. Turn out on floured
board, shape (rolls, or roll out thin, cover with butter and shape
into butterhorn and let rise) Cook 20 minutes at 350 degrees.

Hostess: Una Jarvis
Displayer: Gesele Ross

PEG ROLLS

3/4 cup shortening
2 eggs
2/3 cup sugar
1 cup warm mashed potoates
1 yeast cake in 1/2 cup lukewarm water
1 teaspoon salt
1 cup warm water
7 1/2 cups unsifted flour

Cream shortening and sugar, add eggs to mixture, then add beaten
potatoes. Add yeast cake, salt and water, flour alternately. Let
rise once. Punch down and put in refrigerator if you don't want
to make until the next day. Otherwise let rise once more and
make into biscuits. Let rise again and bake. 375 degrees.

Hostess: Genevieve Bowers
Displayer: Bonnie Laux

HOT ROLLS

1/2 cup sugar
3/4 teaspoon salt
1 package or cake of yeast
1/2 cup shortening
2 eggs
5 cups of flour, approximately
Add sugar, salt and shortening to hot water and let cool. Dissolve
yeast in 1/4 cup of warm water, then add this to the sugar mixture,
also the beaten eggs and 3 cups of flour. Mix well with hands then
put on board and knead well. (Probably will take around 2 cups of
flour.) Roll out, cut with biscuit cutter, put in greased pan to
rise for about 2 hours. Bake at 400 degrees for 12 minutes.

Hostess: Barbara McDonald

PUMPKIN BREAD

Preheat oven to 350 degrees, grease and flour pans
Mix Well:
2 cups pumpkin
4 eggs
1 cup oil
1/3 cup water
Sift together:
3 1/2 cups flour
3 cups sugar
1 tablespoon pumpkin spice
2 teaspoons soda
1 1/2 teaspoons salt
Nuts optional-about 1 cup

Add dry ingredients to pumpkin mixture a little at a time. Mix
well. Place in greased and floured loaf pans. Makes 2 regular
loaves or 3 small loaves. Bake at 350 degrees for 1 hour to 1
hour 20 minutes.

Hostess: Dinah Houfek
Displayer: Margaret Pacheco

PUMPKIN BREAD

2 3/4 cups sugar
2 sticks oleo
3 eggs
2 cups pumpkin
2 3/4 cups flour
1 teaspoon baking soda
2 teaspoons baking powder
1 tablespoon cinnamon
1 tablespoon vanilla
1 teaspoon nutmeg
1 teaspoon cloves
1/4 teaspoon salt
1 cup chopped nuts

Using largest bowl, cream together sugar and oleo. Add 3 eggs one
at a time and beat using electric mixer. Sift flour and measure
accurately. Sift again with the following, baking soda, baking
powder, cinnamon, nutmeg, cloves and salt. Add the flour mixture
to the sugar, oleo, egg mixture. Blend well with a wooden spoon.
Add the pumpkin, vanilla and nuts. Blend well after each addition
but do not beat. Bake at 325 degrees for one hour in loaf or tube
pans which have been lightly greased and floured. Fill pans 2/3
full.

Hostess: Kathy Wallace
Displayer: Bessie Queen

****

God leads, not by miles, but by inches. "Be Somebody" by Mary Crowley

201

CARROT BREAD

1 cup sugar
3/4 cup oil
2 eggs
2 cups flour
1 teaspoon cinnamon
1 teaspoon baking powder
1 teaspoon soda
1 1/4 cups shredded carrots
1/2 cup nuts or raisins

Cream sugar and oil together. Blend in eggs. Add alternately
dry ingredients with shredded carrots. Grease and flour three
6 x 3 inch pans. Bake 1 hour at 325 degrees.

Hostess: Dorothy Cummings

BUBBLE BREAD

1 cup scalded milk
1/2 cup shortening
1/2 cup sugar
1 teaspoon salt
Mix the above ingredients together, cool to luke warm, then crumble
into the mixture,
2 cakes yeast, add
2 beaten eggs
4 1/2 cups flour
Mix to soft dough, turn out on a floured board, knead until smooth
and not sticky. Place in a greased bowl and cover with a damp cloth.
Let rise until double in bulk. Punch down and let set for 10 minutes.
While dough is setting; combine the ingredients below in a bowl.
1 stick butter, melted
1 tablespoon sugar
1 cup sugar
1/2 cup chopped nuts, optional
Make dough into small balls, about the size of a walnut, roll each
ball in butter, then into the sugar mixture. Then place in greased
angelfood cake pan, in staggered rows and layers until all dough is
used. Let rise again, then bake in 350 degree oven about 45 minutes.
Turn out on board or plate, and pull off luscious mouthwatering
pieces one by one.

Hostess: Sharon Wienandt
Displayer: Mildred Yahr

****

God will mend a broken heart if we give Him ALL the pieces.
From "Be Somebody" by Mary Crowley.

****

202

ZUCCHINI BREAD

3 eggs
1 cup oil
2 cups sugar
2 cups peeled and grated zucchini
1 teaspoon vanilla
1/4 teaspoon baking powder
1 cup nuts
3 cups flour
1 teaspoon salt
3 teaspoons cinnamon
1 teaspoon soda

Beat eggs, sugar, oil. Add vanilla, stir in zucchini. Sift
flour, salt, cinnamon, soda and baking powder. Stir into first
mixture. Fold in nuts, pour in 2 well greased 9 x 5 x 3 inch
loaf pans. Bake at 325 degrees, 60-75 minutes.

Hostess: Sally Jerore

ZUCCHINI BREAD

3 cups flour
2 cups sugar
1 teaspoon salt
1 teaspoon baking soda
1 teaspoon baking powder
1 teaspoon cinnamon
3 beaten eggs
2 cups chopped zucchini, fine seeds and all
2 teaspoons vanilla
1 small can crushed pineapple, drained
1 cup salad oil
1 cup nuts

Combine flour, sugar, salt, soda, baking powder, and cinnamon in a
large bowl. Add other ingredients. Mix well, bake in greased & floured
9 x 5 x 3 inch pan for 1 hour at 350 degrees.

Hostess: Clair Griffith
Displayer: Colleen Weitz

****

I like God's mathematics - He can take nine-tenths and do more
with it than I can do with ten-tenths. Tithing takes the worry
our of living.   "Be Somebody" by Mary Crowley

****

BRAN MUFFINS

1 cup Nabisco 100% Bran
2 cups All-Bran-Kelloggs
1 cup boiling water, pour on bran and let stand
1/2 cup oil
1 cup brown sugar
2 beaten eggs
2 cups buttermilk
2 1/4 cups wheat flour
2 1/2 teaspoons soda
1/2 teaspoon salt
2/3 cup chopped dates, optional
2/3 cup walnuts, optional

Bake in oiled muffing tins; 400 degrees for 15 minutes. Cover
unused batter and store in refrigerator. Use as needed, will keep
at least 2 weeks. Yield, 2 dozen.

Hostess: Joanne Roe
Displayer: Carol Craig

CORNMEAL ROLLS

2 cups milk
2/3 cup white corn meal
1/2 cup sugar
1 stick butter or oleo
1 1/2 teaspoons salt
3 eggs, beaten
2 packages yeast
1/2 cup warm water
Scant 6 cups white flour

Add milk to corn meal slowly. Cook until thick, remove from heat.
Add sugar, oleo, and salt. Let cool. Dissolve yeast in water and
let stand 10 minutes. Add yeast to beaten egg and corn meal. Add
flour and knead, it is a very soft dough. Let rise once. Roll out
3/4 inch thick and cut with cookie cutter and let rise. Use for
hamburger buns, dough can also be used for rolls of any type. Bake
at 350 degrees until golden brown.

Hostess: Jane Alexander
Displayer: Wanda A. Fowles,

****

We need society, and we need solitude also, as we need summer and
winter, day and night, exercise and rest.

****

204

MASTER MIX DEVELOPED AT PURDUE UNIVERSITY

INGREDIENTS:
5 pounds all purpose flour
2 1/2 cups dry milk solids
3/4 cup double acting baking powder
3 tablespoons salt
2 tablespoons cream of tartar
1/2 cup sugar
2 pounds vegetable shortening

INSTRUCTIONS:
Sift dry ingredients together. Then cut in shortening until mix looks
like cornmeal. Store at room temperature in giant canister or two
Econo Canisters (Tupperware) Yield: 29 cups

1 DOZEN BISCUITS: 3 cups mix, 3/4 cup water, blend and knead for
10 strokes. Pat out and cut. Bake at 450 for 10 minutes.

18 MEDIUM PANCAKES OR 6 WAFFLES: 3 cups mix, 1 egg, 1 1/2 cups
water. Blend, bake as usual.

1 DOZEN MUFFINS: 3 cups mix, 2 tablespoons sugar, 1 egg, 1 cup water.
Mix water and eggs, add to dry ingredients. Bake at 450 degrees45 min.

8 X 8 GINGERBREAD: 2 cups mix, 1/4 cup sugar, 1 egg, 1/2 cup water,
1/2 cup molasses, 1/2 teaspoon each: cinnamon, ginger, cloves. Beat
egg, water, and molassas, mix with dry ingredients. Bake 350 for 40 min.

9" ROUND COFFEE CAKE: 3 cups mix, 1/2 cup sugar, 1 egg, 2/3 cup water:
Blend, put in pan and cover with topping: 1/2 cup brown sugar, 3
tablespoons melted butter, 1/2 teaspoon cinnamon. Nuts and raisins
(1/2 cup) are optional. Bake at 400 degrees for 25 minutes.

DROP COOKIES: 3 cups mix, 1 cup sugar, 1 egg, 1/3 cup water, 1 teaspoon
vanilla, 1/2 cup nuts and/or chocolate chips. Bake 375 degrees, 10 min.

SHORTCAKE: 2 cups mix, 1/2 cup water, 1/4 cup melted butter, 2 tablespoon
sugar, mix and knead a few strokes. Roll 1/2 inch thick. Cut into
six 3 inch cakes or bake in 8 x 8 inch pan.

2 8" LAYERS, YELLOW OR CHOCOLATE CAKE: 3 cups mix, 1 1/2 cup sugar,
3 eggs, 1 cup water, 1 teaspoon vanilla, (1/2 cup cocoa for chocolate
cake) Blend sugar into mix. Beat eggs and water and add half of mix.
Beat 2 minutes add remainder of mix and beat additional 2 minutes.
For chocolate cake, add cocoa to dry ingredients. Bake at 325
degrees for 25 minutes.

Additional recipes next page.

The Master Mix can be used successfully in any recipe calling for
biscuit mix, using water in the place of milk. Here are a few others:

FRITTERS: 2 cups mix, 2/3 cup water, 1 egg, 2 cups fruit or cooked
vegetable. Mix ingredients. Stir in pineapple chunks, peach chunks,
or whole kernel corn (drained) drop by small teaspoons into hot deep
fat and fry until golden brown. Drain. Serve hot with confectioners
sugar.

1-2-3 COOKIES: 1 cup peanut butter, 1/4 cup margarine, 1/2 cup water
1 cup granulated sugar (or brown sugar) Mix til smooth, then add
2 cups mix. Drop by teaspoon onto lightly greased cookie sheet.
Flatten with fork dipped in flour. Bake 8-10 minutes, 400 degrees.
Makes 6 1/2 dozen.

BANANA COFFEE CAKE: 2 cups mix, 1 egg, 1 tablespoon sugar. 1 cup
mashed bananas fully ripened. No additional liquid is required.
Mix well. Bake in 8 x 8 inch greased pan for 25 minutes, 400 degrees.

MONEY SAVING MILK RECIPE: Mix 5 cups powdered milk and 11 cups water
in the jumbo canister. When mixed, add 1/2 gallon whole milk. Let
stand, sealed in refrigerator overnight. Put into 2 quart beverage
containers for easy serving.

ANGEL BISCUITS: 2 packages dry yeast, dissolved in 1 cup lukewarm water. Add 2 tablespoons sugar, 2 teaspoons salt, 1 teaspoon
soda, 3/4 cup cooking oil or 1 cup crisco. About 5 cups self-
rising flour and 2 cups buttermilk. Mix until consistency of
rolls. Seal and store in the refrigerator, lasts about one week.
pinch off desired amount. Bake at 400 degrees for 10/12 minutes.

SOUR CREAM CORNBREAD

2 cups Martha Gooch complete corn bread mix
1 egg, beaten
1 tablespoon melted shortening
1/2 cup cream style corn
1/2 cup sour cream
1/2 small can green chili peppers, drained and chopped
1/2 cup grated cheese

Preheat oven to 300 degrees. Mix egg and corn bread mix thoroughly
with a fork. Stir in shortening, corn, sour cream, and peppers.
Spoon half of the mixture into a greased piping hot 6 inch heavy
skillet, or an 8 x 8 x 2 inch pan and then spread with cheese, cover
with remaining corn bread mixture. Bake about 40 minutes. Serves 4-6.

Hostess: Evelyn Wood
Displayer: Frances Burger

****

Ring in the love of truth and right,
Ring in the common love of good.
Ring out old shapes of foul disease,
Ring out the narrowing lust of gold;
Ring out the thousand wars of old.
Ring in the thousand years of peace.
Ring in the valiant man and free,
The larger heart, the kindlier hand;
Ring out the darkness of the land,
Ring in the Christ that is to be.

Alfred Lord Tennyson

****

ZUCCHINI BREAD

3 eggs beaten
2 cups sugar
1 teaspoon salt
1/4 teaspoon baking powder
3 teaspoons cinnamon
1 cup oil
3 cups flour
1/2 teaspoon nutmeg
1 teaspoon soda
2 cups peeled and grated zucchini squash

Mix the eggs, oil, sugar and zucchini, add remaining ingredients.
Bake at 325 degrees for 1 hour. Candied cherries, nuts and raisins
may be added for extra festive occasions.

Hostess: Marty Cunningham
Displayer: Joan Niernberger

FOR THE BODY
FOR THE SOUL

For the past seven years it has been my custom and my joy
to take our new managers to Mary's Mountain Lodge on Mt.
Princeton near Buena Vista, Colorado for fellowship,
training, sharing, and getting to know each other. Usually,
the Managers come with some of our Area or Branch Managers
in groups of 20 to 25. The groups come in on Monday and go
home on Friday. We break bread together (along with a lot
of other goodies, as you can see from the recipies.) We use
the book of Proverbs for studies in leadership. We learn
sales and management skills. We shop together; We pray
together; We sing together for days of fullfillment and
blessed memories. I make out all the menues and do the
shopping and prepare the evening meal when our people
arrive. Through the years I have enjoyed fixing exciting
recipies. Some are original, some are borrowed. But all
are delicious and much in demand. The following selections
are called Mary's Mountain Recipies.

GREEN GOOP

I won "Best Cook Award" on this 25 years ago. Unfortunately, this
name got hung on it by my adorable brother-in-law and it has stuck
through the years. This is the size recipe that I always make for
either family or guests because everybody loves it. Please make
exactly as instructed. Do NOT substitute.

40 large marshmallows (approximately)
2 large size packages lime jello
1 large and 1 small size Philadelphia cream cheese
1 large and 1 small size can crushed pineapple
1/2 pint whipping cream
1 cup chopped pecans

Melt marshmallows and lime jello in 7 cups boiling water. Stir
until completely dissolved. Set aside to congeal.

Next day, or later, at least one hour before ready to serve,
whip congealed jello with mixer and add softened cream cheese.
Work cream cheese with a fork to soften it, adding a little
pineapple juice to make it soft enough to whip with jello.

Fold in drained pineapple, and pecans, and whipped cream.

ENJOY!!

SOUR CREAM DELIGHT

2 cups sour cream
3/4 cup sugar
1 teaspoon salt
Mix the above ingredients together. Add:
1 large can crushed pineapple (and juice)
6 bananas, mashed or cut finely
1 tablespoon lemon juice
2 small or 1 large package frozen strawberries, thawed
3/4 cup pecans

Mix and freeze. Serve slightly thawed.
Concocted by Mary C. Crowley

****

"We thank Him for His kindness, We thank Him for His love
We've been in heavenly places, Had blessings from above
We've shared in all the good things the Family could afford
Let's just turn our praise toward heaven and praise the Lord..."
        from "Let's Just Praise the Lord" by Gaither.

****

CHEESE GRITS

Better'n Chocolate Cake!
Serves about 15 people.

7 cups water
2 teaspoons salt
2 cups grits
Cook according to directions on box. I use Quick Grits, do NOT
use Instant Grits. They DO NOT work.

Into hot grits stir:
1/3 cup grated onion
1 small jar cheese whiz
1/2 pound grated cheddar cheese
2 eggs, slightly beaten
1 stick butter
1 teaspoon accent
1 teaspoon garlic salt
dash of red pepper
1 small can of diced green chilies. These are green chili
   peppers and add zest! They are optional.
Sprinkle with paprika and bake at 350 degrees 30-40 minutes.

SOUR CREAM AND RICE RECIPE

Rice
Chicken bouillon
Salt and seasoned salt
Monterey Jack Cheese
Jalepano Peppers
Sour Cream

Cook rice by instruction on box. When cooking, add chicken
bouillon to water with butter and salt. When rice is ready,
pour a layer in a buttered casserole dish. Sprinkle seasoned
salt on top. Put several pats of butter on top of rice.

Put a layer of Monterey Jack Cheese, then a layer of Jalepano
Peppers, then another layer of rice. Top with cheese.
Bake in 350 degree oven until cheese is melted. Take from oven.

Just before serving, spread sour cream on top and serve.
(Use Jalepano Peppers according to taste. If you like lots
of peppers, then use them; but if not, use a few thin strips)

Recipe by Connie Sapien of El Paso, Texas.

CHICKEN BREAST AND SHERRY SOUR CREAM SAUCE

Place chicken in a 9 x 13" pan.
Saute 2 teaspoons onion and 2 teaspoons butter
Add 1 large carton sour cream
2 cans mushroom soup
1 small can mushrooms
and 1/3 cup cooking sherry
Salt and pepper to taste**
Cover chicken with mixture and bake at 325 degrees for one hour.

**I use vege-sal, an all purpose seasoning salt. Now vegetized.
Put out by Modern Products, Inc. Milwaukee, Wisc.

HAWAIIAN CHICKEN

2 cut up fryers (Brown ahead of time or you can use Kentucky
   Fried Chicken.)
1 large can pineapple chunks, drained, reserve juice
1 sliced green bell pepper
1 bunch chopped green onions
Arrange in a baking dish and top with pineapple and bell peppers.

Sprinkle with 1/2 teaspoon ginger.
Pour sauce over top and bake at 350 degrees for 1 hour.
Top with chopped green onions.

SAUCE:
1 cup pineapple juice, drained off chunks
1/2 cup wine vinegar
1/2 cup brown sugar
2 tablespoons conrstarch
2 tablespoons soy sauce
pinch salt.
Combine ingredients and bring to a boil. Stirring until thickened
and clear. Pour over chicken and bake as directed above.

"WILLY'S WINNER" SALAD

1 can french style green beans, drained
1 can small early june peas, drained
1 large tomatoe, chopped
1 medium onion, chopped
1 medium green pepper
2 tablespoons mayonnaise
Mix all the ingredients together. Add mayonnaise, mix well
and serve. 4 to 6 servings.

Hostess: Willean Claybrook
Displayer: Doris Roper

MARY'S VEGETABLE SUPREME CASSEROLE

2 packages frozen baby lima beans
2 packages frozen mixed vegetables
2 packages frozen baby peas

Thaw and drian. Layer in buttered casserole. Add:
Vege-Sal*
Celery Salt

TOPPING:
Into 2 cups whipped cream,
fold 1 cup mayonnaise
1/2 cup grated cheddar cheese
1/2 cup parmesan cheese
Spread on top of vegetables. Bake 1 hour at 350 degrees, until
golden brown.

*An all purpose seasoning salt, now vegetized. Put out by
Modern Products, Inc., Milwaukee, Wisc.

SUPER SALAD

Slice the first 3 items:
1 bunch fresh broccoli
1 bunch green onions
1 pound fresh mushrooms

Cut cherry tomatoes in half, add to above

Pour over all this 1 regular size Wishbone Italian dressing.
Marinate 8 hours.

Recipe by Barbara Hammond

BAKED SQUASH

Use Hubbard Squash.
Wash and cut in serving size, Hollow out, removing seed.

Place on flat pan with 3/4 cup water in bottom of pan.
Cover tightly with foil.
Bake until tender (1 hour on Mountain, less time otherwise.)

Remove foil
Sprinkle with brown sugar (approximately 1 teaspoon for each slice)
Dot with butter.
Sprinkle with nutmeg. (May use cinnamon if you prefer.)

Return to 400 degree oven about 15 minutes, simmer and brown.

Recipe of our beloved Grace Shakes. Loved by Pearl Burns.

212

MEXICAN CASSEROLE

3 pounds ground chuck (I use <u>ground</u> <u>lean</u> <u>meat</u>)
2 chopped onions
Lowery's salt
pepper
garlic powder
2 cans Ranch Style beans
2 cans Ro-Tel tomatoes (or Ortega tomatoes and green chilies)
2 cans cream of chicken soup
Large package of soft tortillas (I use corn tortillas)
2 pounds sharp old English cheese

Brown meat and onions, pour off any excess grease. Add beans, tomatoes, soup. Layer in a large càsserole dish the soft tortillas, then meat mixture, then grated cheese. Do another 3 layers, ending with a lot of cheese. Sprinkle with paprika. Bake at 350 degrees until bubbly, about 35 minutes. Feeds approximately 20 people.

Recipe by Margaret Broyles.

Mary

at

home

Dave

Mary

Tiger

Samantha

Mary

playing

piano

TACO SALAD

1 large bag Fritos, crushed
1 pound hamburger meat, browned
1 cup chopped green onions
1 green pepper
3 garlic buds, or 1 tablespoon garlic salt
1 tablespoon cumin
1/2 teaspoon chili powder
1 pound Velveta cheese
1 large head of shreaded lettuce
2-3 tomatoes, chopped
1 can Rotel tomato sauce
Combine cheese, tomato sauce, garlic, chili powder, and cumin and
lay aside.
In a large bowl, combine lettuce and chopped tomatoes. Add Fritos,
hamburger meat, onions, and green pepper. Pour cheese sauce over
the lettuce and tossed mixture just before serving and toss.

Recipe by Joan Horner

BUENO SNACKS

1 large can whole green chiles
6 eggs
salt
1-2 tablespoons dry minced or chopped onions
1/2 pound or more of grated longhorn cheese

Spread chiles in a buttered 9" pan. Beat eggs, add salt, and
onions, pour over chiles in pan. Top with cheese. Bake at
325 degrees 20-30 minutes or until cheese is melted and golden.
Slice into squares and serve.

Recipe by Karen Baker

214

MAGIC FRUIT COBBLER

1/4 pound butter or margarine
1 large can fruit or 2 medium cans fruit (with juice)

3/4 cup milk
1 cup sugar
1 cup flour
1 1/2 teaspoons baking powder

Melt butter in bottom of baking dish. Mix milk, sugar, flour, and baking powder and pour <u>over</u> butter. <u>Do not stir.</u>

Pour fruit over batter - Do not stir.
Sprinkle sugar over top.

Bake 1 hour at 350-375 degrees. Fruit will sink and batter will rise. Add a little cinnamon to peaches or apples and almond flavoring to cherries. Use your imagination. Never Fails!!

MARY'S GLORIFIED BREAD PUDDING

2 cups brown sugar: PUT IN LARGE DOUBLE BOILER
8 slices "Old Raisin Bread" (or any kind, I use Orowheat)
  BUTTERED LAVISHLY & CUBED
Place over brown sugar. This is a wonderful way to use stale bread deliciously.

6 eggs slightly beaten
4 cups milk
2 teaspoons vanilla
Mix, and pour over bread cubes in double boiler. DO NOT STIR. Sprinkle coconut on top. Place lid on and boil for 1 1/2 hours. Not stirring. Chill in pot and serve with lemon sauce or whipped cream. When dipping up to serve, be sure you dip up some caramel syrup from the bottom.

GOLDEN TASSIES

BASIC CRUST RECIPE:

1 cup margarine
2 3 ounce packages cream cheese
2 cups sifted flour

Let margarine and cream cheese soften. Then work with a wooden
spoon until smooth and creamy. Add flour and blend. Using
fingers, press dough into very small muffin tins (1 3/4" in
diameter.)
USE 1/2 THE BASIC RECIPE WITH THE FILLING BELOW. MAKES 2 DOZEN.

PECAN FILLING:

1 egg, beaten only enough to mix yolk and white. Add:
3/4 cup firmly packed brown sugar: Add:
1 tablespoon melted margarine: Add:
dash of salt
few drops vanilla
3/4 cup chopped pecans (about)

Bake at 350 degrees for 15-18 minutes. Reduce heat to 250
degrees and bake 10 minutes longer. Cool.

Recipe from Margaret Broyles

YUMMY ORANGE BALLS
For fall and winter serving with coffee or hot tea.

1 stick butter melted (or margarine, I guess.)
        I cook with "love and butter" you know!
1 12 ounce package vanilla wafers, crushed.
        Put in a zip-loc bag and crush with a glass rolled over them.
1 pound box powdered sugar
1 cup pecans (or walnuts) finely chopped
1 6 ounce can frozen orange juice, thawed

Mix crushed wafers, powdered sugar, and pecans. Add melted butter
and melted orange juice. Mix well. Roll into small balls and roll
them in finely grated coconut. Store in refirgerator overnight.
They freeze well, if you have any left.

MILKY WAY CAKE

8 Milky Way Candy Bars (1 7/8 ounce size)
1/2 cup melted butter or margarine
2 cups sugar
1/2 cup butter or margarine, softened
4 eggs
1 teaspoon vanilla extract
1 1/4 cup buttermilk
1/2 teaspoon soda
3 cups all-purpose flour
1 cup chopped pecans (not too fine)

Combine candy bars and 1/2 cup melted butter or margarine in
sauce pan. Place over low heat until candy bars are melted,
stirring constantly. Cool. Cream sugar and 1/2 cup softened
butter or margarine until light and fluffy. Add eggs, one at
a time, beating well after each addition. Stir in vanilla
extract. Combine buttermilk and soda. Add to creamed mixture,
alternately with flour, beating well after each addition. Stir
in candy bar mixture with pecans.

Pour into greased and floured 10" tube pan. Bake at 325 degrees
for 1 hour 20 minutes or until done. Let cool in pan 1 hour.
Remove from pan and complete cooling on wire rack.

MILK CHOCOLATE FROSTING:

2 1/2 cups sugar
1 cup evaporated milk, undiluted
1/2 cup melted butter or margarine
1 6 ounce package semi-sweet chocolate pieces
1 cup marshmellow cream

Combine sugar, milk, and butter in heavy saucepan. Cook over
medium heat until small amount dropped in cold water forms a
soft ball. Remove from heat. Add chocolate pieces and
marshmellow cream, stirring until melted. If necessary, add
small amount of milk to make spreading consistency.

This recipe came from Southern Living.

MARY'S TRIFLE

This serves 40 people - or 20 people twice!!
Use large crystal or "see through" bowl, preferably with fairly
straight sides.
Layer:
Sliced angel food cake
thawed frozen strawberries
sliced bananas
repeat layer

Take small package of strawberry jello
dilute with only 1 cup water
add 3 tablespoons lemon juice
Let cool a little. Pour over layers in bowl. Set aside for several
hours or overnight in a cool place (or refrigerator.) Don't
panic if the bananas turn a little dark. When mixture is set:
Fix vanilla custard (I use several packages of instant Jello pudding)
and cover layers about 1 inch at least.
Cover all layers with whipped cream (I use about 3 1/2 pints
whipping cream. Let set up about an hour in refrigerator. This
is absolutely, beautifully delicious.

VANILLA ICE CREAM

6 eggs, whipped in mixer
1 quart real cream, add to eggs and whip

1 1/2 cups sugar

3 tablespoons vanilla
1/2 teaspoon salt
3 cans Eagle Brand Condensed Milk

Add sugar slowly to egg and cream mixture and whip so all sugar
is dissolved. Add 1 can of Eagle Brand and vanilla and salt
and thoroughly blend. Then add 2 more cans of Eagle Brand and
put all in freezer can and fill with regular sweet milk until
you reach the "fill line" on can. Stir well and freeze.
Use a 6 quart freezer.

FRUIT SLUSH

3 cups water
1 1/2 cups sugar
Boil about 3 minutes. Then add:

1 large can frozen orange juice concentrate
1 large can crushed pineapple with juice
2 large packages strawberries, thawed
6 bananas, sliced

Mix and freeze. Serve slightly thawed.

Courtesy of Peggy England.

MARY'S GRAPE AND BANANA SALAD

Grapes - Thompson's seedless grapes, washed and cut in half
Bananas, peeled and sliced
Miniature marshmallows
Nuts are optional

Mix together and add special fruit dressing.

SPECIAL FRUIT DRESSING:
1 can Eagle Brand Milk
1/2 cup lemon juice (I use the Minute-Maid lemon juice, it's 100%
    pure lemon juice that is frozen fresh - available in frozen
    foods department. Put in refrigerator and it will thaw and
    keep well.)
1/2 pint whipping cream

Combine Eagle Brand and lemon juice. Whip cream. Add Eagle
Brand mixture and whip lightly. Put over grape mixture and
toss lightly.

Makes a fabulous, delicious dressing. Serve to HAPPY PEOPLE!

MARY'S ITALIAN CREAM CAKE

1 cup buttermilk
1 teaspoon soda
5 eggs, separated
2 cups sugar
1 stick butter (or margarine)
1/2 cup shortening
2 cups sifted flour
1 teaspoon vanilla
1 small can coconut

Preheat oven to 325 degrees. Combine milk and soda. Cream sugar,
butter (or margarine) and shortening. Add egg yolks one at a time,
beating well after each. Add buttermilk mixture, alternating with
flour, to cream mixture and stir in vanilla. Beat egg whites until
stiff. Fold into batter gently. Fold in coconut. Bake in three
pans 25 minutes.

CREAM CHEESE ICING:

1 package 8 ounce cream cheese
1 stick butter (or margarine)
1 pound box confectioner's sugar
1 teaspoon vanilla
4 mashed bananas (or strawberries**)
1 cup chopped pecans

Mix cream cheese, butter (or margarine) and vanilla. Beat in
sugar a little at a time until spreading consistency. Stir in
3/4 cup pecans. Add mashed bananas (or strawberries) Sprinkle
remaining 1/4 cup pecans on top of cake after frosting.
** If using strawberries, garnish top with luscious fresh
strawberries.

CHOCOLATE CHIP CAKE

I got this recipe from Hannah Till.

1 package yellow cake mix
1 small package vannila instant pudding
1 small package chocolate instant pudding
1 1/2 cups water
1/2 cup cooking oil
Beat all and mix two minutes. Add:
4 eggs all at one time, mix another minute. Add:
1 small package chocolate chips
Bake in greased and floured bundt pan for 1 hour
at 350 degrees.

KENTUCKY JAM CAKE

1 3/4 cup flour
1 1/2 cup sugar
1 cup salad oil
1 cup buttermilk
1 cup blackberry jam
1 teaspoon soda
1 teaspoon baking powder
1 teaspoon each cinnamon, nutmeg, allspice
1 teaspoon vanilla
1/2 teaspoon ground cloves
1/2 teaspoon salt
3 eggs
1 cup finely chopped pecans

Measure all ingredients, except pecans, into mixer bowl. Use low speed until mixed, then high speed and beat about 8 minutes until sugar is completely dissolved. Fold in pecans and pour into pan. Bake 40 minutes at 350 degrees or until cake pulls away from pan. Cool on rack 20 minutes. Bake in 2 9 x 9" pans or 3 9" round pans.

BUTTERMILK ICING:
3 cups sugar   1 cup pecans, for topping
1 cup butter
1 cup buttermilk
2 tablespoons light corn syrup
1 teaspoon baking soda
Combine in 4 quart sauce pan over medium heat, bring to boiling, stirring constantly. Set candy thermometer in place and continue cooking, stirring occasionally until 238 degrees (soft ball stage) Pour in mixer at high speed. Beat 7 minutes until spreading consistency. Fold in 1 cup pecans, ice cake.

This is an old recipe from a good friend of mine, Joe Yoakley.

STRAWBERRY SHERBET

Super delicious and sooooo EASY to make!!

Use a 6 quart freezer.

9 12 ounce cans Strawberry Drink
3 cans Eagle Brand Milk
3 10 ounce cartons frozen sliced strawberries

Mix together and freeze.

This recipe is by Linda Carter.

HEAVENLY DIP

For the Mountain, this is doubled, of course!

2 eggs
2 tablespoons sugar
2 tablespoons vinegar
Lowery's salt

Beat together and cook until thickened. Stir often. Then add to
6 ounces cream cheese. Beat until well blended and smooth. Add
1/2 green pepper
1 onion, chopped. If using fresh onions, toss in green tops and all.

CHOCOLATE SYRUP

1 cup sugar
1/4 cup cocoa
1/4 cup butter or margarine
1/4 cup milk

Bring to boil, boil 2 minutes at least. Test in ice water for
cheweyness.
Add 1 teasponn vanilla - cool. Put on ice cream.

BAKED CHEESE GOODIES

2 cups shreaded sharp cheddar cheese, about an 8 ounce pakcage
1 1/4 cups regular flour
1/2 cup butter, melted

You work the cheese and flour together until crumbly with
your hands. Add butter and mix well with a fork. If the
the dough seems dry, work it with your hands.

SUGGESTED FILLERS:
1) pimento stuffed small olives
2) dates stuffed with sliced almond
3) 1 inch long piece of cooked sausage (I use the small smoked links)

Mold 1 teaspoon of dough around the filler you choose and
shape into a ball. Place 2 inches apart on an ungreased
baking sheet. Chill for 1 hour or longer. Then bake
15-20 minutes in a 400 degree oven. These may be frozen.
(They freeze very well, before or after baking.)

Recipe by Joan Horner

We haven't tried these at the mountain but they sound good!

Beverages

CALIFORNIA PARTY PUNCH

1 large can pineapple juice
2 large cans frozen orange juice
2 large cans frozen lemon aide
Mix frozen juices with water as directed on cans.
1 pint orange sherbert
1/2 gallon vanilla ice cream
1 large can gingerale

Mix all juices together. Cut ice cream and sherbert in two
inch squares and add to fruit juices. Chill. Add gingerale
just before serving.

Displayer: Maida Godwin
Hostess: Marty Rickman

FROZEN FRUIT PUNCH

Juice of 2 lemons
2 ounces citric acid, powdered, get at drug store
3 cans frozen orange juice, diluted
1 quart bottle Tropicano Orange Juice
1 tall can pineapple juice, 46 ounces, sweetened to taste
1 tall can crushed pineapple, No. 3.
7 cups sugar
2 large bottles cherries and juice
Green or red cake coloring

Pour 2 quarts boiling water over acid and sugar. Add 4 quarts
cold water, then other ingredients. Freeze in plastic cartons.
This can be kept frozen 3-4 weeks without change of taste. To
thaw: let melt about 3 3/12 hours in punch bowl, not necessary
to add ice. Serves 100.

Hostess: Irene Noblin

****

Good to know: A decorative ice ring can be made to float
beautifully on your punch. Boil water (so mold won't get
cloudy.) Pour into ring jello mold. Add maraschino cherry,
lemon, lime or orange slices for decoration.

****

SPICED TEA MIX

1 cup instant tea mix with lemon
2 cups orange Tang
3 cups sugar
1 teaspoon cinnamon
1/2 teaspoon cloves, ground

Mix well and keep in tight container. To use: 2 teaspoons
per cup hot water.

Hostess: Sandi Marcum
Displayer: Nancy Evans

ALMOND PUNCH

1 12 ounce can frozen orange juice
1 12 ounce can frozen lemonade
1 cup sugar
1 teaspoon vanilla extract
1 teaspoon almond extract

Add water to make one gallon. Garnish with orange or lemon slices.

Hostess: Donna Gardner
Displayer: Linda K. Case

LIME PUNCH

4 bottles Bubble-Up, 28 ounce size
1 small can of frozen lemon or lime juice, undiluted
1/2 gallon lime sherbert

Ice mold is made from lemonade, lemon slices, and maraschino
cherries. Use both red and green cherries to add color.

Hostess: Chela Cortez
Displayer: June Lackey

PUNCH

1 cup sugar
2 packages Kool-Aid, the color you choose
1 large can sweet pineapple juice
2 quarts of cold gingerale

Mix sugar and Kool-Aid with small amount of water. Add pineapple
juice, finish filling gallon jug almost full with water. Add
gingerale.

Hostess: Barbara McDonald

the story of

the*
happy
*house

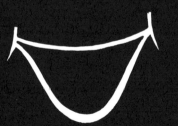

HOME INTERIORS & GIFTS, INC.
4550 SPRING VALLEY   DALLAS, TEXAS 75240

Once upon

Written by Mary C Crowley in 1961 -- first printing 1962

a time. . .

On a quiet, shaded street, in a town like yours, there was a little Red Brick House. He was a fine house; strong and sturdy, warm in the winter, cool in the summer. He had a nice yard with big trees, and little birds came every day to sing to him.

The Little Brick House belonged to a wonderful family.

In fact . . . they *were* the Wonderful family: There was Mr. Wonderful, who gulped his morning coffee and rushed off to the office. And Mrs. Wonderful, who whistled in the kitchen as she cooked. And two little Wonderfuls who filled the house with their happy noise.

It was a good Town. A pleasant Neighborhood. A "Wonderful" Family. And the Little Red Brick House often said: "I'm a pretty lucky house."

And yet . . .

He felt there was *something* missing. He knew he was a good house. He was neat. He was clean. But he had the nagging feeling that he was somehow "incomplete" . . . as though there was no "sparkle" to his personality.

And all because of his best friend . . . the little White Frame House across the street. They were about the same age and had been good friends for a long, long time. It was easy to be friends with the little White Frame; he was such a *friendly* house . . . always cheerful.

When the draperies of the White Frame were open, you could see such exciting things: Interesting pictures on his walls, colorful bowls of flowers on the coffee table, and some fascinating figurines that he wished he could see better! In the evenings, candles glowed inside and made the little White Frame look romantic, cozy and inviting. Everything about the White Frame seemed to say:

"Come on in . . . Happy People live here."

It was when he compared himself to his good friend that the little Brick house felt something was missing . . . he almost felt a twinge of jealousy. He, himself had the big brown painting of Great Grandmother Wonderful on one of his walls and two nail holes on another wall. Although he had a fine mirror over his fireplace, it always seemed cold and harsh.

And that was all he had! He felt so monotonous and bare, he almost wished he could close the shutters over his windows.

He knew the Wonderfuls weren't poor. They had a television, and a new washing machine, and Mr. Wonderful rushed off to work every morning in their shiny new car.

The Wonderfuls were a friendly family; they had lots of friends and often these friends came to visit in the little Brick House. But Mrs. Wonderful always seemed "uneasy," as if she were not quite pleased with the appearance of the house.

Now this really worried the Little Brick House, for he was a truly fine house. He knew Mr. Wonderful worked hard to make the monthly payments, do the little repair jobs outside and keep the lawn neat and green in the summer.

And the little Brick House thought: "If only I could tell Mrs. Wonderful that *she* has a responsibility too. Its up to *her* to make the *inside* of a house look beautiful and interesting and inviting."

He felt she *really* wanted to . . . but just didn't know where to begin. (Why lots of times he had seen her look wistfully through the open windows of his cheerful friend across the street).

If there was some way he could help! *That was the anwer!* He'd ask the little White Frame where his owners got the ideas and decorations that made him look so happy and inviting. So . . . that very night, after all the people were asleep, he talked it over with his friend.

The little White Frame was very understanding and eager to help. "I can remember when I used to feel just like you do," he told the little Brick House. "But one day my lady went to a "Show." It wasn't a "movie-show" . . . it was something different . . . and you should have seen her when she came back! I've never seen her so *excited*. She started re-arranging my furniture . . . and putting nails in my plaster . . . and hanging things on my walls . . . and doing amazing new things with flowers.

"As you know," (the little White Frame went on, proudly but modestly) "I'm a pretty calm sort of house, so although at first I was a little bit worried, I finally decided, 'If it makes her happy, it's fine with me.' Then, next morning Mrs. Mansion-on-the-Hill came to visit (and brought her daughter who lives down the block). You should have seen them going from room to room and *raving* about 'The New Look.' I'll tell you, Old Friend, it made me pretty proud. It made me glad my lady went to that little get-together!"

"But what was this meeting she went to?" asked the Little Brick House excitedly.

The little White Frame said he didn't know, but he promised to listen and try to find out. "Whatever it was, though . . . it's when I really started being happy!"

The little White Frame had the answer the very next night! When all the neighborhood was asleep, he called over to the little Brick House: "I found out! It was a Home Interiors Decorating Show. And here's some good news for you . . . We're having a Home Interiors Decorating Show right here TOMORROW!"

"What's a Home Interiors Decorating Show?"

"That," explained the little White Frame, "Is what the meeting was . . . that's why I'm a Happy House! And tomorrow morning they're having one of these shows here, and this is the best part of all . . . Your Mrs. Wonderful is coming to the show! This may be just what you've been waiting for. Wow! Have I been getting a scrubbing today!"

"Maybe this *is* the answer," said the little Brick House.

"I hope so," said the little White Frame. "Well, good luck . . . and good night." And he settled down comfortably for the night.

"Good night," said the little Brick House. And to himself he said: "I sure hope it doesn't rain."

It didn't!

The next day dawned bright and sunny and by mid-morning, his friend, the White Frame was almost hidden by parked cars and happily chatting women. (Oh, and there was the limousine with Mrs. Mansion-on-the-Hill, so she must have been impressed.)

One car was filled to bursting with interesting looking suitcases and *Baskets* of *Flowers* and the Happy Lady who got out of this car seemed to be bubbling with eagerness to carry these things into the little White Frame.

The little Brick House watched through the living room window of the little White Frame. And oh! What a display of good things! Pictures, plaques, figurines, flowers . . . until he wondered what else would come out of those suitcases! The little Brick House watched with excitement and hope.

"I better settle down," he finally warned himself, "Or, I'll crack my bricks!"

The Happy Lady was showing all the fabulous Home Interiors decorations and telling about them, and he could see the other ladies say: "oooh" and "aaah," and he got a wonderful feeling that this was just what he'd been waiting for!

He could hardly wait until it was over . . . and when Mrs. Wonderful came home, the Cheerful Lady came with her. Their arms were filled with many of the exciting things he'd seen through the window, and Mrs. Wonderful and the Happy Lady were laughing and talking. They went from room to room and excitedly held things up to this wall . . . and then to that wall, and the little Brick House wanted to swell with pride, for they were talking about *his* interior.

At last they came back into his living room still looking and talking. The little Brick House listened . . .

"Everything is just *so* beautiful," Mrs. Wonderful said, "But I just don't know if I can use them as they should be used."

The Happy Lady then spoke very seriously: "Mrs. Wonderful," she said, "*Every woman is a decorator* . . . but some of them are trained. Now you watch . . . and I'll show you this natural talent which *you* have for interior decoration."

"I'm ready," said Mrs. Wonderful, "I've known for a long time that I've needed *something* but only today did I realize how *bare* my walls looked!" But where in the world do we start?"

The Happy Lady said: "First things *first*. Let's go outside and come in the *front door*.

When they stood inside the front door, the Happy Lady said: "Now, wherever our eyes fall *first* . . . that is where we will start to use your decorating dollars wisely. You see . . . *that's where your visitors get their first impression of you, your home and your family.* So when your front door opens, the room should say: "Come on in . . . Happy People live here!" This is one of the basic principles of decoration which we learn at Home Interiors. Now . . . what do you see *first?"*

"That bare, bare wall over the sofa," said Mrs. Wonderful ruefully.

"Right! And that's were we start," said the Happy Lady.

Mrs. Wonderful's eyes began to shine with excitement and she tried first this arrangement and then that, and then she stepped back, puzzled. "Well, how high should we hang a picture or a wall arrangement? "I've always heard they should be at eye level."

"It all depends," said the Home Interiors Lady (for by now, Mrs. Wonderful *and* the little Brick House knew who the Happy Lady was) "Remember this: Pictures should not be at 'standing-eye-level' because most pictures are viewed by people who are seated. Also . . . no picture or plaque should be hung *too high,* or *too low* for the piece of furniture that is under it. Your wall decoration must keep a continuity with the sofa, chair, hutch or table so that both of them become part of a "unit." They must compliment each other. Too often, people make the mistake of hanging a picture or plaque or wall arrangement too high so the eye of the viewer has to *leap* from one to the other. The same is true if pictures are hung too far

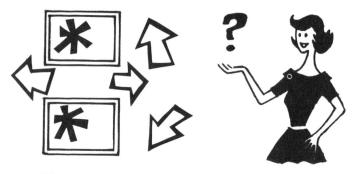

apart. Often a picture is hung on one side of a doorway and its 'mate' is hung on the other side of the doorway. This loses the theme-of-the-story between them and it is almost like watching a ping-pong game as you try to see two things at one time.

"These things give us an uneasy feeling . . . it bothers us and we know something is not "quite right" but often we can't put our finger on what it is.

Our rule of thumb is this: Pictures, plaques or wall decorations should never be hung more than half the diameter of each apart from one another."

"How interesting!" said Mrs. Wonderful, "But how will I know exactly where to place these things on the wall? I always *guess* and step back and close one eye . . . and I always *guess wrong* . . . so the only ornament on my wall is a nail hole."

"Here's your answer," said the Home Interiors Lady, and she winked. She took a large piece of brown paper and spread it on the carpet. Then she took the plaques and the pictures and arranged them 'just so' on the paper. "Next we take our pencil and we mark on the paper just were each item will hang on the wall . . . then we move the paper to the wall . . . and drive a nail through each spot we've marked. And since you have plaster walls, remember to put a small strip of adhesive tape over the spot to keep the plaster from chipping. Now when we hang the arrangements . . . each one will be just exactly right!"

"You're terrific!" said Mrs. Wonderful. "Those are TWO ideas I won't forget! I'm learning so much . . . perhaps you can tell me what's wrong here?"

And she pointed to the big wall mirror above the fireplace mantle. "For some reason it's never seemed right". . . but we didn't know what else to put up in that large vacant space. My husband suggested a mirror because that was the biggest thing he could think of. Why doesn't it look right?"

"Because a mirror has no personality of its own . . . it NEEDS attractive frames, or the placement of sconces or scrolls close by to lend WARMTH and INTEREST. A mirror can reflect only what it sees. And this brings up another 'rule of thumb'. . .

Before hanging a mirror . . . stand where the mirror will be hung. (Of course, you won't *have* to stand on the mantle) . . . but stand so your vision will enable you to see the view that the mirror will reflect from that location. All too often the view is nothing unusual . . . just the other side of the room . . . or worse, a hallway leading to the bathroom. (and whose bathroom door is *always* closed?)

But a mirror is placed perfectly when it reflects a lovely garden . . . an interesting painting . . . or a porch where baskets of real or artificial flowers and ferns are hanging . . . and a mirror 'doubles' this beauty by reflecting it."

For a long moment the Home Interiors lady looked thoughtful and then at last she said: "Perhaps this is a little off the subject, but let me give you a simple illustration as to how we feel about accessories at Home Interiors . . . GOOD ACCESSORIES ARE LIKE THE STATUE OF LIBERTY . . . THEY SHOULD BE ABLE TO STAND ALONE . . . AND THEY SHOULD STAND FOR SOMETHING."

Mrs. Wonderful nodded thoughtfully. "Yes. I see now exactly what you mean."

"And please remember," said the Home Interiors Lady, *"That* little guidepost is true for all of your house . . . for every single room!" She cocked her head at Mrs. Wonderful. "Including your bathroom."

"What?" said Mrs. Wonderful. "Why, nobody pays any attention to a bathroom."

"Oh my dear, if you only knew! The bathroom is always the most neglected room in the house from a *decorating standpoint* . . . and you may take my word for it . . . this is the room that *must* have a touch of glamour in it. Think for a moment . . . this is the room where your guests can "judge" you in complete privacy! For here . . . alone to themselves . . . they can LOOK . . . AND LOOK . . . AND LOOK. And one well chosen, special accessory *absorbs* their attention so they never notice Junior's dirty socks on the floor (you know: the socks with holes in *both* heels!) We have found that the most popular accessory for the bath is a hanging planter filled with Home Interiors *Fabulous Fake foliage* . . . and for added intrigue . . . a china bird perched on a branch is the perfect touch to this special, oft-neglected room!"

Mrs. Wonderful listened in amazement then asked thoughtfully: "I wonder . . . There is another room that is a real problem. If you can give me any help in *that* room . . . I'll think it's just plain magic. I have two sons. They share a room, all their own. Can anything be done there?"

"Why don't we see?" smiled the Home Interiors Lady. "I just have a notion we can. Too often we think that children do not notice the things on their walls and so we let their walls 'just happen.' We forget that we should really decorate a child's room . . . just as we decorate the rest of our home."

Mrs. Wonderful hesitantly opened the door to the two boys' room, and sure enough . . . COMPLETE CHAOS! A hodge-podge of newspaper pictures, school pennants, baseball gloves, and model space ships covered the walls . . . *and* the floor.

"Why this is a fascinating room!" exclaimed the Home Interiors Lady. "Your boys show they're interested in a thousand things! It's wonderful to have two boys. I have two boys myself, you know . . . and I too had a problem of both of them sharing the same room. Believe me, in a small bedroom . . . *Two is a crowd* if they are growing boys!

'Tis said that every room should have a purpose . . . but the problem here is to provide a bedroom for two youngsters which will serve *many* purposes: a place to study . . . a place to play . . . a museum for their hobbies and collections . . . and a place to entertain their friends."

"It's hopeless, isn't it?" sighed Mrs. Wonderful.

"Not a bit! You already have most of the ingredients for a charming room. Here's an idea . . . you can put up a colorful peg board for their clippings and pennants . . . add a few groupings and a few shelves in the right places and . . .'presto'. . . you have a room that's easily adaptable to changing tastes and growing emotions."

"And speaking of emotions . . . because a child's emotions are so easily influenced, leading decorators tell us that *wall decorations* in a child's room are very important. The scenes a child last sees before going to sleep . . . and sees first upon awakening, definitely influences his outlook on life.

That's why a famous professional decorator once recommended one of the Prayer Plaques as a 'must' for a child's room. The Child's Prayer is excellent . . . or The Lord's Prayer . . . or the beloved Psalm of David, The Twenty Third Psalm. Any of these placed on the wall or on a night table is perfect . . . especially with *a real live candle* in a holder beneath the plaque.

Then when evening Prayer Time comes . . . you make it a 'moment to remember'. . . . a special time . . . by having prayers by candlelight. Children love candles! Candles fill their world with a glow of warmth . . . and there's no thought more comforting to a child as he drifts off to sleep than . . .

THE LORD IS MY SHEPHERD . . . I SHALL NOT WANT . . . or a more vital thrill as he arises to the dawn of a new day!"

Mrs. Wonderful felt a lump in her throat and a glow in her heart. She suddenly realized how rapidly her sons were growing up . . . how short a time she had to teach and guide them and give them love of God and beauty and culture. She vowed she would make her children's room glow with the warmth of her love for them.

"You've been *so* kind to take time to come over. I can see I am going to want to decorate ALL of our home. Could you possibly come again and help me with the rest of the house?"

"I'd love to!" said the Home Interiors Lady. "The greatest reward of my business is sharing my knowledge and training with people like you. I once felt just as you do . . . I had ideas but somehow, I hesitated to turn them into reality. I had what we call an 'Apple-Pie-House.' Did you ever notice how the choice of words on a menu can excite your appetite? The better restaurants never just say: 'Apple Pie,' they say: 'Crusty, Rich, Deep Dish Apple Pie,' or 'Spicy Fresh Apple Pie.' Doesn't that *sound* more inviting?

It's the same with our homes. You don't need to have an ornate recipe of decorative theory . . . just a touch of 'spice' . . . just a fascinating little 'something extra' like the exotic India Brass Pitcher holding a single rose bud . . . placed on the coffee table. The only difference between a Model House and a "House That is a Model" is that little 'Spice of Accessories.' Accessories are to the home what spice is to the apple pie! Our homes must satisfy the emotional and psychological needs of our families as well as the physical needs of a roof overhead.

In the final analysis, your home should reflect *your* ideas and *your way of life* (fitted, of course, within the framework of your family budget). This is why so many women depend on their local Home Interiors Displayer. We try to furnish the *'touch of perfection'* to home decoration . . . and even more important . . . we try to provide you with clever decorating ideas and professional tips which can *help you develop your own decorating personality.*

Just remember . . . Every woman is a decorator *at heart* . . . and I think you and I will have a world of fun developing that talent together as we complete the decoration of your home.

As they walked to the front door, Mrs. Wonderful hesitated a moment by the antique chest which had belonged to Great Grand-mother Wonderful . . .

She started to apologize for its 'antiquity' but before she could speak, the Home Interiors Lady stopped . . . and ran her fingertips lovingly over the glistening patina of the hand-rubbed wood.

"Oh! Isn't this a treasure!" she said. "Such hand work . . . it's so wonderfully reminiscent of the traditions of the past!"

Mrs. Wonderful was encouraged enough to ask: "Do you *really* think so? It was handed down to my husband and he loves it . . . but it doesn't seem to 'go with' anything we have. What should I do with it?"

The Home Interiors Lady glanced at her watch. "Goodness! I must run to another appointment!" She smiled at Mrs. Wonderful. *"To be continued next week,"* she promised. "We'll talk more about that next week when you have your Home Interiors Show! Believe me . . . there are so many beautiful ways to 'blend' furniture that I want to take extra time to tell you about all of them. You'll love learning how you can make this antique chest an important, happy relation to the rest of your furnishings."

With a friendly goodby, and a promise of, "see you next week," the Home Interiors Lady hurried across the street to her car. Mrs. Wonderful watched as she drove away.

"I can hardly wait until next week," she whispered to herself.

"Neither can I," the Little Brick House whispered to himself.

What a day! He felt gay . . . giddy . . . excited! (Indeed, he be-haved in a manner *most* unbecoming to a solid brick house!) But how wonderfully alive he felt! Soon *he* would be a "spicy-apple-pie" house. Soon *he* would be the most impressive house on the block.

It was like magic!

Magic?

Yes . . . it *was* magic, for as all of us know . . . magic and miracles show themselves in wondrous ways . . . and wonder of wonders . . . *Peeking from the chimney of the Little Brick House was a cheerful, provocative flower!*

That is why to this very day . . .
The house
With the chimney
With the flower peeking out
Tells all the world:

Home Interiors Magic
helped this house
to live
happily
ever after

The End